Bhagavad Gītā

*The Beloved Lord's
Secret Love Song*

Graham M. Schweig

HarperOne
An Imprint of HarperCollins*Publishers*

This book is a source and reference text
for the Philosophy, Religion & Ethics curriculum
taught in the Avanti Schools Trust schools in England.

HarperOne

FIRST HARPERCOLLINS PAPERBACK EDITION PUBLISHED IN 2010

Designed by Joseph Rutt

Library of Congress Cataloging-in-Publication Data

Bhagavadgita. English & Sanskrit.
 Bhagavad Gītā : the beloved Lord's secret love song / Graham M. Schweig.
  p. cm.
 In English and Sanskrit (romanized); includes translation from Sanskrit.
 Includes bibliographical references and index.
 ISBN 978-0-06-199730-3
  I. Schweig, Graham M. II. Title.
 BL1138.62.E5 2006
 294.5'92404521—dc22   2006041312

17 18 19 RRD (H) 10

Bhagavad Gītā

Contents

Introduction

The Meaning of the Bhagavad Gītā

The Bhagavad Gītā comes to us from sacred India. Its verses of ancient wisdom on the mysteries of human existence speak to us today as if they had just been spoken. The Bhagavad Gītā is one of the most loved works among the collections of scriptural texts found within the Hindu traditions. It also stands out among the holy books of the major world religions, for its flowing Sanskrit verses present a uniquely vivid portrait of the intimacy between humanity and divinity. Indeed, this divine intimacy is revealed in the form of a dialogue that takes the soul on an inward journey culminating in the ultimate state of yoga, in which souls unite with the heart of God.

The Bhagavad Gītā, often called simply "the Gītā,"[1] is essentially a book on yoga.[2] This profound teaching is the book on yoga par excellence because it presents yoga in the most comprehensive sense of the term and in all its depth. As discussed in "Textual Illuminations," yoga covers a broad range of practices and visions, significantly more than what we encounter in the West, or for that matter more than what a reading of famous treatises on yoga, such as the Yoga Sūtra of Patanjali, may yield. In the Gītā, the concept of the sacred connection of humanity with divinity is gradually introduced and developed, then fully disclosed as the "supreme secret of yoga."[3]

Bhagavad Gītā may be translated as "the song of the Beloved Lord," which conveys a divine yearning. The word *Bhagavad*[4] means "the Beloved Lord," referring to Krishna, whose voice is prominent

---

1 Throughout this discussion, the title Bhagavad Gītā is shortened to "the Gītā." In footnotes and verse references the title is abbreviated as BG. When specific verses are referenced, the chapter number appears first, followed by the verse number.

2 The word *yoga* is found 78 times in the BG, appearing in every chapter except three (chapters 1, 15, and 17). The word *yoga* and related words, such as *yogi* (found 28 times) and *yukta* (found 49 times), appear 155 times. This means that in over 20 percent of the Gītā's verses the word *yoga* or its related forms appear.

3 This phrase is found in the words *guhyam param yogam* in BG 18.75. The "supreme secret" is discussed at length in the "Textual Illuminations."

4 The *g* in *Bhagavad* is pronounced as in *go*; the *a* is pronounced as in *about*. See "Pronunciation of Sanskrit." The word *Bhagavad*, translated as "the Beloved Lord," is a modified form of *bhagavat*, according to the Sanskrit rules of euphonic combination, *sandhi*. The word often appears in other works as *bhagavān*, the word's inflected form in the nominative case.

throughout the work. In the Bhagavad Gītā, Krishna, perhaps the most loved of all manifestations of divinity in India, is identified as the ultimate and supreme Lord, from whom all other divine manifestations emanate. *Gītā*[5] means "song," in this case one coming from Krishna or God. Clearly the text is a philosophical poem and not a song in the literal sense. At a deeper level, however, it is a song issuing forth from the heart of God. It is the secret call of the divinity for all souls to love him, to take the journey to him, to be blissfully united with him.

The Bhagavad Gītā in Context

Although India is the birthplace of a variety of religious traditions, including Buddhism, Jainism, and Sikhism, it is Hinduism that is the dominant religion in India today. Hinduism is composed of several primary and numerous less familiar traditions, all theologically distinctive, yet each acknowledging the revelational authority of a common ancient scriptural source. Possibly the oldest sacred text in the world, dating as far back as 2500 to 1500 BCE, the collection of Sanskrit hymns known as the Vedas are foundational for the myriad traditions that come under the umbrella of Hinduism. These traditions make up the largest constituency of religious practitioners in South Asia. Among these, the traditions that focus upon the supreme divinity of Krishna or his cosmic manifestation of Vishnu are known as Vaishnava, and they constitute the dominant form of religion. The Bhagavad Gītā comes to us from this Vaishnava tradition, which is present throughout India and, in the second half of the twentieth century, around the globe.[6]

This beloved book of India is often called the "bible of Hinduism" in the West. As the Bible is for Christians and the Qur'an

---

5 Pronounced "geet-ah."
6 A. C. Bhaktivedanta Swami Prabhupāda (1896–1977), as an elderly monk, along with his disciples, established the orthodox practice of the Chaitanya school of Vaishnavism (as the modern Krishna movement) in many major cities around the world, beginning with the United States in 1965. His translation and traditional commentary on the Gītā, *Bhagavad-gītā As It Is* (New York: Macmillan Publishing Co., 1972; Los Angeles: Bhaktivedanta Book Trust, 1983, 1989), is by far the most widely read and distributed in the world.

for Muslims, so it could be said that the Bhagavad Gītā is for Hindus, for it is the single most influential philosophical sacred text coming from South Asia. Though it is, since the seventh century, the most widely read and commented on holy text in all of India, it comes from a tradition that reveres many sacred texts, unlike Western religious traditions, which focus on one sacred book of revelation. Moreover, though the Bhagavad Gītā is usually read alone, it is a small section of a substantially larger text, perhaps the largest epic poem in the world, the Mahābhārata. The philosophical verses of the Gītā stand gracefully as an autonomous text with a beginning, middle, and end, despite their original placement within the continuum of this greater epic poem. The Mahābhārata, containing approximately 100,000 verses, is thought by Western scholars to have appeared in its final form sometime between 500 BCE and 200 CE, though traditional dating of events in the text places them in the third millennium BCE. The eighteen chapters of the Gītā appear as chapters 23 through 40 in the Book of Bhīshma, the sixth of the Mahābhārata's eighteen books.

Historically, we first come to know of the divinity of Krishna in the Bhagavad Gītā text. Although his identity as "the divine lover" is not revealed in the Gītā, Krishna is traditionally appreciated as the divinity who sends out a love call to all souls. His call is intended for those who relate to him in loving intimacy, not for those who regard him with reverential awe, worshipping primarily his attributes of cosmic power and majesty. As the supreme divinity, Krishna plays multiple roles, adopts a variety of personae, and displays numerous grand and cosmic manifestations, yet he is also delightfully playful and personal. The various roles that Krishna assumes in his more intimate acts, particularly as a youthful cowherd, are considered the most exquisite, revealing endearing and beautiful visions of the supreme.

Most enchanting and charming, Krishna is loved and worshipped by Hindus in a variety of forms: as a sweet but mischievous child, as the closest friend, or even as the ultimate lover. In these intimate relationships with the divinity, Krishna, famous for his divine love call, sends forth his call by producing captivating music on his flute. He is best known for alluring the lovely cowherd maidens of the paradisal village of Vraja out of

their homes, one serene autumn evening. Upon hearing his irresist-
ibly sweet flute music, the maidens abruptly abandon their families
and household duties to join him in the moonlit forest. On this
sanctified night, the maidens and Krishna enact the famous Rāsa
Līlā, which I have broadly translated as the "dance of divine
love."[7]

In the Bhagavad Gītā, Krishna's call to love, the expression of
his divine longing, is a more hidden feature of the text, though it
carries the Gītā's most powerful message: the heart of God passionately desires to connect with the hearts of humans. Here,
Krishna's love call is directed to Arjuna, his dearest friend, who
already knows Krishna's love but finds himself in a devastating
worldly crisis that distracts him from the heart of God. In the
dialogue that ensues between Krishna and Arjuna, Krishna gently
and compassionately brings Arjuna's heart back to his divine
heart, even in the midst of the most trying of circumstances—
war. As might be expected, the outer conflict that distracts Arjuna
from his relationship with Krishna is accompanied by intense
inner conflict. This personal crisis, however, serves to reunite
Arjuna with the divinity, enabling him to return to the overwhelming challenges of the outer world with renewed strength
and resolve.

Outer and Inner Conflict

When turning to the first verse, the reader steps into a greater
story that is already taking place. The opening words are spoken
by a king, which we discover from his epithetical name, Dhritarāshtra, meaning "powerful ruler." From the background story
that surrounds the Gītā event we learn that this king, significantly,
was born blind. The sons of the king are prepared to lead his army
into battle against the sons of his deceased younger brother, Pāndu,

---

7 This celebrated passage is found in the Bhāgavata Purāṇa, tenth book, chapters 29–33. See my
Dance of Divine Love: India's Classic Sacred Love Story: The Rāsa Līlā of Krishna (Princeton, NJ:
Princeton University Press, 2005) for a translation and comprehensive treatment of this sacred text,
with an introduction.

who inherited the throne from their renowned ancestor, the great King Bharata, due to the older son's blindness. Unfortunately, when the noble and righteous Pāndu passed away, his five sons (the Pāndavas) were too young to assume the throne. Their envious uncle, in his blindness, thus took over the kingdom and ruled for many years, with devastating results. The Pāndavas, led by Pāndu's grown son, the general and archer Arjuna—the mightiest warrior of his time—fervently desire to take charge of the kingdom to restore peace. Their uncle and his sons, however, led by the eldest son, Duryodhana, have refused to surrender the throne. Consequently, a battle is inevitable.

This great classic of some seven hundred Sanskrit verses opens with the tension of imminent battle, as each army, lined up like pieces on a chessboard, looks over the other, setting the stage for the dialogue of the Bhagavad Gītā. The first half of the first chapter can be understood as the narration of Arjuna's outer conflict (BG I.1–I.27) and the second half as the expression of his inner conflict (BG I.28–I.47). The full impact of the looming confrontation weighs on Arjuna as he prepares to lead his men against an enemy army composed of many of his teachers, friends, and even relatives. Anticipating that he will have to fight and slay those whom he loves and reveres, Arjuna is overcome by grief and hurled into debilitating despair:

> My limbs are sinking down
>   and my mouth has
>   become very dry.
> Also, my body trembles
>   and the hairs of
>   my limbs stand on end.
>
> My bow, Gāndīva,
>   falls from my hand
>   and even my skin is burning.
> I also am unable
>   to stand steadily and
>   my mind seems to be reeling.
>
> (BG I.29–I.30)

While experiencing such agonizing symptoms of dread, Arjuna is unable to respond in accordance with his nature as a warrior to the outer conflict he faces.

The Gītā begins, then, by introducing a seemingly irresolvable ethical challenge: should the virtuous Arjuna protect the innocent by fighting an enemy army composed of loved ones and gurus? The ethical codes of ancient India command him to carry out his duty as the leading warrior of his time, to protect the innocent from ruthless forces; yet these same codes forbid a warrior to kill family, friends, and especially a teacher or beloved guru. Indeed, the Gītā informs us that there always will be ethical conflict in the outer world. Consequently, the text does not attempt to resolve the dilemma that befalls Arjuna, at least not directly. Instead it points to something deeper.

This work of Indian spirituality not only raises the question of the appropriate action for Arjuna to adopt, it also defines the existential challenge facing every human being. As struggling souls we ultimately attempt to transform our precarious painful world into a meaningful one. In the first half of the opening verse, spoken by the blind king Dhritarāshtra, the Gītā presents such an existential tension:

> On the field of dharma,
>   on the field of Kuru,
>   assembled together
>   desiring to fight,
> Were my armies
>   and indeed those
>   of the sons of Pāndu—
>   how did they act, O Sanjaya?
>   (BG I.I)

The first two lines, *dharma-kshetre*, "on the field of dharma" and *kuru-kshetre*, "on the field of Kuru," set the stage for this tension. The field of Kuru, the holy place known as Kurukshetra, is presented here as a place of "dharma." Named after the pious King Kuru, the common ancestor of Dhritarāshtra and Pāndu, Kurukshetra is, ironically, the site where the civil war between the sons of these two brothers, along with their respective armies, is about to take place. The reader learns that in the world of human inter-action, we have an opportunity to live a life of dharma—a godly life promoting true happiness in relation to our worldly responsi-bilities and ultimate spiritual goals—or an ungodly life, in which forces destructive to dharma constantly prevail. The armies of the Pāṇḍavas, the sons of Pāṇḍu, represent the life of dharma; Dhritarāshtra's armies, the Kauravas, are destroyers of dharma.

Like Arjuna, we humans often are caught between Pāṇḍava– and Kaurava–like forces, vacillating between thoughts and activi-ties that elevate the spirit, helping us to rise above the destructive forces surrounding us, and those that degrade the spirit and fur-ther embroil us in the perils of worldly existence. The Gītā speaks deeply to each of us, for at some point, doesn't every soul, like Arjuna, face a unique battlefield in the outer world as well as within? Throughout, Krishna proffers not only *that* we must act, but also *how* we must act to fight our individual battles. The axial core of the Gītā is this perpetual existential tension that we encounter—but not without purpose, the Gītā propounds.

The foundational theme for the entire Gītā is dramatically established in the opening verse through the king's inquiry, "How did they act, O Sanjaya?" This question reveals the major theme of action, around which the teaching of the Bhagavad Gītā revolves: what action is, why and how we must act, our relation to action and nonaction, when action is right or wrong, and how we should understand action in all circumstances. The blessings that sur-round us in this world, symbolized by the holy place of Kuru-kshetra as a place of dharma; the struggles that we face in the world, represented by the desire to fight; and the dilemma of how to act in light of the tension between the two, expressed by the king's question, combine to make this opening verse of the Gītā the "seed" verse of the whole text.[8]

The Gītā's ultimate teaching—its response to the question of how souls should act in this world—is that souls should at all

---

8 The practice of implanting the essential idea or "seed," around which the whole text revolves, in an opening passage or verse, often occurs in great Sanskrit works.

times and in every circumstance *act out of love*. By hearing Krishna's call to love, Arjuna discovers a more elevated state of consciousness, then an inner state of transcendence, and finally, a state of eternal freedom in which his heart can fully love God and, consequently, all beings. From this newfound fortitude and love, Arjuna is prepared to act with full-heartedness.[9]

The opening question concerning action is posed by the troubled King Dhritarāshtra. He approaches his minister Sanjaya, who functions as a sage. This forms the outer dialogue of the text. As we have seen, the king is an illegitimate ruler, misguided and selfish. Thus he is emblematic of our human condition, for we all can be, in a sense, blinded by myopic vision, by self-centeredness. We are blind kings ruling over our false kingdoms, misguided and selfish in our individual existences. Our false kingdoms are the very fleeting worlds to which we impute eternal significance, as if our impermanent lives were going to last forever. The king's troubled state leads him to inquire from his minister, who is granted exceptional vision. The Gītā also encourages us in our "blindness" to seek out someone of broad spiritual insight for divine guidance:

> Learn this
> by humble submission,
> by thorough inquiry,
> and by serving.
> They will impart
> this knowledge to you,
> for they are knowers
> and seers of the truth.
>
> (BG 4.34)

Sanjaya, who has a vision of the truth, through his outer dialogue with the king, becomes the narrator of the private inner dialogue between Krishna and Arjuna. This conversation is then meant to be contemplated deeply within the heart and lived by in our challenging worlds.

---

9 Full-heartedness refers to the state of *bhakti* in which the heart is brimming over with love for the divinity and therefore, for all beings in whose hearts the divinity resides.

Literary Dimensions

The journey of the soul to the divinity and the ways in which the divinity embraces the soul are described in the Bhagavad Gītā in narrative, conversational, philosophical, and didactic verse. The Gītā presents a variety of paths leading the soul to the divine, along with various manifestations of divinity. The majority of its verses focus on three concepts: (1) a philosophical vision of the human self and the nature of the precarious "outer world"; (2) the various paths and practices that lead the self to the "inner world" of transcendence and personal presence of the divine; and (3) the "innermost world" of the heart, where divinity is encountered directly in a dialogue between the soul and God, as represented by the heartfelt exchange between Arjuna and Krishna.

In effect, then, the Gītā takes us, along with Arjuna, on an internal journey to the innermost region of the heart. The hardships of the outer world often distract the soul from the inner world, hurling the soul into despondency. The Gītā demonstrates how souls can reconnect with the divine in their hearts, thereby attaining a state of full-heartedness. From this position of inner strength and fulfillment, the soul is able to return to the battlefield of the outer world with courage, fully prepared to act. The inner dialogue between Arjuna and Krishna is private; no one on the battlefield is close enough to hear or directly observe it. This intimate conversation is a deeply loving exchange that discloses the secret love song of the divinity, relieving Arjuna of his insurmountable grief and awarding him a full heart.

The voices of Krishna and Arjuna are heard throughout the Gītā, along with an occasional supporting narrative by Sanjaya. Of these, it is Krishna's voice that is heard the most.[10] Although his voice appears only once in the first chapter, it dominates the other seventeen. Arjuna's voice is prominent in the first and eleventh chapters, and is heard in only twenty-eight verses in twelve other chapters.[11] Sanjaya's voice is heard most frequently in the first chapter and is found in three others. The text concludes with five

---

10 Krishna speaks in 575 verses, roughly 82 percent of the text.
11 Arjuna speaks in 83 verses, roughly 12 percent of the text.

effusive verses spoken by Sanjaya to Dhritarāshtra, thus resuming the outer dialogue, which expresses the bliss the soul derives from recalling the words spoken between Krishna and Arjuna.

For one encountering the work for the first time, it is important to note that Krishna and Arjuna are given numerous epithets in the text. Arjuna is given at least twenty other names and Krishna at least thirty-three. One encounters such names as: Govinda (one who tends the cows), Supreme Person, and Slayer of Madhu for Krishna; and Pārtha (son of Prithā), Mighty-Armed, and Bhārata (descendant of King Bharata) for Arjuna. The devotee of Krishna experiences endless delight in affectionately calling the beloved Lord by any number of these names. Indeed, another section of the Mahābhārata text, known as *Vishnu Sahasra Nāma*, "The Thousand Names of Vishnu," bespeaks this practice.[12] Therefore, it should not surprise the reader to find such variety of nomenclature in the Gītā. (The complete list of epithets for Arjuna and Krishna appears in the "Dramatis Personae.")

The Bhagavad Gītā is reminiscent of other sacred texts, in particular the Vedas and the Upanishads, which contribute to the work's synthetic character. As stated above, Vaishnava traditions, along with other Hindu traditions, revere these scriptural works for their foundational revelations. Beginning with the Vedas, a significant part is dedicated to devotional Sanskrit hymns. To compare, in the following passage Arjuna marvels at the magnificence and divinity of Krishna:[13]

> You are the indestructible,
>   the supreme object of knowledge.
> You are the supreme
>   resting place of all.
> You are the everpresent
>   protector of lasting dharma.
> You are the eternal Person—
>   so it is understood by me.
>
>   (BG 11.18)

---

12 Found in Anuśāsan Parvan of the Mahābhārata and in the Padma Purāna.
13 See BG 10.12–18; 11.15–31.

Here one is reminded of the Vedic worshipper whose voice extols the greatness of the divine in its myriad forms.

The Gītā is also reminiscent of the dialogues between student and teacher found in the Upanishads, the other source mirrored in the text. The following verses of the Gītā remind one of the Upanishads:

Arjuna said:

What is the description
  of one established
  in profound knowledge,
  who is established
  in perfect meditation,
  O Keshava?
How would
  one established
  in thought speak?
  How would one sit?
  How would one move about?

The Beloved Lord said:

When a person gives up
  all selfish desires
  arising from the mind,
  O Pārtha,
Satisfied within the self
  by the self alone,
  then that person
  is said to be established
  in profound knowledge.
                    (BG 2.54–2.55)

The dominant literary structure of the Bhagavad Gītā text is a dialogue, comprised of both inner and outer dialogues. The voice of the master is by far the most prominent within the inner dialogue and reflects an important dimension of Krishna's relationship with Arjuna, that of the compassionate teacher with the submissive student. Arjuna asks several questions in the text, and Krishna responds with didactic words. Arjuna submits to Krishna as his humble student in the following words: "I am your student—instruct me, for I have offered myself unto you" (BG 2.7). This paradigm of the student inquiring from the spiritual guide, characteristic of the Upanishads, is present early on and throughout the Gītā. It is no wonder that the Gītā is sometimes called Gitopanishad, expressing its close relationship to the Upanishads.

I have presented briefly some key literary and philosophical aspects of the Bhagavad Gītā to facilitate the reader's encounter with this great dialogue. The "Textual Illuminations" provides a more elaborate discussion of the complex theology of the work, as well as an exploration of various dimensions of the "secret love song" of the divinity. Because the Bhagavad Gītā engages many traditions of spiritual practice and philosophy and is framed within a complex epic, it is challenging for any reader to penetrate its essential message. Indeed, traditional schools of India often have taken minor practices or philosophies engaged in the text to be the whole intent of the text's message. And Western readers typically have grasped only that part which reflects something familiar from the Abrahamic traditions, thereby ignoring essential themes of the Gītā.

My purpose, therefore, is to offer the reader an overall vision derived directly from the text that allows one to appreciate every aspect of the work. This vision is one of love, beginning with God's heart yearning for the love of souls. For now, I invite the reader to encounter the ideas and messages of this complex text with an open heart. As you consider the predicament of the softhearted Arjuna, take the journey along with him into your own heart, where you will begin to experience an authentic ancient voice of spiritual wisdom that for millennia has moved the hearts of countless millions the world over.

Bhagavad Gītā

Dramatis Personae

(in order of appearance)

Dhritarāshtra

Speaker of the first verse; the king to whom the whole text is narrated, for whose throne the war is being fought

Sanjaya

Narrator; the king's minister, who has been given special power to hear and see events on the battlefield and the great dialogue between Arjuna and Krishna

Duryodhana

A leading general of the Kauravas; cousin of Arjuna; eldest son of Dhritarāshtra; the prime instigator of the fratricidal conflict

Arjuna

A leading general of the Pāndavas; cousin of Duryodhana; son of Pāndu (the younger brother of Dhritarāshtra), who speaks with Krishna throughout the text (see Epithets below)

The Beloved Lord

Krishna, Arjuna's chariot driver, who imparts teachings and engages in personal dialogue with Arjuna for the greater part of the text (see Epithets below)

The Setting

Geographic location: the holy site of Kurukshetra ("the field of Kuru"), a rural area located in central northern India about one hundred miles north of Delhi.

The scene on the Kurukshetra battlefield: The massive opposing armies, composed of the righteous army of the sons of Pāndu, the Pāndavas, led by Arjuna, and the unrighteous army of the sons of Dhritarāshtra, the Kurus, led by Duryodhana, the eldest son. On his chariot, Krishna drives Arjuna into the middle of the battlefield, between the armies, to survey the warriors and battle scene.

Epithets

ARJUNA

Pāndava	Leader of the Bharatas
Dhananjaya	Subduer of the Enemy
Gudākesha	Best of the Kurus
Pārtha	Son of Pāndu
Son of Kuntī	Son of Kuru
Scorcher of the Enemy	Best of the Bharatas
Bhārata	Best of the Embodied
Best Among Men	Destroyer of the Enemy
Mighty-Armed	Hero of the Kurus
Kaunteya	Masterful Archer
Descendant of Kuru	Fighter of the Enemy
Conqueror of Wealth	Tiger Among Men
Blameless One	Holder of the Bow

THE BELOVED LORD, KRISHNA

Mādhava	Hari
Hrishīkesha	Divinity
Achyuta	All-Pervasive Supreme Lord
Keshava	Mighty Self
Govinda	Mighty-Armed
Madhusūdhana	Lord of Divinities
Janārdana	Vishnu
Descendant of Vrishni	Best of Divinities
Slayer of the Enemy	Extraordinary Self
Vārshneya	Unlimited Lord
Ultimate Person	One of Unlimited Form
Supreme Person	Everything
Source of Beings	Yādava
Divinity of Divinities	Friend
Master of the Universe	Unfathomable One
Yogi	One of Incomparable Being
One with Lotus-like Eyes	Thousand-Armed One
Highest Supreme Lord	Universal Form
Ultimate Person	Vāsudeva
Supreme Lord of Yoga	Majestic One
Lord	Slayer of Keshi

Translation

I

Arjuna's Conflict and Despair

Dhritarāshtra said:
On the field of dharma,
on the field of Kuru,
assembled together
desiring to fight,
Were my armies
and indeed those
of the sons of Pāndu—
how did they act, O Sanjaya?[1]   I

---

1 Dhritarāshtra: The hard-hearted king of the Kurus, blind from birth, while sitting in his palace, desires to know what is occurring on the battlefield, where a civil war between his sons and nephews, the heroic sons of his brother Pāndu, is about to begin.

On the field of dharma: Translates *dharma-kṣetre*. This phrase tells the reader that the field of Kuru, or Kurukshetra, is a holy place, a place of dharma (see meaning of *dharma* below).

On the field of Kuru: Translates *kurukṣetre*, the name of the holy place Kurukshetra, about 100 miles north of Delhi, India's modern capital city.

Dharma: A state of righteousness, a personal calling to goodness, cosmic harmony, sound ethical law, or justice. The very first word in the opening Sanskrit verse.

Kuru: Name of a common ancestral king for the leaders of both armies, the sons of Dhritarāshtra and the sons of his brother, Pāndu.

The sons of Pāndu: Also known as the Pāndavas, the five sons of King Pāndu, whose names are presented in verses 15 and 16 below; also, the name of the army led by Arjuna.

Pāndu: The younger brother of Dhritarāshtra, who was king before his untimely death.

How did they act: The word *act* translates an active form of the verbal root *kr*, which means "to act." The noun form, *karma*, meaning "action," is a major theme of the BG. All words that derive from this verbal root are here translated with some form of the word *act*.

Sanjaya: The king's minister, endowed by Vyāsa with the power to see what is transpiring on the battlefield at every moment, recounts these events to the king.

Sanjaya said:

Now seeing the armies
of the Pāndavas arrayed
in battle formation,
King Duryodhana,
approaching his teacher,
spoke these words:[2]   2

[Duryodhana said:]

Behold these mighty warriors
of the sons of Pāndu,
O Revered Teacher,
Arrayed in
battle formation
by the son of Drupada,
your own skillful student.[3]   3

Here are their heroes,
powerful archers equal
to Bhīma and Arjuna in battle:
Yuyudhāna and Virāta,
and King Drupada,
the great chariot warrior;[4]   4

---

2 Pāndavas: The sons of the Pāndus and the army led by Arjuna. Beginning with this verse, Duryodhana reviews the powerful warriors on the opposing side.

King Duryodhana: The oldest son of King Dhritarāshtra and the leading general of the Kuru warriors who oppose the righteous Pāndavas. The name Duryodhana means "dirty fighter." This is the first of nine consecutive verses spoken by Duryodhana (BG 1.3–11).

His teacher: Refers to Dronacharya, the great teacher of warfare for both Arjuna and Duryodhana.

3 In verses 3 through 6, Duryodhana, the leader of the unrighteous Kurus, observes the powerful warriors in the opposing army, led by Arjuna, his cousin. In verses 7 through 11, he then speaks about the superior power of his own men.

The son of Drupada: Dhristadyumna, the leading commander of the Pāndavas.

4 Bhima: One of five Pāndava brothers known to be a great warrior.

Arjuna: One of five Pāndava brothers who lead the Pāndava army; the loving friend of Krishna to whom the teachings of the BG are spoken.

Yuyudhāna and the other men named in this verse, as well as in the following two verses, are all well-known and powerful warriors in the Pāndava army.

Dhrishtaketu, Chetikāna,
    and the heroic king of Kāshi;
Purojit and Kuntibhoja,
    and Shaibya, leader among men;   5

And the courageous
    Yudhāmanyu, also
    the valorous Uttamaujas;
The son of Subhadrā
    and the sons of Draupadi—
    all certainly great chariot warriors.[5]   6

However, our own men,
    the most distinguished—
    learn about them,
    O Best of the Twice-Born.
To inform you,
    I will tell you the names
    of those who are
    the leaders of my forces.[6]   7

They are yourself and Bhīshma,
    also Karna and Kripa,
    victorious in battle;
Also Ashwatthāma
    and Vikarna, and indeed,
    the son of Somadatta;[7]   8

---

5 Son of Subhadrā: Refers to Abhimanyu; Subhadrā is Krishna's sister.

Sons of Draupadi: Draupadi is the wife of each of the five Pāndavas, each with whom she has a son.

6 O Best of the Twice-born: Translates *dvijottama*, addressing Duryodhana's teacher, Drona, as the best of the Brahmins.

7 Bhīshma: The most venerated of the Kaurava warriors, who is the grand uncle of the Pāndavas.

Karna: A half-brother and chief rival of Arjuna and a highly skilled bowman.

Kripa and the other warriors mentioned here are all prominent in the opposing Kaurava army.

And many other heroes
who are willing to relinquish
their lives for my sake—
Wielding various weapons,
all are highly skilled in battle.   9

Unlimited are our forces
protected by Bhīshma,
Whereas limited are their forces
protected by Bhīma.[8]   10

Thus in all maneuvers
from your respective positions,
You must certainly guard Bhīshma—
indeed, every one of you.[9]   11

[Sanjaya continued:]

Giving him [Duryodhana] a thrill,
the revered elder
of the Kurus [Bhīshma]
Cried out the roar
of a lion and blew
his conch with great vigor.   12

Then conches and kettledrums,
cymbals, drums, and trumpets
Were all sounded at once—
the vibration became tumultuous.   13

---

8 Unlimited: Translates the word *aparyāptam,* also meaning paradoxically, "inadequate." Similarly, "limited," in the second half of the verse, translates *paryāptam,* the positive form of this word, which also means "adequate." This double meaning expresses how Duryodhana's overconfidence compensates for his insecurity regarding the outcome of the battle.

9 Duryodhana, after directing his words to his teacher, now turns to his men to instruct them.

Thereupon, standing
    in a magnificent chariot
    yoked with white horses,
Mādhava [Krishna]
    and the Pāndava [Arjuna]
    sounded their divine conch shells.[10]   14

Hrishīkesha [Krishna]
    blew the conch Panchajanya;
Dhananjaya [Arjuna]
    blew the conch Devadatta;
And Bhīma,
    the voracious eater
    who is terrifying in action,
    blew the great conch Paundra.[11]   15

King Yudhishthira,
    the son of Kuntī,
    blew his conch Anantavijaya;
While Nakula and Sahadeva
    blew their conches,
    Sughosha and Manipushpaka.[12]   16

---

10 Mādhava: Name of Krishna meaning "a descendant of Madhu" (of the Yadu dynasty). This name indicates Krishna's distant family relationship with Arjuna, whose ancestry goes back to Puru. Yadu and Puru were sons of the great king Yayāti. This name is also associated with Krishna as the husband of the Great Goddess, Lakshmī Devī, the embodiment of all auspiciousness, success, prosperity, and happiness. This is the first verse in which Krishna is introduced.

11 Hrishīkesha: Name of Krishna meaning "the lord of the senses."

Dhananjaya: Name of Arjuna throughout the BG, meaning "conqueror of wealth."

Bhīma: One of the five Pāndavas and brother of Arjuna. The other three brothers are named in the next verse.

12 Yudhishthira: The eldest of the Pāndava brothers.

Nakula and Sahadeva: Two Pāndava brothers.

Also, the king of Kāshi,
   an expert archer,
   and Shikhandī,
   a great chariot warrior;
Dhrishtadhyumna and Virāta,
   along with Sātyaki,
   the unconquerable;   17

Drupada and the sons
   of Draupadī,
   grouped together,
   O Lord of the Earth;
And the mighty-armed
   son of Subhadrā—
   all of them blew
   their conches one by one.[13]   18

That sound shattered the hearts
   of the sons of Dhritarāshtra,
And indeed, the tumult caused
   the heavens and earth to resound.[14]   19

---

13 The son of Subhadrā: Abhimanyu, the son of Arjuna's second wife.

O Lord of the Earth: An epithet for Dhritarāshtra, the king to whom Sanjaya narrates this text.

14 The sons of Dhritarāshtra: Sanjaya identifies Dhritarāshtra's sons using a slightly altered Sanskrit form of the king's name while narrating the events occurring far from the king. Thus Sanjaya is not ignoring the fact that the king sits before him by speaking of him in the third person. Rather, in Sanskrit, offspring are identified by a slightly altered form of the father's name, here as Dhārtarāshtra.

Thus observing
  the sons of Dhritarāshtra
  lined up in battle formation,
The Pāndava [Arjuna],
  his chariot displaying
  the banner of the monkey,
  lifted his bow as weapons
  began to clash.[15]   20

Then, O Lord of the Earth,
  to Hrishīkesha,
  he spoke these words:
Between the two armies
  place my chariot,
  O Achyuta [Krishna],[16]   21

So that I may look upon those
  who are standing here
  desiring battle—
With whom
  must I battle while
  engaging in this war?   22

I look upon those
  about to engage in battle,
  who are assembled here
Desiring to please
  the evil-minded son
  of Dhritarāshtra in battle.[17]   23

---

15 The Pāndava: A son of King Pāndu, referring to Arjuna.

  The banner of the monkey: The particular monkey referred to here is Hanumān, the great monkey servant of Rāma, a manifestation of Vishnu.

16 O Lord of the Earth: This epithet refers to Dhritarāshtra.

17 The evil-minded son of Dhritarāshtra: Duryodhana, who leads the Kuru army.

[Sanjaya continued:]

Hrishīkesha, thus addressed
   by Gudākesha [Arjuna],
   O Bhārata [Dhritarāshtra],
Placed his magnificent chariot
   between the two armies.[18]   24

Facing Bhīshma, Drona,
   and all the kings
   of the earth,
He [Krishna] said,
   "O Pārtha [Arjuna],
   behold these Kurus
   assembled here!"   25

Pārtha saw,
   standing there—
   fathers, then grandfathers,
Teachers, maternal uncles,
   brothers, sons, grandsons,
   as well as companions;   26

Fathers-in-law,
   and even dear friends,
   present in both battalions.
The Son of Kuntī [Arjuna],
   observing all of them,
   his kinsmen arrayed for battle;   27

---

18 O Bhārata: Son of Bharata, here referring   Gudākesha: "The full-haired one."
to Dhritarāshtra.

Filled with deep compassion
  and falling into despair,
  he spoke the following:
Seeing my own relations,
  O Krishna, standing
  nearby ready to fight,[19]   28

My limbs are sinking down
  and my mouth has
  become very dry.
Also, my body trembles
  and the hairs of
  my limbs stand on end.   29

My bow, Gāndīva,
  falls from my hand
  and even my skin is burning.
I also am unable
  to stand steadily and
  my mind seems to be reeling.   30

And I perceive signs of chaos,
  terrible reversals,
  O Keshava [Krishna],
And I foresee
  no benefit in slaying
  my own relations in battle.[20]   31

---

19 With deep compassion: Translates *kṛpayā parayā*.
  Falling into despair: Translates *viṣīdan*.

20 Keshava: Name of Krishna meaning "the one with beautiful hair."

I do not desire victory,
  O Krishna,
  nor a kingdom,
  nor happiness.
What use is a kingdom to us,
  O Govinda [Krishna]?
  What is the use of pleasures
  or purpose in living?[21]   32

Those persons for
  whose sake we desire
  such kingdom, pleasures,
  and happiness—
They stand here arrayed
  in battle readiness,
  relinquishing
  their lives and wealth: 33

Our teachers,
  fathers, and sons;
  also grandfathers,
Maternal uncles,
  fathers-in-law,
  grandsons,
  brothers-in-law,
  and other kinsmen.   34

---

21 Govinda: Name of Krishna meaning "the one who herds the cows." Considered to be an especially endearing and intimate name for Krishna.

I do not wish to slay them,
    even those who are
    about to slay,
    O Madhusūdana [Krishna],
Even for the rule
    of the three worlds—
    how much less, then,
    for the rule of the earth?[22]   35

What joy would there be for us,
    O Janārdana [Krishna],
    in slaying the sons
    of Dhritarāshtra?
Certainly misfortune
    would fall upon us
    having slain them
    whose bows are drawn.[23]   36

Therefore, we are not entitled
    to slay the sons of
    Dhritarāshtra,
    our kinsmen.
Indeed, in slaying
    our own relations,
    how could we realize
    happiness, O Mādhava?[24]   37

---

22 Madhusūdana: "Slayer of the demon Madhu," a well-known name for Krishna. Arjuna's use of this name suggests, "You slay demons, but even you don't slay persons whom you love and revere!"

23 Janārdana: Name of Krishna meaning "one who inspires human beings."

Misfortune: Translates *pāpa*, often rendered as "sin," which carries too much of the narrower Christian sense. I have chosen to translate as "misfortune" or "trouble," indicating both the unfortunate things that can befall a person as well as something unfortunate that a person has caused. The word *pāpa* means anything disturbing that creates conflict internally and externally, an impediment in one's spiritual evolution causing effects that impede one's progress. The word *sin* has a much narrower application that carries a particular Christian sense not present in the Sanskrit word *pāpa*.

24 Happiness: Translates *sukhinaḥ*.

Even if, with their thoughts
    overcome by greed,
    they do not perceive
The harm caused by acts
    that destroy the family,
    nor the crime in
    harming a friend;[25]   38

Still, how can we not know
    to turn away from
    this wrongdoing,
With our understanding of
    the harm caused by acts
    that destroy the family,
    O Janārdana?[26]   39

In destroying the family,
    the eternal dharma
    of the family is lost.
When dharma is lost,
    whatever opposes dharma
    also overcomes the entire family.[27]   40

Because of the prevalence
    of that which opposes dharma,
    the women of the family
    become degraded.
When the women are degraded,
    O Descendant of Vrishni [Krishna],
    disorder between
    classes of society arises.[28]   41

---

25 Greed: Translates *lobha*.
  Destroy the family: Translates *kula-kṣ aya*.
  Crime in harming a friend: Translates *mitra-droha*.
26 Wrongdoing: Translates *pāpa*.
  Harm: Translates *doṣa*.

27 Dharma of the family: Translates *kula-dharma*.
  Whatever opposes dharma: Translates *adharma*, meaning lawlessness, chaos, or evil.
28 Disorder between classes of society: Translates *varṇa-saṁkaraḥ*. Sometimes taken as "confusion of caste."

This disorder certainly leads
  to a place of torment
  for destroyers of the family
  and the family itself.
Indeed, the spirits of
  their ancestors fall,
  deprived of their ritual
  offerings of rice and water.   42

By these wrongdoings of
  the destroyers of the family,
  which produce disorder
  between the classes of society,
The dharmas of
  lineages are ruined,
  along with the eternal
  dharma of the family.²⁹   43

When the family dharma
  of human beings
  has been ruined,
  O Janārdana,
Dwelling in a place of torment
  certainly becomes their fate—
  so we have heard
  from sacred sources.   44

Ah yes!
  what great misfortune
  we are resolved to enact,
For which, out of greed
  for the happiness of royalty,
  we are prepared to slay
  our own people.   45

---

29 The dharmas of lineages: Translates *jāti-dharmāḥ*, meaning the "dharmas of the castes." The BG focuses, however, mostly on varṇa, or the four major classes of society.

If without my acting
    in opposition
    and without any
    weapons for myself,
The sons of Dhritarāshtra,
    with weapons in their hands,
    should slay me in battle—
    that would be
    a greater peace for me!   46

Thus speaking
    in the midst of conflict,
    Arjuna sat upon
    the seat of the chariot.
Casting aside
    his bow and arrow,
    his mind was
    tormented by sorrow.   47

2

The Way of Discernment

Sanjaya said:

To him who was thus
    overwhelmed by compassion,
    whose troubled eyes were
    full of tears,
Who was deeply depressed,
    Madhusūdana
    spoke these words.   1

The Beloved Lord said:

From where
    does your weakness
    come at this time of crisis?
It is not befitting
    the noble-minded,
    nor does it lead
    to celestial realms—
    it causes disgrace, O Arjuna.[1]   2

---

1 The Beloved Lord: Translates *bhagavān*
or *bhagavat,* the same word as in the title —
an epithet that refers to Krishna, which introduces Krishna's words throughout the text.

This is the first verse in which the words of
Krishna are introduced.

Do not yield to
　　this weakness, O Pārtha;
　　it is inappropriate for you.
Relinquishing this poor
　　faint-heartedness,
　　stand up,
　　O Scorcher of the Enemy!　　　　　　3

Arjuna said:

How shall I,
　　in battle against
　　Bhīshma and Drona,
　　O Madhusūdana,
Fight back with arrows
　　against those who
　　are worthy of respect,
　　O Slayer of the Enemy?　　　　　　4

Indeed, rather than slaying
　　greatly revered gurus,
It would be better
　　to subsist in this world
　　by begging for alms.
For slaying such gurus,
　　though they desire
　　selfish gain in this world,
Surely would taint
　　with their blood
　　any pleasures I might enjoy.²　　　　5

---

2 Desire: Translates the word *kāma*. "selfish" or "worldly" desire throughout
This word, simply, means "desire," but the BG.
most often carries the negative sense of

And we know not
    which of the two is better:
Whether we should conquer them
    or they should conquer us.
For having slain them
    we should not wish to live—
They who are standing here before us,
    the sons of Dhritarāshtra.³   6

My very being
    is afflicted by a piteous
    weakness of spirit.
My thoughts on dharma
    are completely bewildered.
I ask you, tell me what
    is definitely better for me!
I am your student—
    instruct me, for I have
    offered myself unto you.   7

Indeed, I cannot foresee
    what would dispel
This grief that is
    drying up my senses,
Even if achieving an unrivaled
    flourishing kingdom on earth,
Or the sovereignty
    of celestial beings.⁴   8

---

3 Up until this verse, Arjuna has been speaking in the first person singular; here Arjuna speaks in the first person plural, "we," referring to himself and the leading generals of his army.
4 Celestial beings: Translates the plural form of *sura*.

Sanjaya said:

Thus having spoken
   to Hrishīkesha,
   Gudākesha,
   the subduer of the enemy,
Said to Govinda,
   "I shall not fight!"
Having spoken thus,
   he fell silent.   9

Hrishīkesha,
   as if about to laugh,
   O Bhārata [Dhritarāshtra],
In the midst of the two armies,
   spoke these words to him
   who was feeling despondent.   10

The Beloved Lord said:

You have grieved for that
   which is not worthy of grief,
   and yet you speak words
   of profound knowledge.
The learned grieve
   neither for those
   who have passed on,
   nor for those
   who have not departed.⁵   11

---

5 Krishna's teachings commence with this   Profound knowledge: Translates *prajñā*,
verse.   often rendered as "wisdom."

Never, truly,
    have I ever not existed—
    nor you, nor these kings
    who protect the people,
And never
    shall any of us
    ever cease to be,
    now or forevermore.   12

Just as the embodied
    while in this body
    passes through childhood,
    youth, and old age,
So also the embodied
    attains another body—
    the wise person
    is not bewildered by this.   13

Certainly, contact
    of the senses with matter,
    O Kaunteya [Arjuna],
    which results in cold, heat,
    happiness, and suffering,
Comes and goes,
    and is impermanent—
    you must strive
    to tolerate this,
    O Bhārata [Arjuna].   14

Indeed, the person whom
    these do not trouble,
    O Best Among Persons,
The wise one for whom
    suffering and happiness
    are the same—
    that one is prepared
    for immortality.   15

Of the impermanent
   one finds no being;
   one finds no nonbeing
   of the permanent.
Indeed, the certainty
   of both of these
   has been perceived
   by seers of the truth.   16

Now, know that
   to be indestructible
   by which all this
   is pervaded.
No one is able
   to bring about
   the destruction
   of the everpresent.   17

These bodies,
   said to have an end,
   belong to the embodied,
   which is eternal,
Indestructible,
   and immeasurable—
   therefore fight,
   O Bhārata!   18

One who considers
   it [the self] a slayer,
   and one who thinks
   it is slain,
Both of these
   fail to understand—
   it does not slay,
   nor is it slain.   19

It does not take birth,
   nor does it ever die.
Such a being has never
   come into being,
   nor shall it ever
   come to be.
It is unborn, eternal,
   everlasting,
   and primeval.
It is not slain
   when the body is slain.[6]   20

One who knows this [self]
   to be indestructible,
   eternal, unborn,
   and everpresent—
How and whom does
   that person slay, O Pārtha?
And whom does
   that one cause to slay?   21

When abandoning
   worn-out garments
A person acquires
   different new ones;
So abandoning
   worn-out bodily frames,
The embodied comes
   together with other new ones.   22

---

6 This verse continues the chapter's theme on the self's eternal presence of being. The self has not come into existence at any time in the past nor does it have any end in the future (BG 2.12). If the self were not to exist at any time, then it would have no true being; and of the self's being there can be no nonexistence (BG 2.16). In the first quarter of this verse, the self does not take birth nor does it die. In the second quarter, it is a being (*bhūya*) that is eternally present, which has never come into being (*bhūtvā*) and shall never come into being (*bhavitā*). Although the noun "being," referring to the self (*bhūya*), can be taken as a verb or an adverb, the most compelling translation as a noun is dictated by its philosophical context found in the two previous aforementioned verses.

Weapons do not pierce it,
    fire does not burn it,
And water does not moisten it;
    nor does wind wither it.   23

It cannot be pierced;
    it cannot be burned,
    moistened, or
    even withered;
Eternal,
    present everywhere,
    stationary, immovable—
    it is everlasting.[7]   24

This [self] is unmanifest,
    it is inconceivable,
    it is spoken of
    as unchangeable.
Therefore,
    knowing this to be so,
    you should not grieve.   25

Further, if you think
    of this [self] as
    always being born
    or always dying—
Even then,
    O Mighty-Armed,
    you should not
    grieve for this.   26

---

7 Present everywhere: Translates *sarva-gataḥ*. This phrase can mean that the self is present everywhere in the body, or that selves permeate the whole universe. It can also refer to the Self, namely the divinity, who is present everywhere in the universe. Thus the BG's idea of self can indicate either the individual or the supreme self. The Sanskrit word *ātman* is translated as "self" to indicate the self of the living being, or "Self" to indicate the supreme divinity present within the very self of every living being (as first seen in BG 4.6). Many verses can be taken as speaking about both simultaneously.

Indeed, for one who is born
   death is certain,
   and for one who has died
   birth is certain.
Therefore, since this
   process is inevitable,
   you ought not to grieve.   27

Unmanifest are the beginnings
   of beings; manifest are
   their interims, O Bhārata;
Then again, unmanifest
   are their endings—
   what is lamentable about this?   28

Rarely, someone
   perceives this [self];
Rarely, another
   also speaks of it.
And rarely, indeed,
   another hears about it;
Even having heard about it,
   no one truly knows it.   29

The embodied,
   eternally indestructible,
   dwells within the body
   of everyone, O Bhārata.
Therefore you
   should not grieve
   for any living being.   30

Moreover, considering
  your own dharma,
  you should not waver.
Truly, for a warrior,
  nothing better exists
  than a battle fought
  according to dharma.   31

And if by good fortune
  what is gained
  is an opened door
  to the celestial world,
Happy are the warriors,
  O Pārtha,
  who obtain such a fight.   32

Now, if you should not
  undertake this battle,
  which is in accordance
  with dharma,
Then, abandoning
  your own dharma
  and reputation,
  you shall meet
  with misfortune.   33

Also, people certainly will speak
  of your undying infamy.
And for one who has been honored,
  such infamy is worse than death.   34

The great chariot warriors
   will believe you have retreated
   from battle out of fear.
And among those who once
   held you in high esteem,
   you shall come to be taken lightly.   35

And many unspeakable words
   your enemies
   will speak of you,
Deriding your ability—
   now what could be
   greater misery than this?   36

Either having been slain
   you shall reach the celestial world,
   or conquering
   you shall enjoy the earth.
Therefore, rise up,
   O Kaunteya,
   acting with firm
   resolve for battle.   37

Acting the same in
   happiness and suffering,
   gain and loss,
   victory and defeat,
Then prepare for battle—
   thus you shall not
   suffer misfortune.   38

This discernment
    has been explained to you
    in [the philosophy of] Sānkhya;
    now hear about this
    in [the practice of] yoga.
Be absorbed in yoga
    with discernment, O Pārtha,
    by which you shall throw off
    the bondage of action.[8]   39

Here there is no loss of effort,
    nor is any diminution found.
Even a little of this dharma
    delivers one from great danger.   40

Discernment that is resolute in nature
    is singular in this world,
    O Descendant of Kuru [Arjuna],
For many-branched and endless
    is the discernment
    of those who are irresolute.   41

---

8 Discernment: Translates *buddhi,* an important word that appears fifty-three times in the text. The word can have the meanings of "intelligence," "wisdom," "insight," or "understanding." *Discernment* is used here because it gives the active sense engaged in the BG.

Sānkhya: This term refers to the theistic system of Sānkhya, which shares much of its philosophy with the nontheistic Sānkhya school, focusing on the ultimate elements and objects of this world. It is one of six primary philosophical systems, including Yoga, Mīmāmsā, Vedānta, Nyāya, and Vaisheshika.

Yoga: Refers to the process that connects the individual self to the supreme Self. It is a complex term that can either refer to any one of the various means for achieving union with the divine or any one of the various perfectional states achievable in union with the divine. This is the first appearance of this word in the BG. It appears seventy-eight times in its noun form.

Absorbed in yoga: Translates *yukta,* the verbal form of the well-known word *yoga,* which has the essential meaning of "connection" or "union," referring to the connection of the self to the Supreme. This word appears thirty-six times in the BG. I have consistently translated it as "absorbed in yoga."

Those who lack understanding
  speak this flowery language,
Delighted by the words
  of the Vedas, O Pārtha,
  declaring, "There is nothing else."⁹   42

For the self full of desire,
  whose intent is on
  the celestial world,
  [this flowery language]
  bestows another birth
  as the fruit of action.
Preoccupied with
  various ritualistic acts,
  [this self] is directed
  toward the goal of worldly
  pleasure and power.   43

For those attached to
  worldly pleasure and power,
  whose thoughts are stolen
  away by this [flowery language],
Discernment that
  is resolute in nature
  is not discovered
  in perfect meditation.¹⁰   44

---

9 The Vedas: The original sacred writings of
India, consisting of numerous Sanskrit hymns
that were originally transmitted orally by
priestly families, and then later preserved in
written form.
10 Perfect meditation: Translates *samādhi*,
the attainment of total absorption in which
the meditator becomes self-forgetful and is
only aware of the object of meditation. This
perfect meditative state in yoga is the eighth
"limb" in the Ashtānga Yoga system as
described by Patanjali.

The domain of the Vedas
  is the three essential 'qualities';
  be free of these three
  'qualities', O Arjuna,
Beyond duality,
  always established
  in pure existence, beyond
  acquisitions and security,
  in possession of one's self.[11]   45

As much value
  as there is in a well
  when all about it
  waters flow abundantly,
Such is the value
  of all the Vedas
  for a Brahmin who
  has realized knowledge.[12]   46

It is in action alone
  that you have a claim,
  never at any time to
  the fruits of such action.
Never let the fruits of action
  be your motive;
  never let your attachment
  be to inaction.   47

---

11 Three 'qualities': Translates *traigunya*. The word *guṇa*, or 'quality', can also mean "strand" or "string" or "rope," expressing how these primary qualities arising from primordial nature bind one like a rope. It is a technical term used in Sānkhya philosophy that is a recurring theme in the BG.

12 Brahmin: The priestly or learned class of society, one of four *varṇas* that make the social order whole and complete. Note that this word is not to be confused with Brahman, meaning the ultimate reality or supreme spirit.

Established in yoga,
   perform actions,
   having relinquished attachment,
   O Conqueror of Wealth [Arjuna],
While remaining the same
   in success and in no success—
   such sameness is said to be yoga.   48

Still, action is by far inferior
   to the yoga of discernment,
   O Conqueror of Wealth.
Seek shelter in discernment—
   miserly are those
   who are motivated
   by the fruits [of action].   49

One absorbed in
   the yoga of discernment
   casts off in this world
   both good and bad acts.
Therefore,
   be absorbed in yoga,
   for yoga is skillfulness
   in action.   50

Indeed, those wise ones
   who are absorbed
   in the yoga of discernment,
   relinquishing the fruits
   born of action,
Who are freed
   from the bondage
   of repeated births,
   go to a place beyond suffering.   51

When your discernment
    crosses beyond the jungle
    of bewilderment,
Then you shall become
    completely indifferent
    to that which is to be heard
    and that which has been heard.[13]   52

When this [discernment]
    is no longer perplexed
    by the heard scriptures,
    when it shall remain
    without change,
When discernment
    is unchanging within
    perfect meditation—
    then you shall attain yoga.   53

Arjuna said:

What is the description
    of one established
    in profound knowledge,
    who is established
    in perfect meditation,
    O Keshava?
How would
    one established
    in thought speak?
How would one sit?
How would one move about?   54

---

13 That which has been heard: Refers to *śruti*, the Vedas. Another term for the Vedas found in the BG is *śabda-brahma*, "the sound of Brahman." The Vedas offer worldly results, but superficial reading of this text is discouraged in the BG; Krishna encourages a more esoteric reading that reveals himself: "And by all the Vedas only I am to be known" (BG 15.15).

The Beloved Lord said:

When a person gives up
   all selfish desires
   arising from the mind,
   O Pārtha,
Satisfied within the self
   by the self alone,
   then that person
   is said to be established
   in profound knowledge.   55

One whose mind is
   undisturbed in suffering,
   who is free from desire
   in all kinds of happiness,
Whose passion, fear,
   and anger have departed—
   such a person,
   established in thought,
   is said to be a sage.   56

One who, everywhere,
   is without sentimentality
   upon encountering this or that,
   things pleasant or unpleasant,
Who neither rejoices nor despises—
   the profound knowledge
   of such a person
   is firmly established.   57

And when one withdraws
   completely,
   as a tortoise
   all of its limbs,
The senses from
   their sense objects—
   the profound knowledge
   of such a person
   is firmly established.   58

Sense objects fade away
     for the embodied who
     does not partake of them,
Except for the taste—
     for one who has
     seen the Supreme,
     even this taste fades.   59

Indeed, even for one
     who is striving,
     O Kaunteya,
     for the person
     of discrimination,
The impetuous senses
     forcibly carry away
     the mind.   60

Restraining all these [senses],
     one should be seated
     while absorbed in yoga,
     wholly intent on me.
For one whose senses
     are under control—
     for that one,
     profound knowledge
     is firmly established.[14]   61

For a person dwelling
     on the objects of the senses,
     attachment to them develops;
From attachment,
     selfish desire develops;
     from desire, anger develops.   62

---

14 This is the first verse in which Krishna   him, with the words *mat-paraḥ*, "wholly
introduces the practice of meditation on   intent on me."

From anger comes
    bewilderment;
    from bewilderment,
    disturbed memory;
From disturbed memory,
    loss of discernment;
    from loss of discernment
    one becomes lost.   63

Without being absorbed
    in attraction and repulsion
    as the senses are moving
    toward their objects—
With self-restraint,
    the self that
    can be governed
    attains calmness.   64

In calmness,
    the cessation of all
    one's suffering occurs.
Indeed, for one whose
    thought has been calmed,
    discernment is quickly established.   65

There is no discernment for one
    who is not absorbed in yoga;
    and for one not absorbed in yoga,
    there is no meditative state;
And for one who has
    no meditative state,
    there is no peace—
    for one who is not peaceful,
    from where is happiness to come?   66

Indeed, when the mind
　　is being pulled
　　by the roaming senses,
Then just one of them
　　can carry away one's
　　profound knowledge,
　　as wind does a ship at sea.　　　　　67

Therefore,
　　O Mighty-Armed,
　　whosoever has
　　completely withdrawn
The senses from
　　the objects of the senses—
　　the profound knowledge of
　　such a person is firmly established.　　68

During that which is night
　　for all beings,
　　the deeply meditative
　　person is awake.
During that time in which
　　beings are awake,
　　that is night for
　　the insightful sage.[15]　　　　　69

---

15 The deeply meditative person: Translates the word *saṁyamī,* meaning a person absorbed in the yoga processes of *saṁyama.* The term *saṁyama* refers to the final three "limbs of yoga" in the Patanjali Yoga Sūtra: *dhāraṇa* ("concentration"), *dhyāna* ("meditation"), and *samādhi* ("total absorption in perfect meditation"). See Yoga Sūtra 3.4.

Continually being filled,
    the ocean remains
    unmoved;
It stands still,
    though waters
    enter into it.
That person into whom
    all desires enter
    in this same way
    attains peace—
Not the one
    who is desirous
    of fulfilling such desires.   70

Abandoning all selfish desires,
    a person moves through life
    free from worldly longings,
Without the sense of 'mine',
    without the notion
    of 'I am acting'—
    that one attains peace.[16]   71

---

16 Without the sense of 'mine': Translates *nirmama,* meaning literally, "without mine." This term conveys a state of being that is without the false sense of possessiveness. Because of the temporary nature of things in this world, no one actually possesses anything permanently, yet one holds on to such a conception.

    Without the notion of 'I am acting': Translates *nirahamkāra,* meaning literally, "without I am acting." The phrase "I am acting" connotes egocenteredness; an essential message of the BG is the need for the self to develop a vision of theocenteredness, one centered upon the divinity, implied by the phrase "without the notion of 'I am acting'." The term "I am acting" (*ahamkāra*) conveys the idea that a person falsely thinks oneself to be acting independently of the various physical, cosmic, and spiritual aspects of "action,"

explained in later verses. It conveys the false confidence of mistaken identity, wherein one feels oneself to be in complete control, falsely identified with the body and the impermanent roles one assumes in this world. In a realized state, a person "without the notion of 'I am acting' " (*nirahamkāra*) no longer identifies with anything temporary, including one's body, gender, family, country, race, etc., nor does one claim ownership or possession of anything (*nirmama*).

    The added single quotation marks for "mine" and for "I am acting" are meant to distinguish this type of translated word or phrase from those containing double quotation marks, assigned because they are indicated in the text itself.

This is the state of
the feminine energy
of Brahman, O Pārtha,
having attained which
one is not bewildered.
Being established in this,
even if only at
the end of one's life,
one reaches
the Nirvāna of Brahman.[17]   72

---

[17] The feminine energy of Brahman: Translates the word *brāhmī*. Quite literally, it is the *śakti,* or "female energy," of Brahman. This word is most often taken as a neutered adjective in this verse, meaning simply a Brahman-like state. However, this latter approach ignores the strong feminine presence in the verse, expressed by three feminine gendered words: a pronoun (*eṣā*), and two nouns (*brāhmī* and *sthiti*), all found in the first quarter line. Note that the key words of this chapter, namely *buddhi,* "discernment," and *prajñā,* "profound knowledge," are also feminine gendered. Thus this chapter concludes that the state of Brahman's feminine energy supports the nature of the discernment and the profound knowledge of the self.

Nirvāna: Literally, "blown out," meaning "the extinguishing of any worldly existence or experience whatsoever," a spiritual state found within the Brahman that entails a complete calming of the senses, often described as a state of serenity and peacefulness.

Brahman: Supreme spiritual existence, the eternal ultimate reality or the whole of reality. This word is to be distinguished from the words Brahmin and Brahmā. A Brahmin is a person of the priestly or educator class belonging to traditional Indian society, and its first instance is in BG 2.46. Brahmā is the cosmic deity of creation (see BG 8.16), whose counterpart is Shiva, the deity of cosmic transformation or dissolution.

3

The Way of Action

Arjuna said:

If you consider discernment
  to be better than action,
  O Janārdana,
Then why do you engage me
  in dreadful action,
  O Keshava?   1

With very confusing words,
  you seem to bewilder
  my intellect.
Therefore, speak definitely
  of that one thing by which
  I may attain the greater good.   2

The Beloved Lord said:

In this world
  the established path is twofold,
  as stated previously by me,
  O Blameless One:
The yoga of knowledge
  for the followers of Sānkhya,
  and the yoga of action
  for the yogis.[1]   3

---

1 Yogis: Plural of *yogi*, meaning a practitioner of yoga. The word appears twenty-eight
times in the BG, and is also in the English
lexicon.

Not by avoiding actions
   does a person gain
   freedom from action,
And not by renunciation
   alone does one
   attain perfection.   4

Certainly no one,
   not even for a moment,
   ever lives without
   performing action.
Indeed, against one's will,
   everyone is forced
   to perform action
   by the 'qualities' born
   of primordial nature.²   5

Having controlled
   the senses of action,
   one who continues
   with the mind to dwell
On the objects of the senses—
   that one,
   whose self is bewildered,
   is called one with false behavior.   6

---

2 The 'qualities': Translates the plural form of *guṇa*, which is translated by this word throughout this translation. The plural of *guṇa* refers to the three primary qualities of nature, *sattva, rajas,* and *tamas,* which are first presented in BG 7.12. In general, these fundamental distinctions describe degrees of self-centeredness and conditions of the heart: self-giving, selfish, self-destructive; or capacities of the soul to illumine the worldly condition: transparency, translucency, opacity; or levels of consciousness: conscious, subconscious, unconscious. The Gītā's teachings on the essential qualities encourage the soul to attain its original state beyond these qualities, a state of pure *sattva,* to establish a relation- ship with transcendence and the divine in a state of selflessness, pure transparency, or super-consciousness, respectively.

   Primordial nature: Translates the word *prakṛti,* referring to the original source of the physical world or the world of matter, from which the essential qualities arise. The word can mean more generally the original nature of something, and is also applied in some verses below to the divinity himself. The word in Sanskrit is of feminine gender, and the BG presents *prakṛti* as part of the divine feminine energy that complements the ultimate *puruṣa,* or the supreme masculine divinity, Krishna.

But one who,
    with the mind
    controlling the senses,
    O Arjuna, engages in
The yoga of action
    with the senses of action,
    remaining unattached—
    that person is superior.   7

Perform your prescribed actions,
    for action is certainly better
    than inaction.
And even the subsistence
    of one's body cannot be
    accomplished without action.   8

Other than action
    that has sacrifice
    as its purpose,
    action is bondage
    in this world.
Perform action
    for this purpose,
    O Kaunteya,
    free from attachment.   9

Having previously sent forth
    created beings
    along with sacrifice,
    the Lord of Created Beings said:
May you flourish
    by this [sacrifice]!
    Let this be the sacred cow
    that fulfills your desires.[3]   10

---

3 The sacred cow that fulfills your desires: *kāmadhuk*, "sacred cow," in verse 10.28.
Translates *iṣṭa-kāmadhuk*. See the word

With this [sacrifice] give
   pleasure to the divinities;
   may those divinities
   please you.
By pleasing one another,
   you shall attain
   the greatest good.[4]   11

Indeed, the divinities,
   satisfied by sacrifice,
   will give you desired pleasures.
Without giving back to them,
   one who enjoys these gifts
   is only a thief.   12

Virtuous persons
   who eat the remnants
   of sacrifice are
   freed from all faults,
Whereas wretched persons
   only ingest suffering
   when they cook
   for their selfish motives.   13

---

4 Divinities: Translates the plural of *deva*. Divinities are not beings with eternal functions, as is the supreme Divinity. Rather, they are superior beings, functioning under the supreme Divinity, Krishna. They are beings who preside over the natural elements, divine only in the sense that they function on behalf of the divine.

From foodstuffs
 beings come into being;
 from rain
 foodstuffs manifest;
From sacrifice
 rain comes into being;
 sacrifice arises
 from action.   14

Understand that action arises
 from Brahman, the Vedas;
 this Brahman arises originally
 from the Imperishable.
Therefore eternal Brahman,
 which pervades everything,
 is established in sacrifice.[5] 15

Thus the [sacrificial] cycle
 has been set into motion;
 one who does not
 keep it turning in this world,
Whose life is impure,
 who delights in the senses—
 such a person lives in vain,
 O Pārtha.   16

However, the human being
 who delights
 only in the self,
 who is self-satisfied
And finds full contentment
 in the self alone—
 for that person
 there is nothing to be enacted. 17

---

5 The Imperishable: Translates *akṣara*, the most prominent utterance in mantras.
which can also mean the sacred syllable "OM,"

Surely, such a person
   has no [selfish] motives,
   either in acting
   or in not acting
   in this world.
And nor has such a person,
   in relation to all beings,
   any need whatsoever
   for [selfish] motives.   18

Therefore, without attachment,
   constantly perform action
   that is to be enacted.
Indeed, by performing action
   without attachment,
   a person attains the Supreme.   19

For by action alone,
   King Janaka and others
   attained full perfection.
Even if only considering
   the welfare of the world,
   you are obliged to act.[6]   20

Whatever the greatest one does,
   that very thing
   other persons will do.
Whatever standard
   the greatest one enacts,
   that the world follows.   21

---

6 King Janaka: Known to have attained perfection by his actions as a king. He is the father of Sītā, the queen consort of the divine manifestation of Vishnu as Rāma.

For me, O Pārtha,
   there is nothing
   whatsoever to be enacted
   in the three worlds,
Nor is there anything
   not attained that is
   to be attained—
   even so, I engage in action.   22

Indeed, if ever I should not
   engage in action untiringly,
Human beings everywhere
   would follow my path, O Pārtha.   23

These worlds would perish
   if I should not perform action,
And I would be the cause of chaos—
   I would destroy these procreated
     beings.   24

As the ignorant act,
   attached to action,
   O Bhārata,
So the wise should act
   without attachment,
   desiring to act for
   the welfare of the world.   25

One should not cause
confusion in the discernment
of those attached to action,
who are without knowledge.
One should leave them
to pursue all actions—
one who is thus wise,
performing all actions
while fully absorbed in yoga.   26

Actions are being carried out
in every instance
by the 'qualities'
of primordial nature.
The self, bewildered by
the notion of 'I am acting',
thinks, "the creator of action am I."[7] 27

However, O Mighty-Armed,
one who knows the truth
about the distribution
of the 'qualities'
and their actions,
Being mindful that
"the 'qualities'
are operating on
those very 'qualities'"—
that one is not attached.[8]   28

---

7 The creator of action: Translates *kartā*,
which can mean "the doer," "the agent of
action," or literally, "the one who acts." The
word can also refer to cosmogenesis: "the creator of the universe." The sense here is that
the soul depends upon much beyond itself,
such as the workings of the essential qualities
of nature, in order to act in the world, and
ego-centeredness prevents the soul from
knowing this, giving it a false sense of power.

8 Distribution of . . . actions: Refers to the
types of social obligations in the *varṇas*.
Distribution of the essential qualities: As
they are found in numerous permutations and
combinations, and the ways they affect souls
in determining their *varṇas*.
See BG 4.13, which also contains the
phrase *guṇa-karma-vibhāgaśaḥ*.

Those deluded
  by the 'qualities'
  of primordial nature
  are attached to the actions
  of those 'qualities'.
One whose knowledge
  is complete should not
  disturb those who are dull,
  whose knowledge is incomplete.   29

Renouncing all actions in me,
  with one's thought on
  the 'principle of self',
Without longings,
  without a sense of 'mine'—
  fight, with grief cast off.[9]   30

Those persons who
  constantly follow
  my teaching,
Who are full of faith
  and envy no one,
  also are freed from
  [the effects of] action.   31

However, those who are
  envious of my teaching,
  who do not follow it,
Bewildered by all knowledge—
  know them to be lost
  and thoughtless.   32

---

9 Following BG 2.61, this is the next instance
that introduces the ultimate message of the
BG, with the words "renouncing all actions
in me." These two verses anticipate the
beginning of chapter 4, in which Krishna
boldly declares his secret of divine love and
his identity as the Divinity.

The 'principle of self': Translates
adhyātmā, which is introduced more thor-
oughly beginning in BG 7.29.

One acts according
    to one's own nature,
    even a person of knowledge,
For beings
    follow their nature—
    what shall repression accomplish?   33

For any one of the senses,
    upon the object of that sense,
    both attraction and
    aversion are placed.
One should not come
    under the control
    of either of these, for
    indeed they block one's path.   34

Better is one's own dharma
    even if imperfect
    than another's dharma
    followed perfectly.
Better is death in following
    one's own dharma,
    for another's dharma
    brings danger.[10]   35

Arjuna said:

By what, then, is a person
    compelled to behave
    in unfortunate ways,
Even against one's will,
    O Vārshneya [Krishna],
    as if driven by force?   36

---

10 Better is one's own dharma...: The first
half of this verse is repeated as the first half
of BG 18.47.

Dharma: The word is used here more generally, carrying over the sense of "path" from
the last word of the previous verse.

The Beloved Lord said:

It is selfish desire,
   it is anger, arising from
   the 'quality' of *rajas*.
All-consuming and
   greatly calamitous,
   know it to be
   the enemy in this world.   37

As fire is covered by smoke
   and a mirror by dust,
As an embryo is covered by a womb,
   so this world is covered by this.   38

The knowledge of the knower
   is obscured by
   this constant enemy
In the form of selfish desire,
   O Kaunteya,
   a fire that indeed
   is impossible to satisfy.   39

The senses, the mind,
   and the faculty of
   discernment
   are said to be
   the resting place
   of this [enemy];
Through these
   it bewilders
   the embodied,
   obscuring knowledge.   40

Therefore, first having
    controlled the senses,
    O Leader of the Bharatas,
You must strike down this vice
    that destroys knowledge
    and realized knowledge.   41

The senses are beyond
    [matter], they say;
    beyond the senses
    is the mind;
Still beyond the mind is
    the faculty of discernment—
    yet that which is beyond all else,
    above the faculty of discernment,
    is indeed this [self].   42

Thus having discerned what
    is higher than the faculty
    of discernment,
    sustaining the self
    by the self,
Destroy the enemy,
    O Mighty-Armed,
    in the form
    of selfish desire,
    so difficult to overcome.   43

4

The Way of Knowledge

The Beloved Lord said:

Unto Vivisvān
  I have spoken this yoga,
  which is everlasting.
Vivisvān spoke it to Manu,
  and Manu imparted it
  to Ikshvāku.[1]   I

Thus received through
  a line of succession,
  the royal seers
  understood it.
By the powerful effect
  of time, this yoga was lost
  [to this lineage] in the world,
  O Subduer of the Enemy.   2

1 Vivisvān: The presiding deity of the sun.
  Manu: The name means "man," referring
to the first progenitor of humankind; the son
of Vivisvān.

Ikshvāku: The name of an ancient king of
eastern India; son of Manu.

This same ancient yoga
is now spoken
by me to you:
"Having offered your love,
you have also
become my friend"—
truly, this is the ultimate secret.[2]   3

Arjuna said:

Your birth
came later,
Vivisvān's birth earlier.
How then should I
understand this—
that you, in the beginning,
"have spoken"?[3]   4

The Beloved Lord said:

Through many births
have I passed,
as have you, O Arjuna.
I know all of them—
you know them not,
O Subduer of the Enemy.   5

---

2 Having offered your love: Translates *bhakta*: "devoted," "lovingly devoted," or simply "one who is devoted [to the Lord]," or "a devotee." The word can also mean "one who is loved [by the Lord]." Thus it is a verb that can also act as a noun. This is the first of fifteen instances. The first appearance of the noun form *bhakti* is found in BG 7.17 and it appears fourteen times in the text.

Friend: Translates the word *sakhā*. Krishna states that Arjuna has offered his heart to him, and that he also loves Arjuna as a friend.

3 "Have spoken": Arjuna is quoting Krishna's precise words from verse 1 of this chapter: "Unto Vivisvān I *have spoken* . . ."

As the one without birth,
    the everpresent Self,
    as the supreme
    Lord of beings
Presiding over
    my own nature,
    I become fully
    manifest by Māyā,
    the very power of my Self.[4]   6

Indeed, whenever there is
    a decline of dharma,
    O Bhārata,
And an emerging
    of what opposes dharma—
    at that time I send forth my Self.   7

For protection of the virtuous
    and for destruction of evil acts,
For the purpose of establishing dharma,
    I become fully manifest age after age.[5]   8

One who thus truly knows
    the birth and acts
    of my divine being,
Upon relinquishing the body,
    does not come to another birth—
    such a person comes to me,
    O Arjuna.   9

---

4 Māyā, the very power of my Self: Translates *ātma-māya*. Māyā is the supreme feminine power of Krishna by which he reveals himself to souls, as expressed in this verse, or conceals himself from souls who are not yet ready to know him (see BG 7.14–15). Māyā is Krishna's divine illusive power, which either bewilders souls to facilitate their forgetfulness of divinity or facilitates the revelation of the intimate form of divinity. In BG 18.61, Māyā is the force that facilitates the movement of all beings while in their bodies.

My own nature: Translates *prakṛtim svām*. Here, *prakṛti* refers to the nature of divinity, which is feminine, and in this instance, could include primordial nature as well.

5 Age: Translates the word *yuga*. A *yuga* is a vast period of time, stretching over part of the cosmic cycle.

Freed from passion,
    fear, and anger;
    immersed in me,
    taking full refuge in me,
Many, purified by
    the austerity of knowledge,
    have come to my
    loving state of being.   10

In the way they offer
    themselves to me,
    in just that way
    I offer my love
    to them reciprocally.
Human beings
    follow my path
    universally,
    O Pārtha.   11

Desiring success
    from their actions,
    persons here on earth
    offer sacrifice to deities.
For in the world of humans,
    quickly comes success
    that is born of
    [sacrificial] action.⁶   12

---

6 Deities: Translates the plural form of *devatā*, meaning "deity," while *deva* is translated throughout as "divinity." Krishna is *the* divinity in the singular, and when the plural of the word is used, it refers to those Vedic deities or divinities, superior entities, who preside over the natural phenomena of this world. This word appears in the plural in two other places, BG 7.20 and BG 9.23.

The four social orders
   are sent forth by me,
   with divisions based on
   'qualities' and actions.
Of this know me
   as the creator, yet
   also as the non-creator,
   who is everpresent.   13

Actions do not taint me,
   nor do I aspire
   to the fruit of actions.
One who understands me
   in this way is never
   bound by actions.   14

Having known this,
   the ancient seekers
   of liberation also
   performed action.
Indeed, perform action
   as the ancient ones
   enacted previously,
   in ancient times.   15

"What is action?
   What is inaction?"—
   even the wise are
   perplexed by this subject.
I shall describe
   action to you,
   knowing which
   you shall be freed
   from misfortune.   16

Indeed, the nature of action
    is to be discerned;
    the nature of unfit action
    is to be discerned;
And the nature of inaction
    is to be discerned—
    the ways of action
    are profound.   17

One who can perceive
    inaction within action,
    and action within inaction—
That one among human beings
    possesses discernment,
    is absorbed in yoga,
    and performs all action.   18

One whose every
    endeavor is without
    the intention of
    selfish desire,
Whose actions
    have been consumed
    by the fire of knowledge—
    those of discernment
    call that person learned.   19

Relinquishing attachment
   to the fruits of action,
   always satisfied and
   without dependence
Even while
   engaged in action—
   indeed, one does not
   enact anything whatsoever.   20

Without desire, with self
   and thought restrained,
   having relinquished
   all possessiveness;
Acting only for maintaining
   the activities of the body,
   one incurs no fault.   21

Satisfied with gain
   that comes spontaneously,
   crossing beyond duality,
   free from envy,
The same in success and
   in the absence of success—
   even though acting,
   such a person is not bound.   22

Freed from attachment,
   liberated, with thought
   established in knowledge,
Acting for the sake of sacrifice—
   for such a person,
   action is completely dissolved.   23

Brahman is the ritual instrument;
Brahman is the offering,
which is poured by Brahman
into the fire of Brahman.
Brahman alone
is to be attained by one
who is in perfect meditation
on the actions of Brahman.[7]   24

Indeed, some yogis
worship the divinities
through sacrifice.
Into the fire of Brahman,
through sacrifice itself,
others make sacrificial offerings.   25

Others offer the senses,
those of hearing and the rest,
into the fires of perfect discipline.
While others offer
the objects of the senses,
sound and so forth,
into the fires of the senses.[8]   26

Still others offer the actions
of all the senses and
actions of the life-breath
Into the fire of yoga,
the perfect discipline of self
kindled by knowledge.   27

---

7 Five components of the Vedic sacrifice are presented here: the ritual instrument or ladle, the butter offering, the pouring, the fire, and perfect meditation. These components represent essential elements of religious principles and are found in the next nine verses, through BG 4.33. To understand these principles, Krishna states that one should consult a seer of the truth (BG 4.34).

Perfect meditation: Translates *samādhi*. The state of one who is "completely absorbed" in the object of meditation; sometimes translated simply as "trance." The eighth and last limb of Patanjali's "eight limbs" of yoga in the Yoga Sūtra (2.29).
8 Perfect discipline: Translates the word *saṁyama*. This word first appears in BG 2.69, translated as "the deeply meditative person."

Those whose sacrifice
   is of material possessions,
   those whose sacrifice
   is of austerity,
   also those whose sacrifice
   is of yoga,
And those whose sacrifice
   is of knowledge in
   the study of scripture—
   such persons are
   striving ascetics who
   observe strict vows.   28

Still others offer
   the incoming breath
   into the outgoing breath,
   likewise, the outgoing breath
   into the incoming breath.
Having restrained
   the movements of incoming
   and outgoing breaths,
   they are wholly focused upon
   control of the life-breath.   29

And others,
   who have restricted
   their intake of food,
   offer the life-breath
   into the life-breath.
Indeed, all of these
   are knowers of sacrifice,
   cleansed of their impurities
   through sacrifice.   30

Those who enjoy
   the immortal nature
   of the remnants of sacrifice
   go to the eternal Brahman.
Even this world is not meant
   for one without sacrifice—
   how then the next,
   O Best of the Kurus?   31

Thus, sacrifices of many types
   have been prepared for
   the mouth of Brahman.
Know them all
   to be born of action—
   understanding this,
   you shall be liberated.⁹   32

Better than the sacrifice
   of material objects
   is the sacrifice of knowledge,
   O Chastiser of the Enemy.
All [sacrificial] actions,
   without exception,
   O Son of Pritha,
   culminate in knowledge.   33

Learn this
   by humble submission,
   by thorough inquiry,
   and by serving.
They will impart
   this knowledge to you,
   for they are knowers
   and seers of the truth.¹⁰   34

---

9 The mouth of Brahman: Refers to the cen-   10 Knowledge: Refers to the knowledge of
tral arena of the Vedic fire sacrifice.   the Vedas and derivative scriptures.

Knowing which,
    you shall thus never
    again fall into illusion,
    O Pāndava.
By this you shall see,
    without exception,
    all beings within the Self,
    then within me.   35

Even if, among unfortunate persons,
    you are one who performs
    the most unfortunate acts—
By the boat of knowledge,
    you shall indeed
    cross over all affliction.   36

As firewood is
    transformed into ashes
    by a blazing fire, O Arjuna,
So all actions are
    transformed into ashes
    by the fire of knowledge.   37

There is no means of purification
    found in this world
    that is equal to knowledge.
In time, one perfected
    in yoga personally finds
    that [knowledge] within the self.   38

One who is full of faith
    obtains knowledge,
    being devoted to that
    with the senses
    perfectly controlled.
Obtaining this knowledge,
    one achieves
    supreme peace
    without delay.   39

Not knowing,
  and lacking faith,
  the self who is full
  of doubt is destroyed.
Neither this world,
  nor the higher one,
  nor happiness exists
  for the doubting self.   40

For one who has fully
  renounced action in yoga,
  whose doubt is completely
  severed by knowledge,
Who is in possession
  of one's self—
  action does not bind,
  O Conqueror of Wealth.   41

Therefore, that doubt
  which is produced from
  the absence of knowledge
  and resides within the heart—
Having severed this
  with the sword of knowledge
  belonging to the self,
  rise in yoga!
  Rise up, O Bhārata!   42

5

The Way of Renunciation

Arjuna said:

You commend renunciation
   of actions, O Krishna,
   and also yoga.
Tell me which one
   of these two
   is definitely better.   1

The Beloved Lord said:

Renunciation
   and the yoga of action
   both lead to ultimate happiness.
Of the two, however,
   the yoga of action is superior
   to the renunciation of action.   2

One is to be known
   as a steadfast renouncer
   who neither hates
   nor desires.
Indeed, such a person,
   who is without duality,
   O Mighty-Armed,
   is easily freed
   from bondage [of action].   3

Sānkhya and yoga are
    completely separate paths,
    so the childish declare,
    though not the learned.
For perfectly following
    even one [of these],
    one achieves the fruit of both.   4

That stance attained by
    the followers of Sānkhya
    is also reached by
    the followers of yoga.
Sānkhya and yoga
    are thus one—
    one who sees this,
    that one truly sees.   5

However, renunciation,
    O Mighty-Armed,
    is difficult to attain
    without yoga.
The sage absorbed
    in the yoga of yogas
    reaches Brahman
    without delay.   6

One absorbed in yoga
   through yoga practice,
   with the self purified;
   whose self is controlled
   with senses conquered;
Whose self becomes
   connected to
   the self in all beings—
   that one is not tainted
   even while acting.[1]   7

"Never do I act alone"—
   one absorbed in yoga,
   who knows reality,
   is thus mindful.
While seeing,
   hearing, touching,
   smelling, eating, walking,
   sleeping, breathing;   8

While talking, eliminating,
   grasping, even opening
   and closing one's eyes,
One is convinced that,
   "The senses are engaged
   by their sense objects."   9

---

1 Whose self becomes connected to the self of all beings: Consistent with the teachings of the BG as a whole, the self "becomes" (*bhūta*) the self of others empathetically, not ontologically. This statement expresses the BG's version of the "golden rule."

Offering one's actions
　　to Brahman,
　　having relinquished
　　attachment—
For one who thus acts,
　　misfortune does not cling,
　　as water does not cling
　　to the leaf of a lotus.　　　　　　IO

With the body, with the mind,
　　with one's discernment,
　　even with the senses alone—
Yogis enact [all] action,
　　relinquishing attachment
　　for purity of the self.　　　　　　II

One who is absorbed in yoga,
　　having relinquished
　　the fruit of action,
　　attains lasting peace.
One who is not absorbed in yoga,
　　who is attached to the fruit,
　　is bound by action arising
　　from selfish desire.　　　　　　I2

Renouncing all actions
　　within the mind,
　　the master sits happily
As the embodied
　　in the city of nine gates,
　　neither acting nor causing to act.²　　I3

---

2 The city: Refers to the body.
　Nine gates: The nine "gates" consist of the nine bodily passages of generation and evacuation, passages of seeing (the eyes), passages of hearing (the ears), passages of breathing (the nostrils), and the passage of ingestion and speaking (the mouth).

Neither the means of action
　　nor the actions of
　　those in the world
　　does the master create,
Nor the conjunction
　　of actions with their fruits;
　　rather, one's state of being
　　is set forth into motion.³   14

The Omnipresent
　　certainly does not
　　assume anyone's misdeeds
　　or virtuous deeds.
Knowledge is covered by
　　the absence of knowledge,
　　by which living beings
　　are bewildered.   15

But for those in whom
　　this absence of knowledge
　　of the self is destroyed
　　by knowledge—
For them, knowledge,
　　like the sun,
　　causes illumination,
　　as does the Supreme.   16

---

3 The master: Translates the subject noun *prabhu*, which refers to the self within the "city of nine gates," or to the supreme "master." In the following verse, translating the related word *vibhu* (note the verbal stem *bhū* in *prabhu* and *vibhu*, taken here to mean "present"), the subject noun is "the Omnipresent." Here, too, it could be the soul who is "omnipresent" in the body, or it could refer to the supreme Lord, who is omnipresent in all bodies and in everything.

Those whose discernment
  is focused on that [Supreme],
  whose self is absorbed in that,
  whose foundation is that,
  wholly devoted to that—
Such persons proceed
  to that from which
  there is no return,
  their misdeeds shaken off
  by knowledge.[4]   17

In a Brahmin endowed with
  learning and gentle conduct,
  in a cow, in an elephant,
Even in a dog and
  in one who cooks dog—
  wise ones see the same [Supreme].   18

Even here in this world,
  creation has been conquered
  by those whose minds
  are established in sameness.
Indeed, Brahman is flawless
  and [forever] the same;
  therefore they are
  established in Brahman.[5]   19

---

4 That from which there is no return: This is
considered to be a positive statement. When
one has reached the very highest heaven,
where there is no birth and death, one does
not have to return to the lower regions of
birth and death, such as this world.

5 Creation: Translates *sarga*. The part of
creation that is overcome includes birth and
death.

Such a person would neither
    rejoice upon attaining
    what is pleasing,
    nor be shaken upon
    attaining what is not pleasing.
With steady discernment,
    without being bewildered,
    the knower of Brahman
    is established in Brahman.   20

The self who is not attached
    to external contacts,
    who finds happiness
    within the self—
That one, whose self
    is absorbed in the yoga
    of yogas within Brahman,
    attains imperishable happiness.   21

Certainly, pleasures born
    of [sense] contact
    are only sources
    of suffering;
As they have a beginning
    and end, O Kaunteya,
    a wise person does
    not delight in them.   22

One who, in this very life,
    before giving up the body,
    is able to endure
Agitation arising from
    desire and anger—
    that one is absorbed in yoga;
    happy is that person.   23

One whose happiness is within,
    whose pleasure is within,
    and likewise, whose light
    comes only from within—
Such a yogi, being
    united with Brahman,
    attains the Nirvāna of Brahman.   24

The Nirvāna of Brahman
    is attained by those seers
    whose misdeeds
    have been destroyed,
Whose conflict
    has been severed,
    whose self is disciplined,
    who delight in
    the welfare of all beings.   25

Among those seekers
  who are separated
  from desire and anger,
  whose thought is controlled,
The Nirvāna of Brahman
  exists close at hand—
  for such knowers of the self.   26

Keeping the action of
  the outer sensations outside,
  and one's vision inside,
  just between the eyebrows;
Making the action of incoming
  and outgoing breaths the same
  as they move through the nostrils;   27

The sage with senses, mind,
  and discernment controlled,
  whose highest goal
  is liberation,
From whom desire, fear,
  and anger have departed—
  one who is always so,
  that one indeed is liberated.   28

As the beloved recipient
of sacrifices and austerities,
as the exalted supreme
Lord of all the worlds,
As the innermost heart
of all beings—
thus knowing me
one attains peace.[6]   29

---

6 Innermost heart: Translates *suhṛdam,* so as to provide a more literal and theological meaning of the word, which contains two parts, *su-* (innermost) and *hṛd* (heart). The word is most often translated as "friend," and perhaps could receive a protracted but more dedicated translation as "most kind-hearted [friend]." It is interesting to note that the BG uses another word for friend, *bandhu,* in verses 5, 6, and 9 in the following chapter (also, see its use in BG 1.27). My etymological translation expresses how Krishna is a friend to beings, the closest companion of all creatures: he is intimately present in the hearts of all living beings as "the innermost heart"— the supreme Self within the self. This is one of the most important manifestations of divinity described in the BG.

6

The Way of Meditation

The Beloved Lord said:

One who, without depending
    on the fruits of action,
    enacts that action which
    is a prescribed act—
That person is
    a renouncer and a yogi,
    not one who makes no sacred fire
    nor one who performs no ritual acts.   1

What they call "renunciation,"
    know that as yoga,
    O Son of Pāndu;
For without having
    renounced selfish motive,
    no one becomes a yogi.   2

For the sage who desires
    to ascend to yoga,
    action is said
    to be the means.
Only for that one who
    has ascended to yoga
    is calmness said
    to be the means.   3

When one is not attached
to the objects of the senses
nor to actions,
Renouncing
all selfish motives,
then one is said
to have ascended to yoga.   4

One should raise
the self by the self;
one should not
degrade the self.
Indeed, the self alone
is the self's friend;
the self alone
is the self's enemy.[1]   5

The self is the friend
of that self
by whose self
the very self is conquered.
But for one who is not
truly one's self—
in enmity, that very self
would remain like an enemy.[2]   6

---

1 Self: The self that either ascends, that becomes elevated, or the self that becomes lost in the temporary world; the self that turns toward or away from the true nature of the self. The usage here highlights the free will of the self to ascend to yoga or to "degrade" to selfishness, indicating the dual nature of the self, comprised of a higher and lower self. The higher self can also be taken as the supreme Self or can include the supreme Self.

2 One who is not truly one's self: Translates *anātman*, one who has lost oneself; as commentators state, losing oneself to extensions of the self, such as things of the world and relatives.

Enemy: The enemy here is found in the self and not so much on the battlefield.

For one whose self is conquered,
   who is peaceful—
   that one is fully absorbed
   in the higher self
While in cold and heat,
   happiness and suffering,
   likewise, honor and dishonor.[3]   7

One whose self is
   content in knowledge
   and in realized knowledge,
   who is focused on the highest
   with senses conquered—
That one,
   "absorbed in yoga,"
   is said to be a yogi
   for whom earth, stones,
   and gold are the same.   8

While among intimates, friends,
   enemies, the disinterested,
   mediators, the hateful,
   and family members;
Even among saintly
   and troubled persons—
   one whose discernment
   remains the same is preeminent.   9

---

3 Fully absorbed in the higher self: Translates *paramātmā*, meaning "wholly absorbed (*parama-*) in the self (*-ātmā*)." The word can mean "the higher self" or "the supreme Self," the latter referring to the divinity dwelling within the individual self.

The yogi should absorb
    the self constantly in yoga,
    remaining in secrecy,
Alone, with thought
    and self subdued,
    without cravings and
    free from all possessiveness.   10

In a clean place,
    one should establish
    for oneself a firm seat,
Neither too high nor too low,
    made of kusha grass, then
    covered with a deerskin and cloth.[4]   11

There, having the mind actively
    focused upon a single point,
    with thought and
    sense activity controlled,
Sitting on a seat,
    one should practice yoga
    for purification of the self.   12

With an aligned body,
    head, and neck—
    keeping these steady,
    without movement;
Focusing the vision toward
    the tip of one's nose
    without looking about
    in any direction;   13

---

4 Kusha grass: A type of grass that is considered sacred, utilized in religious ceremonies.

With the self quieted,
    with fear dissipated,
    established in
    a vow of chastity;
Controlling the mind
    with thought
    focused upon me—
    one should be seated
    while absorbed in yoga,
    holding me as the highest.   14

Thus always absorbing
    one's self in yoga,
    the yogi, whose
    mind is subdued,
Achieves peace
    that culminates in
    the highest state of Nirvāna,
    which rests in me.[5]   15

However, for one who
    eats too much
    there is no yoga,
    nor for one who
    does not eat at all,
Nor for one who
    sleeps too much,
    nor for one who
    is ever awake, O Arjuna.   16

---

5 This instance of Nirvāna is the last time it   then in BG 5.24–26. Note that here Nirvāna is
appears, after first appearing in BG 2.72 and   associated with Krishna, in its highest form.

For one who is thus absorbed
   in yoga while eating
   and in recreation,
   who is absorbed
   in the ways of yoga
   while performing actions,
And who is absorbed in yoga
   while sleeping
   and in wakefulness—
   for such a person,
   yoga becomes
   the destroyer of suffering.   17

When, with thought
   fully subdued,
   one abides
   in the self alone,
Without longings
   for any selfish desires,
   then that one is said to be
   "absorbed in yoga."   18

As a lamp standing
   in a windless place
   does not flicker,
   the analogy is recalled
Of the yogi
   with subdued thought,
   who is absorbed
   in practicing the yoga
   of the self.   19

That place where
   thought comes to rest,
   held steady by
   the practice of yoga;
And where,
   seeing the Self
   by the very self,
   one becomes satisfied
   within the self;   20

That boundless happiness
   beyond the senses,
   which is grasped
   through discernment;
That place where
   one knows this,
   indeed, is established in it
   and does not swerve
   from the truth;   21

And which having obtained,
   one is mindful that
   no other gain
   is greater than this;
Situated in which
   one is not shaken
   even by heavy suffering—   22

Let this be understood
   as the disjunction
   from one's conjunction
   with suffering—
   this is called yoga.
One is to be absorbed
   in yoga with determination,
   such yoga being without
   discouraging thought.[6]   23

Relinquishing,
   without exception,
   all desires that arise
   from selfish intentions;
Completely controlling
   the collective senses
   with the mind alone;   24

Little by little,
   one should become
   quieted by discernment
   that is firmly held.
Actively establishing
   the mind in the self,
   one should not
   think of anything else.   25

---

6 Disjunction: Translates *viyoga*, which can also mean "disunion."

   Conjunction: Translates *saṁyoga*, which also means "communion," "perfect union," or "complete union."

Wherever
   the flickering
   unsteady mind strays,
Pulling it back
   from here and there,
   one should bring it
   under control
   within the very self.   26

For such a yogi,
   whose mind is peaceful,
   ultimate happiness
   is attained.
One whose
   passion is calmed,
   who is without impurity,
   becomes united with Brahman.   27

Thus, with the self
   always absorbed in yoga,
   the yogi who is completely
   free from impurity,
Happily enjoys,
   due to contact
   with Brahman,
   boundless happiness.   28

One who sees the Self
  present in all beings
  and all beings present
  within the Self—
That self,
  who is absorbed
  in the yoga of yogas,
  sees the same everywhere.   29

One who sees me everywhere
  and sees all things in me,
To such a person I am never lost
  nor is such a person ever lost to me.   30

One who,
  abiding in oneness,
  offers love to me
  as the One who abides
  in all beings,
In whatever way one
  appears to be living—
  that one is a yogi
  who lives in me.   31

One who sees,
>by comparison to one's self,
>the same in all [beings],
>O Arjuna,
Whether it be happiness
>or suffering—
>that yogi is considered
>to be the highest.[7]   32

Arjuna said:

This yoga,
>which has been described
>as a state of sameness,
>O Madhusūdana—
I do not see the permanent
>establishment of this,
>due to unsteadiness.   33

For the mind
>is unsteady, O Krishna,
>impetuous, powerful,
>and unyielding.
I believe that
>controlling it
>is as difficult as
>controlling the wind.   34

---

7 The yogi is one who exercises a high degree of sympathy, experiencing others' selfhood in comparison to one's own. If one sees one's own higher self in happiness and suffering, then one can see that same higher self in others.

The Beloved Lord said:

Without doubt,
 O Mighty-Armed,
 the mind is unsteady
 and difficult to control.
But with practice,
 O Kaunteya,
 and with dispassion,
 it can be controlled.   35

"For one whose self
 is not striving fully,
 yoga is difficult
 to achieve"—
 this is my opinion.
But for one whose
 self is controlled,
 with striving it is
 possible to achieve
 by the proper approach.   36

Arjuna said:

One who does not strive
    yet possesses faith,
    whose mind has
    deviated from yoga
Without achieving
    full perfection in yoga—
    to what destiny does
    that one go, O Krishna?   37

Having fallen from both,
    does that one not perish
    like a dissipated cloud,
Having no foundation,
    O Mighty-Armed,
    bewildered on
    the path of Brahman?   38

This doubt of mine,
    O Krishna,
    you are able
    to dissipate fully.
Other than you,
    truly there is no
    forthcoming dissipator
    of this doubt.   39

The Beloved Lord said:

O Pārtha, indeed,
    neither in this world
    nor in the next
    is the destruction of such
    a person to be found.
For no one who acts
    in virtuous ways
    ever goes to
    an unfortunate
    destiny, my dear friend.   40

Reaching the worlds of
    those who have performed
    virtuous acts, dwelling
    there for countless years,
Then into the home
    of those who are pure,
    who are prosperous—
    one who has fallen
    from yoga is born again.   41

Or one is born into
    a family of true yogis
    endowed with wisdom.
That is even more difficult
    to attain in the world,
    a birth such as this.   42

There, one attains
   a full connection with
   that discernment from
   the previous body,
And from there
   one strives again
   for complete perfection,
   O Son of Kuru.   43

By that same previous practice,
   one is indeed carried forward
   even without one's effort.
Even one who only
   desires to know of yoga
   transcends the sound of Brahman.[8]   44

However, due to striving
   with great effort,
   completely cleansed
   of all impurities,
The yogi,
   fully perfected
   after many births,
   then goes to
   the supreme destination.   45

---

8 The sound of Brahman: Translates *śabda-brahman*, the Vedas, referring to the sacrificial rituals of the Vedas, for achieving everything the temporary world has to offer. This phrase implies the recitation of mantras in the Vedic sacrifice, an attempt to achieve one's self-interest through ritualistic actions; the Vedas as they are associated with the three essential qualities of nature, as expressed in BG 2.45.

The yogi is superior to ascetics
   and considered superior
   even to those who
   cultivate knowledge;
And the yogi
   is superior to those
   who perform sacred acts—
   therefore be a yogi, O Arjuna![9]   46

Even among all yogis,
   one whose inner self
   has come to me,
Who is full of faith,
   who offers love to me—
   that one is considered by me
   to be the most deeply
   absorbed in yoga.   47

---

9 Ascetics: Translates *tapasvī,* "one who performs *tapas* or rigorous austerity."
   Those who cultivate knowledge: Translates the plural of *jñāni.*
   Those who perform sacred acts: Translates *karmī.*

7

The Way of Realized Knowledge

The Beloved Lord said:

With mind deeply attached to me,
   O Pārtha, practicing yoga
   with dependence on me,
You shall know me
   completely,
   beyond all doubt—
   hear about how this is so.   I

I shall explain this knowledge
   to you, along with
   realized knowledge,
   with nothing left unsaid;
Knowing which,
   nothing further
   in this world
   is left to be known.   2

Among thousands
   of human beings,
   perhaps one may
   strive for perfection.
Even among those
   who strive for
   and achieve perfection,
   perhaps one may truly know me.   3

"Earth, water, fire,
    air, space, mind,
    the faculty of
    discernment,
And indeed the notion
    of 'I am acting'"—
    this is my
    primordial nature,
    which is divided eightfold.[1]   4

This is not the higher [nature],
    for there is another
    nature of mine—
    know it as higher.
It consists of living beings,
    O Mighty-Armed,
    by whom this universe
    becomes animated.   5

This is the cosmic womb
    for beings, for all of them—
    try to understand this.
I am, of the entire universe,
    the coming forth
    into being as well as
    the going forth into
    cosmic absorption.[2]   6

---

1 Faculty of discernment: Translates *buddhi.* Before this, *buddhi* has been presented as an attribute of self, so I have translated as "discernment." As an element of nature, however, *buddhi* is translated as "faculty of discernment."
2 Cosmic womb: Translates the plural of *yoni,* literally "womb." Its neuter gender indicates the cosmic status of this womb. This cosmic sense of the word as source is found in BG 14.3 and 14.4, in relation to the *mahatattva.*
    The coming forth into being: Translates *prabhava,* often translated as "source" or "origin."

My translation here attempts to express the rich etymological sense of the word, which conveys *purāṇic* cosmology: *pra-* ("forth") and *–bhava* ("the coming . . . into being"). See other instances of the word in BG 9.18, 10.2, 10.8, and 18.41.
    The going forth into cosmic absorption: Translates *pralaya,* often given the general and somewhat misleading meaning of "dissolution." In *purāṇic* cosmology, the universe is not dissolved; it is absorbed into a dormant cosmic state until it comes forth into being (*prabhava*) once again.

There is nothing else
   superior to me,
   O Conqueror of Wealth.
On me all this
   [universe] is strung
   like pearls on a thread.   7

I am the taste in water,
   O Kaunteya;
   I am the radiance
   of the moon and the sun,
The sacred utterance
   in all the Vedas,
   the sound in space,
   the prowess in men.[3]   8

The pure fragrance in earth
   and the brilliance
   in fire am I.
The life in all beings
   and the austerity
   in austere persons am I.   9

As the seed of all beings,
   know me to be
   the eternal,
   O Pārtha.
Among the discerning,
   I am discernment;
   of the splendid,
   I am splendor.   10

---

3 Sacred utterance: Translates *praṇavaḥ,* and
refers to the sacred syllable OM.

And among the powerful,
   I am power devoid
   of desire and passion.
In beings, I am desire
   that does not
   conflict with dharma,
   O Best of the Bharatas.   11

And those very states
   of being that are
   of the nature of
   sattva, rajas, and *tamas,*
Know that they
   are from me alone,
   yet I am not in them—
   they are in me.   12

By these three states of being,
   composed of
   the three 'qualities',
   this entire world,
Bewildered,
   does not recognize me—
   I am beyond these
   as the everpresent.   13

For that which consists
   of the 'qualities'
   is my illusive power, Māyā,
   so difficult to cross beyond.
Only those who
   offer themselves to me
   cross over this
   illusive power of Māyā.   14

Maleficent persons are
   those who are bewildered,
   those who do not
   offer themselves to me,
   the lowest of humankind,
Those whose knowledge
   has been stolen by
   the illusive power of Māyā,
   and those who have taken shelter
   of an ungodly existence.   15

Of beneficent persons,
   four types offer
   their love to me,
   O Arjuna:
One who is distressed,
   one desiring knowledge,
   one seeking personal gain,
   and one possessing knowledge,
   O Best of the Bharatas.   16

Among these,
   the person of knowledge,
   who is constantly absorbed
   in yoga that is solely
   an offering of love,
   is exceptional.
For I am so dearly loved
   by the person of knowledge,
   and that person
   is dearly loved by me.[4]   17

---

4 Offering of love: Translates *bhakti,* a word that appears fourteen times in the BG. This is the first instance in which this noun appears. Its verbal form, *bhakta,* "offered love," first appears in BG 4.3.

Certainly all of these are exalted,
   but one who has knowledge
   is my very self;
   this is my opinion.
For one whose self
   is absorbed in yoga
   abides only in me,
   the incomparable goal.   18

At the end of many births,
   one who has knowledge
   offers oneself to me, realizing,
"Vāsudeva is everything!"—
   such an exalted self
   is very rarely found.[5]   19

Persons whose knowledge
   has been carried away
   by desires for this or that
   offer themselves
   to different deities.
Following
   this or that rule,
   they are ruled
   by their own worldly nature.[6]   20

---

5 Vāsudeva: A name of Krishna. The name means "the son of Vasudeva." The word *vāsu* means "the Soul of the universe," and *deva* means "divinity" or "sport" or "play." Thus this name for Krishna can mean "the divine play of the Soul of the universe." It also means "completely pure existence," and is an abbreviation for a person who is beyond primordial nature (*prakṛti*) and the primary 'qualities' of nature (*guṇas*) arising from it.

"Vāsudeva is everything!": Krishna explains here that it is a very rare soul who can exclaim how the divinity is wonderfully omnipresent. See BG 11.40, where Arjuna addresses Krishna as "Everything" and expresses how Krishna is "everything" and pervades "everything."

6 Different deities: Translates *anya-devatāḥ* . The word *sarvam* ("everything") in the previous verse contrasts with the word *anya* ("different") in this verse.

Whoever, with faith,
   has offered love
   to whatever form that
   person desires to worship—
Upon every such person,
   I bestow this
   immovable faith.   21

Such a person,
   absorbed in
   yoga with faith,
   longs to worship that [form]
And obtains one's
   desires from that,
   though they are
   bestowed by me alone.   22

But the fruit
   that comes to those
   of little intelligence
   is temporary.
Those who sacrifice
   to the divinities
   go to the divinities;
   those who offer
   their love to me,
   surely they come to me.   23

The undiscerning
    consider me to be
    an unmanifest existence
    that has become
    visibly manifest,
Not knowing
    my highest being,
    which is everpresent
    and incomparable.⁷   24

I am not revealed to everyone,
    being concealed by
    the divine power of yoga,
    Yoga-Māyā.
This bewildered world
    does not recognize me
    as the unborn and everpresent.⁸   25

I know those beings
    who have passed on,
    those who are living,
    O Arjuna,
And those who
    have yet to come—
    but none of them know me.   26

---

7 Unmanifest existence: Translates *avyak-*
tam, which carries the sense of "indistinct
and formless," that is, the impersonal manifestation of the divine.

    Visibly manifest: Translates *vyaktim*,
which carries the sense of "distinct form and
personality"; that is, "manifest being" refers to
the personal being of the divinity.

    Highest being: Translates *param bhāvam*,
which could be translated as Krishna's
"supreme being" or "supreme heart."

8 Yoga-Māyā: Essentially the word Māyā presented in earlier verses, translated here as "the
divine power of yoga." This divine power
(Māyā) uses "yoga" either to "connect" souls
with the bewildering energy of this world to
conceal such souls from the divinity, or to
"connect" souls with the blissful energy of
Krishna to reveal the divinity to such souls.

With the rising up
  of desire and hatred,
  with the bewilderment
  of duality, O Bhārata,
All beings go to a state
  of complete bewilderment
  at the time of their birth,
  O Scorcher of the Enemy.   27

Now those whose misdeeds
  have come to an end,
  whose actions are virtuous—
Such persons, freed from
  the bewilderment of duality,
  offer their love to me
  with intense devotion.[9]   28

Striving for release
  from aging and death,
  those who have
  taken shelter of me
Know Brahman completely
  and action entirely,
  and the 'principle of self'.[10]   29

---

9 Misdeeds: Translates *pāpam*.
  Virtuous: Translates *puṇyam*.
  Intense devotion: Translates *dṛdha-vratāḥ*.
10 The 'principle of self': Translates *adhyātmā*, introduced again in BG 8.1. The principles of 'becoming', 'divinity', and 'sacrifice' are to follow. As principles, these terms refer to all things pertaining to these essential subject matters for understanding reality.

Those who know me as
the 'principle of becoming',
along with the 'principle of divinity'
and the 'principle of sacrifice',
Even at the time of passing on—
they know me,
for their thought
is absorbed in yoga.[11]　　　　30

---

11 The 'principle of becoming': Translates the term *adhibhūta*.

The 'principle of divinity': Translates the term *adhidaiva*. The word *daiva* means "divine" and can also mean "destiny" or "fate," and most relevantly, carries the sense of the aggregate of the various divine beings within the cosmic government that comprise the ultimate Person, the *puruṣa*. The word is translated here in the most general sense as "divinity," but it pertains to the multiple cosmic divinities. A slight variation of this term appears as *adhidaivatā* in BG 8.4.

The 'principle of sacrifice': Translates the term *adhiyajña*.

8

The Transcendent Brahman

Arjuna said:

What is that Brahman?
   What is the 'principle of self'?
   What is action,
   O Ultimate Person?
And the 'principle of becoming',
   what is said about it?
   The 'principle of divinity',
   what is it declared to be?   I

What is the 'principle of sacrifice',
   and how is it present
   here within this body,
   O Madhusūdana?
And how, at the time
   of passing on,
   are you to be known by
   those who are self-disciplined?   2

The Beloved Lord said:

Brahman is
    the supreme indestructible;
    the 'principle of self'
    is described as one's
    state of intrinsic being.
The activity of beings
    that brings about their
    emerging states of being
    is the creative force
    known as action.[1]   3

The 'principle of becoming'
    is the transitory state of being,
    and the 'principle of divinity'
    is the Person.
Indeed, I am
    the 'principle of sacrifice'
    here in the body,
    O Best of the Embodied.[2]   4

And at the time of one's end,
    remembering me alone
    while giving up the body—
One who thus goes forth,
    goes to my state of being;
    about this there is no doubt.   5

---

1 Emerging states of being: Translates the phrase *bhāvodbhava*, referring here to the successive life-states occurring in reincarnation.

Creative force: Translates *visarga*, referring to the epiphenomenal creative or active process, the actions that create things within this creation.

2 The Person: Translates *puruṣa*, referring to the *virāṭ puruṣa* found in the Vedas, the macrocosmic Person.

Furthermore,
   whatever state of being
   one remembers upon
   giving up the body
   at the end [of life],
To that very state
   one always goes,
   O Kaunteya,
   being conditioned
   by that state of being.   6

Therefore, at all times
   remember me
   and fight!
With your mind and
   discernment offered to me,
   certainly you shall come to me—
   of this there is no doubt.   7

By absorption in yoga
   through the practice of yoga,
   with thought not wandering
   to anything else,
One approaches
   the supreme divine Person,
   O Pārtha, continuously
   focusing one's thought [on him].   8

One should continuously
      remember [him]
As the wise one,
      the most ancient one,
      the perpetual governor,
      the one who is smaller
      than the atom;
As the arranger
      of everything,
      whose form
      is inconceivable;
As the one who is
      luminous like the sun,
      beyond all darkness.   9

At the time
      of passing on,
      with undisturbed mind,
Absorbed in yoga
      by offering one's love
      and by the very power of yoga;
Intently focusing
      the vital life-breath
      between the eyebrows—
One reaches that
      supreme divine Person.   10

The imperishable, which
   knowers of the Vedas describe,
Into which enter the ascetics
   who are free from passion,
Desiring which those persons
   lead a life of chastity—
That place I shall
   briefly explain to you.   11

Controlling all
   the [bodily] gates
   and stopping the mind
   from within the heart,
Placing the self's
   vital life-breath at
   the top of the head,
   one is established
   in yoga concentration.[3]   12

"OM"— thus sounding
   Brahman as a single syllable,
   continuously remembering me,
One who passes away,
   relinquishing the body—
   such a person passes on
   to the supreme destination.   13

3 The [bodily] gates: Refers to the nine passages of the body spoken of in BG 5.13 as the "city of nine gates."

One whose thought
is never on anything else,
who remembers me
continuously—
For that one, O Pārtha,
I am easily attained,
for the yogi who is
constantly absorbed in yoga.   14

Once having come to me,
they do not come
to repeated birth,
to that impermanent
place of suffering;
For those whose selves
are extraordinary
have gone to
the supreme perfection.   15

From the earth up to
the realm of Brahmā,
the worlds undergo
repeated cycles, O Arjuna.
Having come to me,
however, O Kaunteya,
one does not find
repeated birth.[4]   16

---

4 The realm: Translates *bhuvana*, the highest station of this universe.

Brahmā: The cosmic deity who presides over creation within the great cycle of creation and dissolution (the latter presided over by the deity Shiva) in the physical universe. Note that this name is different from Brahman, the ultimate reality, the supreme spirit.

Those who know of Brahmā's day,
    having the duration of
    a thousand ages,
And of his night,
    ending after a thousand ages,
    are persons who know
    what is day and what is night.   17

All manifestations arise
    from the unmanifest
    with the coming of
    the day [of Brahmā].
With the coming of
    the night [of Brahmā],
    they are absorbed,
    then and there, in that
    which is called the unmanifest.   18

This very same totality of beings,
    repeatedly coming into being,
    is reabsorbed helplessly
With the coming of the night,
    O Pārtha;
    it [again] comes forth
    with the coming of the day.   19

Beyond this, however,
    there is another,
    unmanifest state of being
    that is eternal,
Which, when all beings
    perish, itself does
    not ever perish.   20

The unmanifest is called
  "the indestructible";
  they declare it to be
  the supreme destination,
Achieving which,
  they do not return—
  that is my supreme domain.   21

It is the supreme Person,
  moreover, O Pārtha,
  who is attainable
  by offering love
  to none other,
Within whom beings exist,
  by whom all this [world]
  is pervaded.⁵   22

Now, under what
  circumstances do the yogis
  who have passed away
Pass on to the non-repetition
  and also the repetition of birth—
  I shall speak of those circumstances,
  O Best of the Bharatas.   23

---

5 It is the supreme Person: Here Krishna speaks about his cosmic manifestation in the third person. This objectification of his cosmic personal Self, who is approachable by offering love, implies that he who stands before Arjuna is the highest and most intimate Self with whom souls can relate.

Fire, light, day,
   the waxing moon,
   the six-month northern
   course of the sun—
Those who have passed on
   under these circumstances,
   such persons, who are
   knowers of Brahman,
   go to Brahman.[6]   24

Smoke, night, also
   the waning moon,
   the six-month southern
   course of the sun—
Under these circumstances,
   after attaining
   the light of the moon,
   the yogi returns.   25

For these two passages
   from the world,
   light and dark, are
   thought to be perpetual.
By one, the yogi passes on
   with no return;
   by the other,
   the yogi again returns.   26

---

6 These elements—fire, light, day, etc. —in verses 24 and 25 also refer to the guidance of specific divinities on the two paths out of this world. These are the methods of liberation and departure from life found in the Chāndogya Upanishad 4.5, Bṛhadāraṇyaka Upanishad 5.10, and Muṇḍaka Upanishad 2.11. However, Krishna ultimately expresses that offering one's heart transcends these processes, positive or negative. In bhakti, all the technicalities of these paths are unnecessary and even a higher liberation can be achieved in the practice of loving devotion. In this verse and the following, Krishna is acknowledging these various elements for passing on that correspond to the internal dimensions of the self in its passage beyond this life.

Knowing these two paths,
    O Pārtha, the yogi is
    not bewildered in any way.
Therefore, at all times,
    be absorbed
    in the yoga of yogas,
    O Arjuna.   27

In the Vedas, in sacrifices,
    in austerities, and also
In charitable gifts,
    whatever meritorious
    fruit is ordained—
One who goes beyond that,
    having understood all this,
Such a yogi goes
    on to the supreme
    and incomparable realm.   28

9

The King of Secrets

The Beloved Lord said:
Now I shall reveal to you
   this greatest secret,
   for you are without envy.
It is knowledge together
   with realized knowledge,
   knowing which you shall
   be free from inauspiciousness.   I

This is the king of knowledge,
   the king of secrets,
   the ultimate means
   of purification.
Understood by
   direct perception,
   in harmony with dharma,
   it is joyful to enact
   and everlasting.[1]   2

Those persons who have
   no faith in this dharma,
   O Destroyer of the Enemy,
Not achieving me,
   again return to the path
   of recurring death.   3

---

1 "The king of knowledge" and "the king of secrets" are each taken as a special type of *karmadharya* compound, known as *puruṣavyāgra*. The first of these two phrases can thus be understood as meaning, "There is a knowledge that should rule souls just as a king rules his people."

By me this entire universe
  is pervaded, by my
  unmanifest form.
All beings rest on me
  and I do not
  rest upon them.   4

And [yet] beings
  do not rest on me—
  behold my divine
  power of yoga!
Supporting beings
  and not resting on beings,
  my Self causes beings to be.   5

As the mighty wind
  moving everywhere
  rests on space,
"So all beings
  rest on me"—
  understand this!   6

All beings, O Kaunteya,
  enter my
  primordial nature
At the end of a life-cycle
  of the universe;
  again, I send them forth
  at the beginning of
  [another] cycle.²   7

---

2 A life-cycle of the universe: translates the *yugas*, during each of which a manifestation
term *kalpa*, which equals 311 trillion years. A of the Divinity descends to the earth.
kalpa is divided into four subperiods called

Being firmly supported by
   my own primordial nature,
   I send forth again and again
This entire aggregate of beings,
   which is powerless under
   the power of primordial nature.   8

And these actions
   do not bind me,
   O Conqueror of Wealth.
Remaining aloof,
   I am not attached
   to these actions.   9

With my supervision,
   primordial nature
   brings forth the moving
   and the nonmoving.
By this causal force,
   O Kaunteya,
   the universe
   revolves in cycles.[3]   10

The bewildered discount me
   for having assumed
   the limited form
   of a human,
Not knowing
   the supreme nature
   of my Lordship
   over all that exists.[4]   11

---

3 Supervision: Translates *adhyakṣa*, which can also connote "the divine glance," identified as the "causal force." This translation can be justified by the way the word appears in Aitareya Upanishad 1.1.1 and Bṛhadāraṇyaka Upanishad 1.2.5.

4 Limited form. Translates *tanum*, which indicates an insignificant or small form. The sense here is that Krishna possesses an eternal humanlike form that he does not assume at any point in time.

Those who are of vain hopes,
   of vain actions,
   of vain knowledge;
   who are thoughtless,
Demonic, and godless—
   they indeed are enslaved
   by the bewildering
   primordial nature.   12

However, those whose selves
   are extraordinary,
   O Pārtha, who abide
   in the divine nature,
Offer love to me
   with their minds
   focused on none other,
   knowing me as
   the everpresent
   origin of beings.[5]   13

Constantly praising me
   and striving with
   intense devotion,
And honoring me
   with an offering of love,
   always absorbed in yoga,
   they worship me.   14

5 Divine nature: Translates *daivīṁ prakṛtim*. Both words of this phrase are in the feminine gender, indicating that the divine realm is of a feminine nature, as is *prakṛti* ("primordial nature") and Māyā ("divine illusive power").

And there are also others
    who, sacrificing
    with the sacrifice
    of knowledge,
    worship me
In my oneness,
    in my separateness,
    and in my many forms
    facing everywhere.   15

I am the ritual,
    I am the sacrifice,
    I am the oblation,
    I am the healing herb;
I am the sacred mantra,
    I am indeed
    the clarified butter,
    I am the fire, and
    I am the offering.   16

I am the father of this universe,
    the mother, the creator,
    the grandfather;
That which is to be known,
    the means of purification,
    the sacred sound OM,
    and indeed the Rig,
    Sāma, and Yajur [Vedas].⁶   17

---

6 Rig, Sāma, and Yajur: These are the major sections of the Vedic literature. The Rig Veda presents hymns of praise and philosophical reflection; the Sāma Veda focuses primarily on the methods of recitation of the verses in the Rig Veda; and the Yajur Veda emphasizes Vedic ritual performance and practice.

I am the goal, the sustainer,
　　the Lord, the witness,
　　the dwelling, the shelter,
　　the innermost heart;
The coming forth into being,
　　the going forth into
　　cosmic absorption;
　　the continuance of existence,
　　the cosmic receptacle,
　　and the everpresent seed.　　　　　I8

I radiate warmth;
　　I withhold and
　　send forth the rain.
I am mortality
　　and indeed immortality,
　　being and nonbeing,
　　O Arjuna.　　　　　　　　　　　　I9

Those who know the three Vedas,
　　the soma drinkers purified of vice
Who worship me with sacrifices,
　　seek passage
　　to the celestial realm.
Approaching the pious world
　　of the lord of celestials,
Such persons partake
　　of the divine pleasures
　　of divinities, in the divine realm.[7]　　20

---

7 Soma: One of the primary substances utilized as a libation in the Vedic sacrifice. It is a
very intoxicating drink derived from a specific
plant, still unknown.

Celestial realm: In Hindu cosmology, this is
a heavenly realm of celestial beings. The highest abode is beyond even this realm and is the
ultimate, divine realm of Krishna.

Those persons,
    having enjoyed
    that vast celestial world,
Their piety exhausted,
    then [again] enter
    the mortal world.
Thus following
    the dharma of
    the three [Vedas],
Desiring certain
    objects of desire,
    they achieve a state of
    going and coming back.⁸   21

Persons who, meditating
    on none other,
    worship me completely—
For them, who are always
    fully absorbed in yoga,
    I bring prosperity and security.   22

Even those who
    have offered their love
    to different deities,
    who, filled with faith,
    perform sacrifice—
Even they perform
    sacrifice for me alone,
    O Kaunteya,
    though not according
    to injunction.   23

---

8 A state of going and coming back: one, and thus no progress is actually made.
Expresses the futility of this process: one may
go to a higher world but must return to this

For I am the beloved recipient
  and indeed the Lord
  of all sacrifices.
But they do not
  recognize me in truth;
  therefore they fall
  [from the celestial realm].   24

Those who serve divinities
  go to the divinities;
  those who serve ancestors
  go to the ancestors;
Those who sacrifice for spirits
  go to the spirits;
  those who sacrifice for me
  surely come to me.   25

A leaf, a flower,
  a fruit, or water—
  one who, with these,
  expresses devotion to me
  in an offering of love,
That I enjoy, for I am
  brought so near
  by an offering of love
  from one whose
  very self is so devoted.   26

Whatever you do,
  whatever you enjoy,
  whatever you sacrifice,
  whatever you bestow,
Whatever austerity
  you undertake—
  that, enact as
  an offering unto me.   27

Thus you shall be freed
  from the bondage of action,
  which produces
  good and bad fruits.
With the self absorbed in yoga
  by the yoga of renunciation,
  completely liberated,
  you shall come to me.   28

I am the same
  toward all beings;
  no one is either hated
  or dearly loved by me.
Yet those who,
  with an offering of love,
  offer their love to me—
  they are in me
  and I am also in them.   29

Even if one has
  behaved very badly,
  if one offers one's love
  to none other but me,
Indeed, one should be
  considered saintly,
  for such a person
  is rightly absolved.   30

One quickly becomes
  a self who embraces dharma
  and attains eternal peace;
O Kaunteya,
  know this for certain—
  one who offers love to me
  is never lost.   31

For those taking shelter
    of me, O Pārtha,
    whether they come
    from troubled wombs,
Or whether they be
    women, tradespeople,
    or skilled workers—
    even they reach
    the supreme goal.[9]   32

How much more, then,
    for the virtuous Brahmins,
    as well as the saintly kings
    who have offered their love?
Having come to
    this impermanent
    unhappy world,
    offer your love to me.   33

Be mindful of me
    with love offered to me;
    sacrificing for me,
    act out of reverence for me.
Surely you shall
    come to me,
    thus having absorbed
    your self in yoga with
    me as the supreme goal.[10]   34

---

9 Troubled wombs: Translates *pāpa-yoni*.   **10** Be mindful of me . . . come to me: The
first half and part of the third quarter of this
verse are repeated in BG 18.65.

10

The Sublime Presence of Divinity

The Beloved Lord said:

Once again, indeed,
  O Mighty-Armed,
  hear my supreme word,
Which I shall speak to you
  who are so dearly loved,
  with a desire for
  your well-being.   1

Neither the multitude
  of celestial beings
  nor the exalted seers
  understand how I have
  come forth into being,
For I am the beginning
  of the divinities
  and exalted seers—
  every one of them.   2

One who understands me
  as unborn, beginningless,
  and as the exalted supreme
  Lord of the universe—
That person,
  among mortals,
  is unbewildered and
  free from all misfortune.   3

Discernment, knowledge,
   freedom from illusion,
   forbearance, truth,
   restraint, calmness;
Happiness, suffering,
   coming into being
   and cessation of being,
   fear and indeed fearlessness;   4

Nonviolence, sameness,
   contentment, austerity,
   charity, fame, and infamy—
In their various forms,
   these conditions of beings
   arise from me alone.   5

The seven exalted seers,
   the four of previous times,
   and also the Manus,
Having come into being from me,
   are generated from my mind—
   those from whom these progeny
   of the world have come.[1]   6

This abounding power
   and yoga of mine,
   one who knows this in truth—
That one is absorbed in yoga
   through unwavering yoga practice;
   of this there is no doubt.   7

---

1 The seven exalted seers: A group of
unnamed sages first mentioned in the Vedas.
   The four of previous times: The four
Kumāras, whose names are Sanatkumāra, San-
anda, Sanaka, and Sanātana.
   The Manus: *Manu* means "man," here
referring to the primary progenitors of
humankind.

"I am, of everything,
   the coming forth into being;
   from me everything
   is set forth into motion."
Mindful [of these words],
   they offer their love to me,
   the enlightened ones,
   being fully immersed
   in feelings of love.[2]   8

With their thought on me,
   with their life-breath
   offered to me,
   enlightening one another
And conversing about me
   continuously,
   they are satiated and
   also they feel rapturous love.[3]   9

For them, who are constantly
   absorbed in yoga,
   who offer loving service
   with natural affection,
I offer that yoga
   of discernment
   by which they
   come close to me.   10

---

2 The coming forth into being: Translates *prabhavaḥ*, as it is used in a cosmological context. The word is often translated as "source" or "origin."

   Is set forth into motion: Translates the verb *pravartate*, often translated as "emanates."

Being. . . feelings of love: Translates *bhāva*.

3 Life-breath: Translates *prāṇa*, a Sanskrit word adopted by the English language.

For them, truly,
  out of compassion,
  I dispel darkness that comes
  from the absence of knowledge—
For I am the one who dwells
  within the very heart of the self,
  with the light of knowledge
  that glows like the sun.   11

Arjuna said:

You are the supreme Brahman,
  the supreme dwelling place,
  the supreme means of purification;
You are the eternal divine Person,
  the original Divinity,
  the unborn, all-pervading one.   12

All the seers describe you,
  including the divine seer Nārada;
Also, Asita Devala, Vyāsa,
  and now, you yourself tell me.[4]   13

All this that you tell me
  I consider to be true,
  O Keshava.
Indeed, O Beloved Lord,
  neither the divinities
  nor the demons
  know your personality.   14

---

4 Nārada: The wandering mendicant who carries and plays a long stringed instrument (similar to the Indian sitar), who becomes a catalyst for various divine dramas. His name appears again in BG 10.26 below. The legendary author of the Bhakti Sūtra.

Asita Devala: The compiler of divine hymns, some of which are found in the Rig Veda.

Vyāsa: The great sage who is the compiler of the Vedas and other sacred literature, including the Mahābhārata and the Bhagavad Gītā.

Only you personally
    know your Self
    by your Self,
    O Ultimate Person,
O Source of Beings,
    O Lord of Beings,
    O Divinity of Divinities,
    O Master of the Universe!   15

You are able to fully
    describe the divine,
    for boundless are
    the powers of your Self
By which,
    pervading these worlds
    with such boundless powers,
    you are situated.   16

How may I know you,
    O Yogi, while constantly
    meditating upon you?
And in what various states
    of being am I to meditate
    upon you, O Beloved Lord?   17

Elaborating upon the yoga
    and abounding power
    of your Self,
    O Janārdana,
Describe further,
    as there is no satiation
    for me while hearing
    of the immortal.   18

The Beloved Lord said:

Listen! I shall tell you of
    the abounding
    powers of my Self
That are most prominent,
    O Best of the Kurus,
    for there is no end
    to their extent.   19

I am the Self,
    O Gudākesha,
    abiding in the hearts
    of all beings.
I am also the beginning
    and the middle of beings,
    as well as their end.⁵   20

Among the Ādityas,
    I am Vishnu;
    of luminaries,
    I am the radiant sun.
Among the Maruts,
    I am Marīchi;
    of heavenly bodies,
    I am the moon.⁶   21

---

5 All beings: Translates the phrase *sarva-bhūta*. The phrase also can be taken as "All Being," an epithet for the first created being, Brahmā, the deity charged with constructing the cosmos.

6 The Ādityas: The twelve celestial beings who preside over the sun.
    The Maruts: The lords presiding over the wind.

Of the Vedas,
   I am the Sāma;
among divinities,
   I am Vāsava.
Of the senses,
   I am the mind;
and of beings,
   I am consciousness.[7]   22

And among the Rudras,
   I am Shankara [Shiva];
among Yakshas and Rakshasas,
   I am Kuvera, lord of wealth.
Among the Vasus,
   I am fire;
and of lofty mountains,
   I am Meru.[8]   23

And among priests,
   know me to be
   the principal one,
   Brihaspati, O Pārtha.
Among military commanders,
   I am Skanda;
of bodies of water,
   I am the ocean.[9]   24

---

7 Sāma: The section of the Vedas that is
sung.
   Vāsava: The principal deity, whose name is
Indra.
8 The Rudras: The eleven lords who are
involved in cosmic destruction; also the celestial beings of roaring thunder.
   Shankara: Known by the name of Shiva,
the chief of the Rudras; the deity of cosmic
dissolution and transformation.

Yakshas: Spirits.
Rakshasas: Horrific beings.
The Vasus: The eight atmospheric lords.
   Meru: The golden mountain at the center
of the cosmos.
9 Brihaspati: The principal priest of celestial
beings.
   Skanda: The lord of war, who is also the
son of the deity, Shiva.

Among exalted seers,
  I am Bhrigu;
of utterances,
  I am the one sacred syllable.
Of sacrifices,
  I am the sacrifice of
  quietly repeated prayer;
of stationary things,
  I am the Himalayas;[10]   25

Of all trees,
  the sacred Ashwattha;
and among
  divine seers, Nārada;
Among the Gandharvas,
  Citraratha;
among perfected beings,
  the sage Kapila.[11]   26

Of horses, know me
  as Ucchaishravas,
  who arose from the nectar;
Of princely elephants,
  Airāvata;
and among humans,
  the ruler who protects the people.[12]   27

---

10 Bhrigu: The mediator between the divinities.

One sacred syllable: This is the syllable OM.

Quietly repeated prayer: Translates *japa;* understood as softly repeated mantra or prayer.

11 The sacred Ashwattha: Often understood as the banyan or fig tree. The image of this tree is used metaphorically to explain the metaphysics of the BG in the beginning of Chapter 15.

Gandharvas: The celestial singers and musicians.

Kapila: There are two personalities with this name who are associated with the Sānkhya philosophical system: one is the founder of the philosophical school, and the other, here referred to by Krishna, is the divine descent of Vishnu presented in the Bhāgavata Purāṇa.

12 Ucchaishravas: This horse arises from the nectar created by the churning of the ocean, and is associated with Indra and the deity of the sun.

Airāvata: The elephant belonging to Indra.

The ruler who protects the people: Translates Narādhipa, the king.

Of weapons,
    I am the thunderbolt;
    among cows,
    I am the one
    that fulfills desires.
I am also the procreating force,
    Kandarpa;
    and of serpents,
    I am Vāsuki.[13]   28

Of the Nāgas,
    I am Ananta;
    of great aquatics,
    I am Varuna [their lord].
Among ancestors,
    I am Aryaman;
    and among subduers,
    I am Death.[14]   29

And among the Daityas,
    I am Prahlāda;
    I am time of all that
    moves forward in time.
Of animals,
    I am the king of animals;
    of winged creatures,
    the son of Vinatā, Garuda.[15]   30

---

13 The one that fulfills desires: Translates *kāmadhuk*, the divine cow that grants all one's desires (*kāma*).

    Kandarpa: The deity of love, sometimes thought of as India's Cupid.

    Vāsuki: The king of serpents.

14 Nāgas: Celestial serpents.

    Ananta: "The unlimited one." The serpent on whom the cosmic Vishnu lies to sustain the universe.

    Varuna: The lord of the water.

Aryaman: The chief ancestor.

    Death: The lord of death, known as Yama.

15 Daityas: A clan of demons.

    Prahlāda: The saintly son of a demon father.

    The king of animals: The lion.

    The son of Vinatā: Translates *vainateya*, who is Garuda, the divine bird carrier of Lord Vishnu.

Of things that purify,
   I am the purifying wind;
   among wielders of weapons,
   I am Rāma.
Of fish,
   I am the seamonster;
   and of flowing waters,
   I am the Ganges,
   the daughter of Jahnu.[16]   31

Of creations,
   I am the beginning,
   the end, and indeed
   the middle, O Arjuna.
Of knowledge,
   I am knowledge of
   the 'principle of self';
   among those
   professing theories,
   I am the theorem.   32

---

16 Rāma: The manifestation of Vishnu known as Paraśurāma, meaning "the wielder of the ax."

The daughter of Jahnu: The sacred river Ganges, which flows from the toe of Vishnu.

Of letters,
    I am the letter A;
    and of compound words,
    the dual form.
Indeed, I am
    imperishable time;
    I am the world-creator,
    with faces in every direction.[17]   33

I am death, which
    takes away everything,
    and the rising into being
    of all that will be.
Of feminine attributes
    [and their presiding goddesses],
    I am fame, beauty, speech,
    remembrance, intelligence,
    constancy, and forbearance.   34

---

17 Compound words: Translates *sāmāsika*, referring to the grammatical construction in Sanskrit that involves the placing together and construal of two or more words to form a compound phrase.

Dual form: Translates *dvandva*, a certain type of compound word phrase in which each of the two members of the compound are given equal significance and are unified by their relationship. This grammatical construction resonates fundamental philosophical and theistic aspects of Vaishnava thought: embedded within this compound is the idea of "difference" between the two members as well as the "non-difference" of form, or the unity provided by the singularity of the compound itself.

The world-creator, with faces in every direction: The cosmic deity, Brahmā. However, it is Krishna who is the ultimate creator and designer of all the universes.

Also, of hymns,
   I am the great hymn, Brihatsāma;
   of poetic meters,
   I am the Gāyatrī,
   recited by saintly priests.
Of months,
   I am Mārgashīrsha;
   of seasons,
   I am the season
   that abounds in flowers.[18]   35

I am gambling
   among cheaters;
   I am splendor
   of the splendid.
I am victory,
   I am firm resolve,
   I am courage
   among the courageous.   36

Among the descendants of Vrishni,
   I am Vāsudeva;
   among the Pāndavas,
   [you] the Conqueror of Wealth.
Also, among sages,
   I am Vyāsa;
   among poets,
   the poet Ushanā.[19]   37

---

18 Brihatsāma: The "great hymn" for Indra found in the Sāma Veda.

   Gāyatrī meter: A meter with eight syllables per quarter verse.

   Mārgashīrsha: The span of time that corresponds to the months of November and December.

   The season that abounds in flowers: Spring.

19 Vrishni: The dynasty in which Krishna appears.

   Vāsudeva: A name for Krishna meaning "the son of Vasudeva." See BG 7.19. This name can also refer to Krishna's older brother, Balarāma.

   Ushanā: A famous sage, frequently mentioned in the Vedas, who composed four hymns.

I am the taming rod
   among those who tame;
   I am moral conduct
   among those who seek victory.
And indeed,
   I am the silence of secrets;
   I am knowledge
   among those who have knowledge.   38

And I am also that which is
   the seed of all beings,
   O Arjuna.
There is nothing that
   can exist without me—
   no moving or nonmoving being.   39

There is no limit
   to my boundless powers,
   O Scorcher of the Enemy.
What has been described
   by me is merely
   an example of the extent
   of my boundless power.   40

Whatever form of existence
   possesses abounding power,
   contains the beautiful,
   or is well-endowed
   with excellence—
Understand that
   every such form
   has become fully manifest
   from but a part of my splendor.   41

But what is the necessity
  of your knowing
  so many things,
  O Arjuna?
I support
  this whole universe
  continuously,
  with one part [of myself].   42

11

Vision of the Universal Form

Arjuna said:

Due to your grace upon me,
    your supreme secret
    known as the 'principle of self',
Which has been spoken
    by you in these words,
    has dispelled this
    bewilderment of mine.   1

For the becoming and
    the passing on of beings
    has been heard by me
    in great detail
From you,
    O One with Lotus-like Eyes,
    as well as [knowledge]
    of your everpresent supreme Self.   2

Thus as you have described
    this about your Self,
    O Highest Supreme Lord,
I desire to see your
    supremely powerful form,
    O Ultimate Person.   3

If you think it is possible
for me to see you
in this way, O Lord,
O Supreme Lord of Yoga,
then reveal to me
your everpresent Self.[1]   4

The Beloved Lord said:

Behold my forms,
    O Pārtha,
    by the hundreds,
    or by the thousands—
Divine, of various types,
    and of various colors
    and appearances.   5

Behold the Ādityas,
    the Vasus, the Rudras,
    the two Ashvins,
    also the Maruts.
Many of these never
    have been seen before—
    behold these wonders,
    O Bhārata.[2]   6

---

1 Supreme Lord of Yoga: Translates *yogeśvara*. This epithet appears in another instance within this chapter, and in two other instances in the final chapter. It consists of the words *yoga* and *īśvara* (the "Supreme Lord").
2 The Ādityas: Celestial beings related to the sun.

The Vasus: Celestial beings of fire and light.
    The Rudras: Celestial beings of roaring thunder.
    The two Ashvins: Celestial beings of soothing dawn.
    The Maruts: Celestial beings of wind and lightning.

Before you, in one place,
 behold now
 the entire universe,
 with every moving
 and nonmoving being
Within my body,
 O Gudākesha,
 and whatever else
 you desire to see.   7

But you are unable to see me
 with only this, your own eyes.
I [therefore] give divine eyes to you—
 behold my supremely powerful yoga!   8

Sanjaya said:

Thus having spoken,
 O King, the exalted
 Supreme Lord of Yoga, Hari,
Then revealed to Pārtha
 his supremely powerful
 majestic form: 9

Of numerous mouths and eyes,
 of numerous extraordinary
 appearances;
Of numerous divine ornaments,
 of numerous upraised
 divine weapons;   10

Wearing divine garlands
 and garments, with divine
 perfumes and ointments;
Consisting of all wonders—
 the Divinity, endless,
 facing in all directions.   11

If a thousand suns
  were to have risen
  in the sky at once,
Such brilliance as this
  might resemble
  the brilliance
  of that supreme Self.   12

There, in one place,
  the entire universe
  was unlimitedly divided.
The Pāndava then
  saw this in the body of
  the Divinity of divinities.   13

Then struck with amazement,
  the hairs of his limbs
  standing on end,
  the Conqueror of Wealth,
Bowing his head
  to the Divinity,
  with palms joined
  in prayerful gesture, spoke.   14

Arjuna said:

I see the divinities
  in your body, O Divinity—
All of this, and also various
  assemblages of beings,
Lord Brahmā sitting
  on the seat of the lotus,
As well as all the seers
  and divine serpents.   15

With many arms, bellies,
    mouths, and eyes,
I see you everywhere
    in your unending form—
No end, nor middle,
    nor even beginning
    of yourself
Do I see, O All-Pervasive
    Supreme Lord,
    of all-pervading form.   16

Wearing a crown,
    bearing a club,
    and holding a disc,
A mass of light
    shining everywhere—
I see you, so difficult
    to perceive all at once,
With the brilliance of
    the sun and blazing fires,
    which is immeasurable!   17

You are the indestructible,
    the supreme object of knowledge.
You are the supreme
    resting place of all.
You are the everpresent
    protector of lasting dharma.
You are the eternal Person—
    so it is understood by me.[3]   18

---

3 Indestructible: Translates *akṣara*, which is   manifestation of the divinity.
the name of the sacred syllable OM, the sonic

Having no beginning,
   middle, or end,
   of unlimited prowess,
Of unlimited arms,
   with the moon and sun
   as your eyes—
I behold you, whose mouths
   are of blazing fire,
Burning this entire universe
   with your own splendor.   19

Indeed, that which is between
   heaven and earth
Is pervaded by you alone
   in all directions.
Seeing this wondrous
   terrible form of yours,
The three worlds tremble,
   O Mighty Self.   20

For over there, multitudes
   of celestial beings
   enter into you.
Some, daunted,
   sing praises to you with
   palms prayerfully joined.
Crying out "Glory!"
   multitudes of great seers
   and perfected beings
Praise you with abundant
   prayerful hymns.   21

The Rudras, Ādityas,
 Vasus, and Sādhyas;
The Vishva deities,
 the two Ashvins, the Maruts,
 and the forefathers;
The multitudes of Gandharvas,
 Yakshas, Asuras,
 and perfected beings—
All behold you
 and are truly amazed.[4]   22

Your exalted form of
 numerous mouths
 and eyes,
O Mighty-Armed,
 of numerous arms,
 thighs, and feet,
Of numerous bellies,
 with numerous
 frightful teeth—
Seeing this, the worlds
 are trembling,
 so also am I.   23

Touching the blazing
 sky of many colors,
With mouths opened wide
 and expansive blazing eyes—
Truly having seen you,
 my inner self trembles,
And I find neither stability
 nor tranquility, O Vishnu.   24

---

4. Sādhyas: A class of celestial beings mentioned in Vedic literature.

 The Vishva deities: Refers to at least ten minor deities, according to Puranic literature.

Asuras: Within the celestial realm, those "ungodly" beings who oppose the benevolent celestial beings and divinities.

And having seen your mouths
    with frightful teeth,
Resembling the fires
    of the end of cosmic time,
I know not any sense of direction
    and I find no shelter—
Be merciful,
    O Lord of Divinities,
    dwelling place of the universe!   25

And [rushing] toward you,
    over there, are all the sons
    of Dhritarāshtra,
Indeed, along with multitudes
    of protectors of the earth
Such as Bhīshma, Drona,
    and even the son
    of the charioteer—
Also along with our
    own chief warriors.[5]   26

In haste they enter
    your mouths,
Which are terrible
    with frightful teeth.
Some, clinging
    between your teeth,
Are vividly seen with
    their heads crushed.   27

---

5 Bhīshma: The great Kaurava elder and lead-
ing warrior.
    Drona: The teacher of warfare for both
Arjuna and Duryodhana, who fights for the
Kauravas.
    The son of the charioteer: Karna.

As the rivers' many
    currents of water
Rush forward
    toward the sea alone,
So, over there,
    those heroes
    of the world of men
Enter into your
    wildly flaming mouths.   28

As moths,
    with great velocity,
Enter a blazing fire
    unto their destruction,
Similarly,
    the worlds also
Enter your mouths
    with great velocity,
    unto their destruction.   29

Devouring them
    from every side,
    you lick up
All the worlds with
    your flaming mouths.
Filling the entire
    universe with splendor,
Your fierce rays burn,
    O Vishnu.   30

Tell me, who are you,
    of such terrifying form?
Respects unto you,
    O Best of Divinities—
    be merciful!
I wish to truly know you,
    the Original One,
For I do not fully
    understand what you have
    set forth into motion.   31

The Beloved Lord said:

Time I am,
    acting to destroy the worlds,
    advancing forward
To completely annihilate
    the worlds here,
    ever turning forward.
Even without you [acting],
    they shall all cease to be—
Those who are warriors
    arrayed on the opposing side.   32

Therefore you must rise up,
    aspire to glory;
Conquering your enemies,
    enjoy prosperous kingship!
By me these very men
    have already been slain—
Merely be the instrument,
    O Masterful Archer.   33

Drona and Bhīshma
   and Jayadratha,
And also Karna,
   as well as other
   warrior heroes,
Are already slain by me;
   do not hesitate—
   you must slay them!
Fight, for you
   shall conquer
   your rivals in battle!   34

Sanjaya said:

Having heard these
   words of Keshava,
With palms joined in
   prayerful gesture, trembling,
   the diademed one [Arjuna],
Offering obeisance,
   spoke yet again to Krishna.
While stuttering,
   timid and terrified,
   he bowed down.   35

Arjuna said:

It is appropriate, O Hrishīkesha,
   that by declaring your fame
The world loudly rejoices
   and is overjoyed.
Demons, terrified,
   flee in every direction,
And all the multitudes of
   perfected beings shall bow down.   36

And why should they not
    bow down to you,
    O Extraordinary Self?
More venerable even than Brahmā,
    you are the original creator.
O Unlimited Lord of Divinities,
    dwelling place of the universe,
You are the indestructible,
    the existent, the nonexistent,
    and that which is beyond.   37

You are the original Divinity,
    the ancient cosmic Person.
You are the highest
    resting place
    of this universe.
You are the knower,
    what is to be known,
    and the highest domain.
By you this universe is pervaded,
    O One of Unlimited Form.   38

You are Vāyu, Yama, Agni,
    Varuna, the moon,
Prajāpati, and
    the Great-Grandfather.
Obeisance! Obeisance unto you
    a thousand times over,
And again, even more—
    obeisance, obeisance unto you!⁶   39

---

6 Vāyu: A Vedic deity and personification of "the wind."

Yama: A Vedic deity and the personification of "death."

Agni: The powerful Vedic deity of "fire."

Varuna: The Vedic deity of law and order; also identified as the ruler of the universe.

Prajāpati: The "progenitor" of humankind.

The Great-Grandfather: The deity of creation, Brahmā.

Obeisance unto you
    from the front
    and from behind.
May there also be obeisance
    unto you from all sides,
    O Everything.
Of immeasurable prowess,
    of unlimited might,
You complete everything—
    therefore, you are everything.   40

Thus thinking of you as "friend,"
    whatever has been spoken
    inappropriately by me,
Such as "O Krishna,
    O Yādava, O friend,"
Without knowing
    this magnificence of yours,
Due to my carelessness
    or even out of affection;   41

And if in sporting together
    you were treated
    disrespectfully by me,
During play or rest,
    while sitting or dining,
When alone, O Achyuta,
    or even before others' eyes—
For that I beg
    your forgiveness,
    O Unfathomable One!   42

You are the Father of the world,
    of the moving
    and the non-moving,
And you are to be honored
    as its most worthy guru.
There is no other equal to you—
    how could there be
    anyone greater,
Even in all the three worlds,
    O One of Incomparable Being?   43

Therefore, bowing down,
    prostrating my body before you,
I ask you, the worshippable Lord,
    to bestow your grace.
As a father is to a son,
    as a friend to a friend,
As a dearly loved one
    to a dearly beloved—
    be pleased to show your
    loving kindness, O Divinity.   44

Having seen what never
    has been seen before,
    I am exceedingly pleased,
Yet my mind is distressed
    and filled with fear.
O Divinity, allow me to see
    that very [intimate] form.
Bestow upon me your grace,
    O Lord of Divinities,
    dwelling place of the universe.   45

Adorned by the diadem,
    bearing the club,
    with disc held in hand,
I desire to see you
    just as before.
In that very form
    having four arms,
Please become manifest,
    O Thousand-Armed One,
    O Universal Form!   46

The Beloved Lord said:

Bestowing my grace
    upon you, O Arjuna,
This supreme form
    has been manifested
    from the yoga of my Self.
Consisting of splendor,
    it is all-pervasive,
    unending, and original—
[This form] which has
    not been seen before
    by anyone other than you.   47

Not by the Vedas,
    sacrifice, or study,
    nor by giving [in charity],
Nor even by rites,
    nor by severe austerities
Am I able to be seen
    in such a form,
    within the world of humans,
By anyone other than you,
    O Hero of the Kurus.   48

Do not fear
and do not be confused,
Having seen such
a frightful awesome form
as this one of mine.
As one whose fear
has been dispelled,
with mind appeased,
Once again
you may behold
my very [intimate] form.⁷   49

Sanjaya said:

Thus having spoken
this to Arjuna,
Vāsudeva revealed his
own form as before.
And he calmed that
frightened one,
Assuming once again
the gentle appearance
of the exalted Self.   50

Arjuna said:

Seeing this gentle
humanlike form
of yours, O Janārdana,
I am now fulfilled,
with thought restored
to a normal state.⁸   51

---

7 Frightful, awesome: Translates *ghora*, which has both negative and positive senses. I have attempted to include both in this compound phrase.

8 Janārdana: Name for Krishna meaning "one who excites humans."

The Beloved Lord said:

Very rarely seen
    is this form of mine
    that you have seen.
Even the divinities
    are always desiring
    a vision of this form.   52

Not by study of the Vedas,
    nor by austerity,
    nor by giving,
    nor by sacrifice
Am I able to be seen
    in such a form
    as you have seen me.   53

Only by the offering of
    one's love to none other,
    O Arjuna, am I able,
    in such a form,
To be known and
    to be truly seen,
    and to be attained,
    O Fighter of the Enemy.   54

Acting for me
  in one's actions,
  being devoted to me,
  offering love to me,
  having no attachments,
Free from enmity
  toward all beings—
  this is the one
  who comes to me,
  O Son of Pāndu.   55

12

The Way of Love

Arjuna said:

Those who are thus
    constantly absorbed in yoga,
    who fully worship you by
    offering their love,
And also those who [worship]
    the imperishable unmanifest—
    which of these is the greatest
    among those who know yoga?   1

The Beloved Lord said:

Directing the mind to me,
    those who are always
    absorbed in yoga
    worship me.
Endowed with the highest faith,
    they are considered by me
    to be the most
    absorbed in yoga.   2

But those who worship
    the imperishable,
    the uncontainable,
    the unmanifest;
The all-pervading,
    the inconceivable,
    the unchanging,
    the immovable,
    and the constant: 3

Having fully controlled
   the aggregate of the senses,
   having the same discernment
   in all instances—
They also attain me,
   delighting in
   the welfare of all beings.   4

Difficulty is greater
   for those whose thought
   is attached
   to the unmanifest.
Certainly, the goal of
   reaching the unmanifest
   is very hard to attain
   by the embodied.   5

However, for those who,
   having fully renounced
   all actions in me,
   are devoted to me
Through this yoga
   and by no other means;
   who, meditating on me,
   offer worship;   6

For them, I soon
   become the one who
   completely lifts them up
   from the ocean
   of the cycle of death,
O Pārtha,
   for their thought
   has been drawn
   to enter into me.   7

Place your mind on me alone;
   let your discernment
   enter into me.
You shall dwell
   only in me
   from now forevermore—
   of this there is no doubt.   8

Moreover, if you are
   unable to fully absorb
   your thought in me
   with steadiness,
Then, with the practice of yoga
   seek to attain me,
   O Conqueror of Wealth.   9

If you also are incapable
   of practicing this,
   become wholly devoted
   to me in action;
For even by
   enacting such
   actions for my sake,
   you shall attain perfection.   10

If even this you
   are unable to enact,
   then, relying on me
   through yoga,
With the relinquishment
   of the fruits of all action—
   act with restraint,
   in possession of the self.   11

For knowledge is better
　　than practice;
　　meditation
　　is preferred
　　over knowledge;
From meditation comes
　　the relinquishment
　　of the fruits of action;
　　from relinquishment
　　comes peace, immediately.　　　　12

One who has no disdain
　　for any being,
　　who is amicable
　　as well as compassionate;
Who is without
　　the sense of 'mine',
　　without the notion
　　of 'I am acting';
　　who is the same in
　　suffering and happiness,
　　who is patient;　　　　　　　　13

The yogi who is
　　always fully satisfied,
　　whose self is controlled,
　　being of firm resolve;
Whose mind and discernment
　　are focused on me,
　　whose love is offered to me—
　　that one is dearly loved by me.　　14

One before whom the world
　　is not disturbed,
　　and who is not disturbed
　　by the world;
Who is freed from elation,
　　impatience, fear,
　　and anxiety—
　　that one also
　　is dearly loved by me.   15

One who is impartial, pure,
　　capable, detached,
　　free from anxiety;
Who has completely
　　relinquished all undertakings—
　　that one, who offers love to me,
　　is dearly loved by me.   16

One who neither
　　relishes nor loathes,
　　who neither
　　laments nor desires,
Relinquishing the pleasant
　　and the unpleasant—
　　that one, who is filled
　　with offerings of love,
　　is dearly loved by me.   17

The same toward both
　　enemy and friend,
　　honor and dishonor;
The same in cold and heat,
　　happiness and suffering;
　　freed from attachment;   18

One for whom blame
   and praise are equal,
   who is disciplined in speech,
   satisfied with whatever
   comes of its own accord;
Who is without
   [attachment to] home,
   who is of steady mind,
   replete with offerings of love—
   such a person is dearly loved by me.   19

Indeed, this is the immortal
   essence of dharma,
   which has been declared;
   those who participate in
   this worship fully,
Who have faith,
   who are devoted to me,
   who have offered their love—
   they are most dearly loved by me.   20

13

Primordial Nature and the Person

Arjuna said:

Primordial nature
and also the person,
the field as well as
the knower of the field,
Knowledge and
the object of knowledge—
I desire to learn about these,
O Keshava.[1]

The Beloved Lord said:

This body,
O Son of Kuntī,
is considered "the field."
One who realizes this—
such a one they call
"a knower of the field,"
those who are realized in that.   I

---

1 This verse is often not included in editions of the BG. When it is presented, it typically appears unnumbered.

Primordial nature: translates *prakṛti*.

The person: Translates *puruṣa*. It is often translated simply as "spirit" and understood as the antonym of the term *prakṛti*, often taken simply as "matter." However, in the BG, the word *puruṣa* is more fully translated as "person," denoting the "self," an individual spiritual being, a particular center of consciousness. Like the word "self," it can incorporate the sense of the embodied condition of a "per-

son" in this world, or it can refer to the "person" liberated from this world, situated in the highest realm (BG 15.16). The BG also presents the "Person," the divinity personally present in all beings, or "the ultimate Person," the supreme divinity of Krishna, also referred to as "the everpresent supreme Lord" (*avyaya īśvara*) (BG 15.17).

The field: translates *kṣetra*.

The knower of the field: translates *kṣetra-jña*.

Understand me also to be
the knower of the field
in all fields, O Bhārata.
Knowledge of both the field
and the knower of the field—
this is considered to be
knowledge by me.   2

This field—what it is
and what its nature is,
what its transformations are
and from where they [originate];
And who one [the knower] is
and what one's powers are—
hear briefly about these from me.   3

It has been sung
in numerous ways by seers,
in various types of
sacred hymns,
And indeed,
in the aphoristic phrases
concerning Brahman,
which are full of reasoning
and firm resolve.²   4

The gross elements,
the notion of 'I am acting',
the faculty of discernment,
and also the unmanifest;
The senses,
which are ten and one, and
the five regions of the senses;   5

---

2 Various types of sacred hymns: Refers to the Vedas.

The aphoristic phrases concerning Brahman: Translates *brahma-sūtra*, also the name of a famous philosophical text (the Vedānta Sūtra) that presents a vision of the essential philosophy of the Upanishads.

Desire, aversion,
  happiness, suffering,
  the aggregate whole,
  thought, and constancy—
This is described in brief
  as the field, along with
  its transformations.   6

Absence of pride,
  absence of deceit,
  nonviolence,
  patience, honesty;
Service to the guru,
  purity, stability,
  control of the self;   7

Dispassion for the objects
  of the senses, and also,
  absence of the notion
  of 'I am acting';
Foreseeing the perils
  of birth, death,
  old age, disease,
  and suffering;   8

Absence of attachment
  and excessive affection
  for children, spouse,
  home, and so on;
Also, constant
  same-mindedness in
  desirable and undesirable
  circumstances;[3]   9

---

3 Children: Translates *putra*, literally "a son,"   Spouse: Translates *dāra*, literally "a wife."
taken here as children in general.

And absorbed in me
  with no yoga other than
  the unwavering
  offering of love;
Dwelling in
  a secluded place,
  having disregard
  for crowds of people;   10

Continuity in knowledge of
  the 'principle of self',
  with a vision of the object
  of that knowledge
  of the truth—
This is declared
  to be knowledge;
  the absence of knowledge
  is whatever is contrary to this.[4]   11

I shall describe
  what is to be known,
  knowing which one
  attains immortality:
Beginningless,
  subordinate to me,
  Brahman is said to be
  neither existent
  nor nonexistent.   12

---

4 Truth: Translates *tattva,* which can also
mean "reality."

Having hands and feet everywhere,
   with eyes, heads, and faces
   everywhere,
Hearing everywhere in the world,
   surrounding everything,
   it remains constant.   13

Having the appearance
   of the 'qualities' of
   all the senses,
   though devoid
   of all the senses;
Unattached yet
   supporting everything;
   free of the 'qualities'
   though the experiencer
   of the 'qualities';   14

Outside and inside of beings,
   not moving
   and yet moving,
Due to its subtle nature
   it is unknowable—
   it is both far away and near.   15

And among beings it is
   undivided, though
   remaining as if divided.
It is to be known
   as the sustainer of beings,
   and as the one who absorbs them
   and sends them forth into being.   16

Also, of luminaries,
   it is said to be
   the luminary
   beyond darkness.
It is knowledge,
   what is to be known,
   and the purpose of knowledge—
   it is seated in the heart of everyone.   17

Thus the field,
   as well as knowledge
   and the object of knowledge,
   have been briefly described.
One whose love
   is offered to me,
   who realizes this knowledge,
   comes forth to my state of being.   18

Primordial nature
   and indeed the person—
   know for certain that both
   are without beginning,
And know that the 'qualities'
   and also their transformations
   become manifest
   from primordial nature.   19

In that which involves
    the object of action,
    the means of action,
    and the cause of action,
    primordial nature
    is said to be the cause.
[Whereas] the person,
    while experiencing the states
    of happiness and suffering,
    is said to be the cause.   20

For the person situated
    in primordial nature
    experiences the 'qualities'
    born of that primordial nature.
Attachment
    to the 'qualities'
    is the cause of one's birth
    into pure and impure wombs.   21

The observer and consenter,
    the supporter,
    the beloved recipient,
    the exalted supreme Lord,
Or even the "supreme Self"
    is declared to be
    the highest Person
    in this body.   22

Whoever thus knows the Person
    and primordial nature,
    along with the 'qualities'—
That one, though existing
    in any condition whatsoever,
    does not take birth again.   23

By means of meditation,
   some perceive the Self
   within the self, by the self;
Others, by the yoga of Sānkhya,
   and even others,
   by the yoga of action.   24

Still others,
   having no knowledge,
   thus only hearing
   from others, offer worship.
And indeed they also
   cross beyond death,
   devoted to what
   they have heard.   25

As for any being,
   stationary or moving,
   it takes birth
Due to the union of the field
   with the knower of the field,
   O Best of the Bharatas.   26

Situated as the same in
   all beings is the highest
   supreme Lord,
Who is not perishing
   when they are perishing—
   one who sees this,
   that one [truly] sees.   27

Indeed, seeing the same
    supreme Lord fully
    established everywhere,
One does not harm
    the self by the self—
    from there one reaches
    the highest goal.   28

By primordial nature alone,
    actions are being
    completely enacted.
One who sees this,
    and thus sees that the self
    is not the creator of action—
    that one [truly] sees.   29

When one perceives
    the various states of being
    as abiding in one place,
And from that alone
    their emanation,
    then one fully
    attains Brahman.   30

Due to having no beginning,
    free from the effect
    of the 'qualities',
    that everpresent supreme Self,
Though situated in the body,
    O Son of Kuntī,
    does not act—
    nor is it tainted [by action].   31

Just as all-pervasive space
    is not tainted
    due to its subtle nature,
Similarly, the Self
    abiding in every body
    is not tainted.   32

As the sun alone
    illuminates
    this entire world,
So the one who
    resides in the field
    illuminates
    the entire field, O Bhārata.   33

Thus the difference
    between the field
    and the knower of the field,
    [seen] with the eye of knowledge,
And the release of beings
    from primordial nature—
    those who know of these,
    it is they who attain the Supreme.   34

14

The Qualities of Nature

The Beloved Lord said:

I shall describe further
   the best of knowledge,
   the ultimate knowledge,
Knowing which, all seers
   have gone from here
   to the highest perfection.   I

Taking refuge in this knowledge,
   having come to a state
   of likeness with me,
Even during creation
   they do not take birth—
   nor do they tremble
   during cosmic absorption.   2

The great Brahman
   is my womb;
   in this I place
   the [cosmic] embryo.
The coming forth
   of all beings becomes
   manifest from that,
   O Bhārata.   3

In all wombs, O Son of Kuntī,
   for whatever forms
   come into being—
For them, the great Brahman
   is the [cosmic] womb;
   I am the father
   who gives forth the seed.   4

"Sattva, rajas, and tamas,"
   the 'qualities' arising
   from primordial nature,
O Mighty-Armed,
   bind the everpresent
   embodied to the body.   5

Among these, sattva,
   due to its untainted nature,
   is illuminating,
   free from contamination.
It binds one by
   attachment to happiness,
   also by attachment
   to knowledge,
   O Blameless One.   6

Know that *rajas*
   is of the nature of
   passion, arising from
   thirst and attachment.
It tightly binds
   one who is embodied,
   O Son of Kuntī,
   by attachment to action.   7

Moreover, know
    that *tamas* is born of
    the absence of knowledge,
    bewildering all
    who are embodied;
With negligence,
    lethargy, and sleep,
    it binds tightly,
    O Bhārata.   8

Sattva causes attachment
    to happiness
    and *rajas* to action,
    O Bhārata.
Obscuring knowledge,
    however, *tamas*
    causes attachment
    even to negligence.[1]   9

Dominating *rajas* and *tamas*,
    sattva becomes
    prominent,
    O Bhārata;
Likewise *rajas*,
    with *sattva* and *tamas*;
    and also *tamas*,
    with *sattva* and *rajas*.   10

---

1 Negligence: Translates *pramāda,* also
meaning madness or "intoxication."

When in all
   the gates of this body,
   illumination gives rise
To knowledge,
   then it should be
   understood that, indeed,
   "*sattva* is dominant."   11

Greed, exertion,
   the undertaking of actions,
   disquietude, and desire—
These are produced
   when *rajas* is dominant,
   O Best of the Bharatas.   12

The absence of light,
   also inactivity, negligence,
   and even bewilderment—
These are produced
   when *tamas* is dominant,
   O Son of Kuru.   13

Now when, under
   the dominance of *sattva,*
   the embodied goes
   to cosmic absorption,
Then one attains
   the pure worlds
   of those who
   know the highest.   14

Having gone forth
    to cosmic absorption
    in the state of *rajas,*
    one is born among
    those attached to action.
Likewise, being absorbed
    into the cosmos while
    in the state of *tamas,*
    one is born into the wombs
    of bewildered persons.   15

Of action that is
    virtuous when enacted,
    they say the fruit is untainted,
    having the nature of *sattva.*
The fruit of *rajas,*
    however, is suffering;
    the absence of knowledge
    is the fruit of *tamas.*   16

From *sattva,*
    knowledge is born,
    and indeed from *rajas,* greed.
Negligence and bewilderment
    arise from *tamas,* as well as
    the absence of knowledge.   17

Those established in *sattva*
    progress upward;
    those attached to *rajas*
    remain in the middle;
Those established
    in the lowest state
    progress downward—
    those attached to *tamas.*   18

When the observer [self]
  perceives no agent of action
  other than the 'qualities',
And knows what is
  higher than the 'qualities'—
  that one attains my state of being.   19

Transcending these
  three 'qualities'
  emerging from the body,
  the embodied one,
Freed from birth,
  death, old age,
  and suffering,
  attains immortality.   20

Arjuna said:

By what characteristics
  does one become identified
  once having transcended
  these three 'qualities',
  O Majestic One?
What is one's conduct,
  and how does one
  transcend these
  three 'qualities'?   21

The Beloved Lord said:

Both illumination
   and activity, and
   even bewilderment,
   O Son of Pāndu—
One neither despises
   these states when they occur
   nor desires them when
   they cease to occur.[2]   22

One who is seated
   as if seated apart;
   who is not disturbed
   by the 'qualities',
Thinking only
   that "the 'qualities'
   [of nature] are at work";
   who remains fixed,
   who is not shaken;   23

For whom suffering and
   happiness are the same,
   being in one's natural state;
   for whom a lump of earth,
   a stone, and gold are the same;
For whom the dearly loved
   and the unloved are equal;
   who is grave, equal in blame
   and praise of one's self;   24

---

2 Illumination: Translates *prakāśam*, describing *sattva*.
   Activity. Translates *pravṛttim*, describing *rajas*.

Bewilderment: Translates *moham*, describing *tamas*.

Who is equal in both
    honor and dishonor,
    equal to friendly
    and rival factions,
Completely relinquishing
    all undertakings—
    that one is said
    to have transcended
    the 'qualities'.   25

And one who, unfailingly,
    with the yoga of
    offering love,
    serves me—
That one, transcending
    these 'qualities',
    prepares oneself for
    being united with Brahman.   26

Truly, of Brahman,
    I am the foundation—
    and of the immortal
    that is everpresent,
Also, of dharma
    that is everlasting,
    and of happiness
    that is extraordinary.   27

15

The Ultimate Person

The Beloved Lord said:

With its roots upward
   and its branches downward,
   they speak of the everlasting
   Ashwattha tree,
Whose leaves
   are the Vedic hymns—
   one who knows this
   is a knower of the Vedas.[1]   1

Extending downward and upward,
   its branches are nourished
By the 'qualities' [of nature],
   with its fresh shoots
   as the objects of the senses.
Also stretched downward
   are its roots,
Promoting action
   in the world of humans.   2

---

1 Ashwattha tree: Understood as a kind of fig tree, first mentioned in BG 10.26. Some commentators understand this name to refer to the banyan tree.

The form of this [tree]
  here in the world
  cannot be perceived—
Not its end
  nor beginning
  nor foundation.
Cutting this Ashwattha tree,
  whose roots
  are fully grown,
With the strong
  ax of detachment;   3

Then that place
  is to be sought
To which having gone
  such persons
  never again return,
[Declaring]: And to that,
  indeed I offer myself,
  to that original Person
From whom cycles
  of cosmic activity have
  issued forth in former ages.   4

Without pride or bewilderment,
   having conquered
   the faults of attachment;
Constantly situated
   in the 'principle of self'
   with desires turned away;
Liberated from
   the dualities known
   as happiness and suffering—
Those who
   are not bewildered
   attain that everlasting place.   5

Neither the sun,
   nor the moon,
   nor fire illuminates
   that realm
To which having gone
   they do not return—
   that is my supreme dwelling.   6

A part of me alone
   in the world of the living
   is the living being,
   which is eternal.
It draws to itself the senses,
   the mind being the sixth,
   all of which are situated
   in primordial nature.   7

When one acquires a body
    and also,
    when one departs from it,
    its master [the self],
Carrying these [senses],
    moves on,
    as the wind carries
    scents from their source.   8

The senses of hearing,
    sight, and touch,
    as well as taste
    and smell—
Presiding over these
    and the mind,
    one pursues the objects
    of the senses.   9

Whether departing from
    or remaining in [the body],
    or experiencing [sense objects],
    affected by the 'qualities',
Those who are very bewildered
    do not perceive this [self]—
    those with the eye
    of knowledge see this.   10

And upon striving,
   yogis see that [Self]
   which exists
   within the self.
But those who are
   not self-actualized,
   even though striving,
   cannot see this,
   being unthoughtful.   11

The splendor that comes
   forth from the sun,
   which illuminates
   the entire universe;
That which
   is in the moon
   and in fire—
   know this splendor
   as belonging to me.   12

And entering the earth,
   I sustain beings
   by my potency.
And I nourish all vegetation
   by becoming the moon,
   which contains
   the essence of taste.[2]   13

---

2 Taste: Translates *rasa*, which also means
"juice" or "flavor."

I, becoming the digestive fire
    dwelling in the bodies
    of breathing beings,
In conjunction
    with the incoming
    and outgoing breaths,
    digest the four types
    of foodstuffs.[3]   14

And I have fully entered
    into the hearts of all;
From me come remembrance,
    knowledge, and forgetfulness.
And by all the Vedas
    only I am to be known;
I am the author of Vedānta
    and truly the knower of the Vedas.[4]   15

The two types of persons
    in the world are these:
    the perishable and
    also, the imperishable.
The perishable
    consists of all beings;
    the imperishable is described
    as those who are situated
    in the highest [state].[5]   16

---

3 Four types of foodstuffs: The four ways in which foods are eaten: licked, chewed, sucked, and swallowed.

4 Forgetfulness: Translates *apohanam*, which can also mean "the removal [of remembrance and knowledge]." For commentators, forgetfulness can be seen as both positive and negative.

Vedānta: Meaning "the end of the Vedas," referring to the Upanishads or to the Vedānta Sūtra, a work composed of a comprehensive interpretation and synthesis of Upanishadic philosophy.

5 The perishable: Translates *kṣara*, which can mean "destructible" or "alterable," referring to the bodies of all beings in this world.

The imperishable: Translates *akṣara*, referring to persons who are not bound to this world, liberated even while in it.

Yet there is another—
an ultimate person
called "the supreme Self,"
Who, entering into
the three worlds,
maintains them
as the everpresent
supreme Lord.[6]   17

Because I am beyond
the perishable
and am even higher
than the imperishable,
Therefore, I am celebrated
in the oldest texts
and in the Vedas
as the Ultimate Person.   18

One who,
unbewildered,
thus knows me
as the Ultimate Person—
That one, who is
a knower of all,
offers love to me with
all of one's being, O Bhārata.   19

---

6 The three worlds: Refers to the upper, lower, and middle worlds of this universe.

Everpresent supreme Lord: Translates *avyaya īśvaraḥ*, presented in the third person. The supreme Lord who enters the worlds and the living beings is a third type of *puruṣa*, or "person," indeed the "ultimate person," a distinctive manifestation of Krishna's supreme divinity. This manifestation is identical with what is described in the following verse, spoken of in the first person, which is Krishna himself as he stands before Arjuna.

Thus it is the greatest secret
   of the revealed scriptures—
   this has been disclosed by me,
   O Faultless One.
Having discerned this,
   one would possess
   discernment,
   and would have enacted
   all that is required
   to be enacted, O Bhārata.   20

16

The Divine and Ungodly Natures

The Beloved Lord said:

Fearlessness, complete
    purity of existence,
    steadfastness in
    the yoga of knowledge;
Acts of giving and restraint,
    sacrifice, study of scripture,
    austerity, and sincerity;   1

Nonviolence, truthfulness,
    freedom from anger,
    relinquishment, peacefulness,
    absence of slander;
Compassion for all beings,
    freedom from longing,
    gentleness, humility,
    absence of agitation;   2

Vitality, patience, tenacity,
    purity, freedom from envy,
    absence of excessive pride—
These become the attributes
    for those of divine birth,
    O Bhārata.   3

Deceitfulness, arrogance,
   and excessive pride;
   wrath, and indeed harshness,
Also absence of knowledge—
   these are the attributes,
   O Pārtha, for those
   of ungodly birth.   4

The divine attributes move one
   toward complete freedom;
   the ungodly attributes,
   it is thought, toward bondage.
Do not worry—
   you are wellborn
   with divine attributes,
   O Son of Pāndu.   5

The creation of beings
   in this world is only
   of two types: the divine
   and the ungodly.
The divine has been
   described in detail,
   O Pārtha;
   now hear from me
   about the ungodly.   6

Both activity and inactivity
   ungodly persons
   do not understand.
Neither purity
   nor good behavior
   nor truth is found in them.   7

Without reality,
   without foundation,
   the world, they say,
   is without the supreme Lord,
That the one is not brought
   into being by the other—
   then by what?
   It is caused by selfish desire.   8

Supporting this view,
   persons whose self is lost,
   having little discernment,
Whose actions are cruel—
   they come forth into being
   as enemies of the world
   for its destruction.   9

Resorting to insatiable desire,
   filled with deceitfulness,
   pride, and arrogance;
Due to bewilderment,
   holding onto notions
   that are held as untrue—
   they proceed with impure resolve.   10

And subjected to
    immeasurable anxiety,
    which continues until
    one's final death;
Having gratification
    of selfish desires as
    one's highest aim,
    convinced that
    "this is all there is"—   11

Bound by a hundred
    chains of hope,
    devoted to desire
    and wrath,
With the aim of
    indulging in desires—
    those persons seek
    the accumulation of wealth
    by unjust means.   12

"Today this has been
    acquired by me;
    this desire I shall fulfill.
This belongs to me—
    even more wealth
    shall become mine."   13

"That enemy
  has been slain by me,
  and I shall also slay others.
I am the supreme lord,
  I am the enjoyer;
  I am perfect, powerful,
  and happy."   14

"I am wealthy,
  of high birth;
  who else is there
  like me?
I shall sacrifice,
  I shall offer gifts,
  I shall rejoice,"
  say those bewildered
  by a lack of knowledge.   15

Carried away by many thoughts,
  enveloped in a snare
  of bewilderment,
Very attached to the enjoyment
  of selfish desires—
  they fall into an unclean
  place of torment.   16

Self-centered, stubborn,
    full of pride and conceit
    coming from wealth,
They perform sacrifices
    in name only, with deceit—
    not according to what
    previously has been enjoined.[1]   17

The notion of 'I am acting',
    also power, arrogance,
    selfish desire, wrath—
    completely attached to these,
Such envious persons
    loathe me
    in their own bodies
    and in the bodies of others.   18

Those who hate,
    who are cruel,
    low persons caught in
    the cycle [of birth and death]—
I repeatedly hurl
    such impure persons
    only into the wombs
    of the ungodly.   19

---

1 What previously has been enjoined: Refers
to what was stated in the Vedas.

Having come
  into an ungodly womb,
  those who are bewildered
  birth after birth,
Not ever attaining me,
  O Son of Kuntī—
  they then go
  to the lowest place.   20

This is the threefold passage
  of a tormented existence,
  which destroys the self:
Desire, anger, also greed—
  therefore, it is these three
  that one should relinquish.   21

Completely freed
  from these three
  passages of darkness,
  O Son of Kuntī,
A human being does
  what is best for the self,
  then goes to the highest place.   22

One who, abandoning
  scriptural injunction,
  acts according to one's
  own selfish desires—
That person does not
  attain perfection,
  nor happiness,
  nor the highest place.   23

Therefore, let scripture
be your authority
for understanding what
action should be performed
and what action should
not be performed.
Knowing the prescribed
scriptural injunctions,
you are obliged to enact
such action in this world.   24

The Three Types of Faith

Arjuna said:

Those who,
   having abandoned
   scriptural injunctions,
   engage in sacrifice,
   endowed with faith—
What indeed is
   their condition,
   O Krishna:
   is it *sattva, rajas,* or *tamas?*   I

The Beloved Lord said:

The faith of the embodied
   is of three types,
   arising from one's
   particular state of being:
"That of the nature of *sattva,*
   or of the nature of *rajas,*
   or even of the nature of *tamas*"—
   now hear about this.   2

According to the degree of *sattva*,
   the faith of everyone
   becomes manifest,
   O Bhārata.
A person is made of this faith—
   whatever the faith,
   that is indeed
   what one is.[1]   3

Those of the nature of *sattva*
   offer sacrifice to divinities;
   those of the nature of *rajas*
   offer sacrifice to spirits
   and demonic beings.
To ghosts and multitudes
   of departed beings,
   the others, those humans
   of the nature of *tamas*,
   offer sacrifice.   4

Those persons
   who perform terrible
   austerities not enjoined
   in the scriptures,
Who are fully united
   with deceit and the notion
   of 'I am acting',
   who are full of selfish
   desire, passion, and power;   5

---

1 According to the degree of *sattva:* Translates the phrase, *sattvānurūpāḥ,* meaning the greater the degree of *sattva,* the more pure the faith. Every combination of the essential qualities contains some degree of *sattva.*

Faith: Translates *śraddhā,* which means literally, "where one places one's heart."

A person: Refers to the embodied soul as it is influenced by the essential qualities of nature, and not the soul proper.

Mindless ones,
   causing torment
   to the aggregate of elements
   existing within the body,
And thus to me,
   who am also existing
   within the body—
   know them to be
   of ungodly resolve.   6

Indeed, the food
   that becomes dear
   to each person
   is even of three types,
As well as one's sacrifice,
   austerity, and also
   one's acts of giving—
   hear of their differences.   7

Promoting life, energy,
   strength, good health,
   happiness, and satisfaction;
Flavorful, appealing,
   substantial, and hearty—
   such foods are dear to those
   of the nature of *sattva*.   8

Bitter, sour, salty,
  very hot and acidic,
  astringent and burning,
Causing misery,
  sorrow, and disease—
  such foods are desired
  by those of the nature of *rajas*.   9

Food that is no longer fresh,
  that is tasteless, putrid,
  and stale,
That has been rejected
  and is also impure—
  eating such foods is dear
  to those of the nature of *tamas*.   10

Sacrifice offered as observed
  in scriptural injunctions
  by one who does
  not desire its fruits,
Whose mind is completely
  absorbed in the thought that,
  "only sacrifice is to be made"—
  this is of the nature of *sattva*.   11

But that which is offered
    with a motive for the fruit,
    and indeed, even with
    a deceitful purpose,
O Best of the Bharatas—
    know that this sacrifice
    is of the nature of *rajas*.   12

Sacrifice that is lacking
    in scriptural foundation,
    with no offering of grains,
    with no recitation of mantras,
    without monetary donations,
Completely devoid of faith—
    this they regard as having
    the nature of *tamas*.   13

Respect for the divinities,
    the twice-born, the gurus,
    and for those who possess
    profound knowledge;
    purity, sincerity,
Chastity, and
    nonviolence—
    this is called
    austerity of the body.[2]   14

_____

2 Twice-born: Translates *dvija*, referring to a Brahmin, a member of the priestly and educated class. The Brahmin is born twice, first through a physical birth, and then through the initiatory rite-of-passage.

Words that do not cause distress,
    that are truthful,
    endearing, and beneficial;
And further, the practice
    of reciting sacred texts—
    this is called
    austerity of speech.   15

Calmness of mind,
    gentleness, silence,
    control of the self,
"Complete purity of being"—
    this is called austerity
    in relation to the mind.   16

That threefold austerity
    practiced by humans
    who possess the highest faith,
Who do not desire its fruits,
    who are absorbed in yoga—
    they regard that as having
    the nature of *sattva*.   17

That austerity which is enacted
    with pretense, and indeed
    with the aim of receiving
    kind treatment, respect,
    and honor—
That is declared
    in this world to be
    of the nature of *rajas*,
    vacillating and unstable.   18

That which is enacted
   with bewildered notions,
   with self-inflicted pain,
Or with the aim of
   destroying another—
   that austerity is said to be
   of the nature of *tamas*.   19

That gift which is given
   with the thought that,
   "this should be given,"
   to one who may not
   act reciprocally,
At an appropriate
   time and place,
   and to a worthy person—
   that gift is to be
   remembered as having
   the nature of *sattva*.   20

But that gift which is given
   with the aim of gaining
   a returned favor, or
   further, aspiring
   for the fruit,
Or which is given
   reluctantly—
   that gift is to be
   remembered as having
   the nature of *rajas*.   21

That gift which is given
  at an inappropriate
  time and place,
  to unworthy persons,
Without acting respectfully
  or with contempt—
  that is declared to be
  of the nature of *tamas*.   22

"OM TAT SAT"—
  these are the designations
  of Brahman, which are
  remembered as threefold.
By this, the Brahmins
  and the Vedas
  and sacrifices were
  ordained in ancient times.   23

Therefore, with the sounding
  of [the syllable] "OM"—
  acts of sacrifice, giving,
  and austerity,
Which are prescribed
  by scriptural injunction,
  are always set into motion
  by those who profess Brahman.   24

Uttering "TAT" without
   the aim of the fruit—
   acts of sacrifice and austerity,
And various acts of giving
   are enacted by those
   who desire liberation.   25

In the meaning
   of 'eternal truth'
   and in the meaning
   of 'truth-seeking sage'
   this word "SAT"
   is properly engaged.
When action
   is praiseworthy,
   O Pārtha,
   the word "SAT"
   is also engaged.   26

Steadfastness in sacrifice,
   in austerity, and in giving
   is also called "SAT,"
And any action for
   the sake of such purposes
   is likewise explained as "SAT."   27

Without faith,
    that which is sacrificed,
    given, performed as
    intense austerity,
    or enacted
Is called "*asat*" [not SAT],
    O Pārtha, and is not
    truly that [as it seems]—
    for those having passed on,
    or for us remaining here
    in this world.[3]   28

---

3 "*Asat*" [not SAT]: Meaning literally, "not true" or "what is not the supreme truth."

Not truly that: Translates *tat,* the correlative pronoun of *yat* ("which") found in the first half of the verse; "that" refers to that which is "sacrificed, given, etc.," echoing the efficacious TAT presented in BG 17.25.

18

The Supreme Secret of Yoga

Arjuna said:

About renunciation,
   O Mighty-Armed,
   I desire to know the truth,
And about relinquishment,
   O Hrishīkesha;
   also the distinctions
   between them,
   O Slayer of Keshi.　　　　　1

The Beloved Lord said:

The renouncing of acts
   arising from selfish desire
   wise ones understand
   to be renunciation.
The relinquishing of
   the fruits of all action
   seers declare
   as relinquishment.　　　　　2

"It is to be relinquished
   for it is full of fault,"
   certain thoughtful persons
   declare of action.
"Actions of sacrifice,
   giving, and austerity
   are not to be relinquished,"
   yet others declare.　　　　　3

Hear my conclusion
  on this subject
  of relinquishment,
  O Best of the Bharatas.
For relinquishment,
  O Tiger Among Men,
  is widely proclaimed
  to be of three types.   4

Actions of sacrifice,
  giving, and austerity
  are not to be relinquished;
  rather, they are to be enacted.
Sacrifice, giving, and austerity
  are certainly sources
  of purification for
  thoughtful persons.   5

"These actions, however,
  only after relinquishing
  attachment to them
  and their fruits,
Should be enacted,"
  O Pārtha—
  this, without doubt,
  is my highest opinion.   6

So renunciation
  of prescribed action
  is not appropriate.
Complete relinquishment
  of such due to bewilderment
  is proclaimed to be
  of the nature of *tamas*.   7

Who deems action as "difficult,"
   only due to fear
   of bodily suffering—
   one who should
   relinquish in this way,
Enacting relinquishment
   of the nature of *rajas*,
   certainly would not obtain
   the fruits of such relinquishment.   8

"It should be enacted,"
   indeed, that action
   which is enacted
   because it is prescribed,
   O Arjuna.
Relinquishing attachment
   and certainly the fruit,
   such relinquishment
   is thought to be
   of the nature of *sattva*.   9

One who is not adverse
   to disagreeable action
   nor attached to that
   which is agreeable—
Such a relinquisher
   is fully absorbed in *sattva*;
   the doubts of that
   learned person are severed.   10

For one who bears a body
    is not able to relinquish
    actions entirely;
Yet one who relinquishes
    the fruits of action—
    that one is said to be
    "one who relinquishes."   11

Undesirable,
    desirable, and mixed
    are the threefold
    fruits of action,
Which continue
    to come into being
    for those who
    do not relinquish,
    even after passing on,
    but never for those
    who are renouncers.   12

The five causes of action,
    O Mighty-Armed—
    learn from me about these,
Which have been declared
    in the enacted conclusions
    by the followers of Sānkhya
    for success in all actions: 13

[They are] the physical basis,
    also the agent of action,
    and the various
    means of action,
And the different types
    of various movements,
    and even the divine forces,
    the fifth of these.   14

With one's body,
   speech, or mind,
   whatever action
   a human undertakes,
Whether it be normal,
   or contrary to the norm—
   these are its five causes.   15

This being so,
   one who perceives
   the self alone as
   the agent of action,
Due to one's
   inner discernment
   not being active—
   that one does not
   truly perceive things,
   being weak-minded.   16

One whose state of being
   is free from the notion
   of 'I have acted',
   whose discernment
   is not contaminated—
That one,
   even though having
   slain these people,
   does not slay;
   nor is that one bound.   17

Knowledge,
   the object of knowledge,
   and the knower
   are the three factors
   that compel one to act.
The means of action,
   action itself, and
   the agent of action
   are the three factors
   that constitute action.   18

Knowledge and action
   and the agent of action
   are [all] of three types,
   determined by the divisions
   of the 'qualities'.
This is declared
   in the Sānkhya theory
   of the 'qualities'—
   hear also about these,
   as they are.   19

That by which one
   perceives in all beings
   one everpresent being,
Who is undivided
   among divided beings—
   understand that knowledge
   to be of the nature of *sattva*.   20

But with a view of separateness,
  that knowledge
  which understands
  various states of being
As having been separately
  formed in all beings—
  understand that knowledge
  to be of the nature of *rajas*.   21

However, that [knowledge]
  wherein one thing
  is taken to be the whole—
  being attached, without reason,
  to the performance of
  [a single] activity
Having no true value
  or significance—
  that is said to be
  of the nature of *tamas*.   22

Disciplined,
  free from attachment,
  acting without
  passion or repulsion,
Without desiring to obtain
  the fruit of action—
  that is said to be
  of the nature of *sattva*.   23

But that action which,
   with the hope of
   fulfilling selfish desires,
   or further, with the notion
   of 'I am acting',
Is enacted
   with great effort—
   that is declared to be
   of the nature of *rajas*.   24

Disregarding consequences,
   loss, harm, and also
   personal capacity—
Such action, undertaken
   due to bewilderment,
   is said to be of
   the nature of *tamas*.   25

Freed from attachment,
   not speaking of oneself,
   fully endowed with
   energy and steadfastness,
Unaffected by both success
   and lack of success—
   such an agent of action
   is said to be of
   the nature of *sattva*.   26

Passionate, desirous of
   gaining the fruits of action,
   having an aggressive nature,
   greedy, unclean,
Filled with joy and sorrow—
   such an agent of action
   is proclaimed to be of
   the nature of *rajas*.   27

Not absorbed in yoga,
    vulgar, stubborn, deceitful,
    denouncing others, lethargic,
Despondent, and procrastinating—
    such an agent of action is said
    to be of the nature of *tamas*.   28

The different types of discernment
    and also of determination,
    according to the 'qualities'
    are divided into three—
    now hear of these
Expounded upon separately,
    with nothing left out,
    O Conqueror of Wealth.   29

Positive engagement
    and disengagement,
    what is to be enacted
    and not to be enacted,
    what is to be feared
    and not to be feared,
Bondage and freedom—
    one who perceives these,
    that one's discernment
    is of the nature of *sattva*,
    O Pārtha.   30

Dharma and what
    opposes dharma,
    and what is to be enacted,
    and also, what is not
    to be enacted—
That discernment
    which incorrectly
    understands these
    is of the nature of *rajas*,
    O Pārtha.   31

"What opposes dharma
    is dharma"—
    that which thinks this
    is covered by *tamas*,
And that which completely
    reverses all meaning;
    such discernment is of
    the nature of *tamas*, O Pārtha.   32

That determination by which
    one is able to hold steady
    the activities of the mind,
    the breath, and the senses
Through the undisturbed
    practice of yoga—
    that determination, O Pārtha,
    is of the nature of *sattva*.   33

But that by which one
   holds steadily to dharma,
   desires, and wealth,
   with determination,
   O Arjuna,
With attachment,
   desirous of the fruits—
   that determination is
   of the nature of *rajas*,
   O Pārtha.   34

That by which an ignorant person
   does not let go of sleep, fear,
   lamentation, depression,
   and even madness—
That determination,
   O Pārtha, is of
   the nature of *tamas*.   35

But now hear from me
   about the three
   types of happiness,
   O Leader of the Bharatas,
In which one experiences
   [such happiness]
   through repetition,
   then finally comes
   to the end of suffering.   36

That which in the beginning
  seems like poison
  but in the end
  resembles the immortal—
That is declared
  to be happiness
  of the nature of *sattva*,
  born from the serenity
  of the discerning self.   37

Due to the conjunction
  of the senses with their objects,
  that which in the beginning
  resembles the immortal
But in the end
  seems like poison—
  that happiness is understood
  to be of the nature of *rajas*.   38

Happiness which in the beginning
  and consequently in the end
  is bewildering for the self,
Which arises from sleep,
  lethargy, and confusion—
  that is declared to be
  of the nature of *tamas*.   39

There is nothing
  either on this earth
  or in the divine realm,
  even among the divinities,
With an existence
  that is freed from
  these three 'qualities'
  born of primordial nature.   40

Among Brahmins,
   rulers, tradespeople,
   and skilled workers,
   O Scorcher of the Enemy,
Actions are determined
   by the coming forth into being
   of their particular natures,
   according to the 'qualities'.   41

Calmness, restraint,
   austerity, purity, patience,
   and also sincerity;
Knowledge, realized knowledge,
   and strong faith in the divine
   are the active traits of Brahmins,
   born of their own nature.   42

Heroism, prowess,
   steadfastness, skill, and
   also, not fleeing in battle,
Generosity, and lordliness
   are the active traits of rulers,
   born of their own nature.   43

Cultivating the fields,
   protecting cows, and
   engaging in commerce
   are the actions
   of tradespeople,
   born of their own nature.
Characterized by performing
   all kinds of service for others
   are the actions
   of skilled workers, also
   born of their own nature.   44

Being practiced in one's
   own specific activity,
   a person attains
   full perfection.
How one who is practiced
   in such activity
   finds perfection—
   hear about this.   45

That one from whom the activity
   of beings comes forth,
   by whom this [universe]
   is pervaded—
Worshipping that one
   by one's own action,
   a human being
   finds perfection.   46

Better is one's own dharma
   even if imperfect
   than another's dharma
   followed perfectly.
Performing action
   determined by
   one's own nature,
   one does not incur fault.   47

Action born of one's nature,
O Son of Kuntī,
even if faulty,
should not be relinquished.
For all undertakings
are covered by faults,
as fire is by smoke.   48

With one's discernment
unattached in all circumstances,
with the self conquered,
longings having vanished,
One attains
the supreme perfection
of actionlessness
through renunciation.[1]   49

Once having attained perfection,
how one also attains Brahman,
learn from me through
Just a brief summary,
O Son of Kuntī—
this is the highest
culmination of knowledge.[2]   50

---

1 Actionlessness: Translates *naiṣkarmya*, which means literally, "action without any binding consequences [for the one who acts]."

2 This verse begins Krishna's summary of the greater secret, which is a transcendent state of being that focuses upon Brahman and Purush-ottama. From the beginning of this chapter up to the present verse, Krishna's summary of his great secret is presented.

Absorbed in yoga
  with pure discernment
  and subduing the self
  with steadfastness;
Relinquishing
  the objects of the senses,
  such as sound and so forth,
  casting away attraction and repulsion; 51

Dwelling apart from others,
  eating lightly,
  controlling one's speech,
  body, and mental activity;
Constantly devoted
  to the yoga of meditation,
  taking full refuge
  in dispassion;   52

Being completely freed from
  the notion of 'I am acting',
  from aggressiveness, pride,
  selfish desire, anger,
  and possessiveness;
Without a sense of
  'mine', peaceful—
  that one is prepared
  to be united with Brahman.   53

Being united with Brahman,
  one whose self is tranquil,
  who neither laments
  nor desires,
Who is the same
  toward all beings—
  that one attains the highest,
  the offering of love to me.   54

By offering love
   one recognizes
   me fully and
   who I am in truth.
Once knowing
   me in truth,
   one comes to me
   immediately.[3]   55

Even though continually
   enacting all activities,
   fully taking refuge
   in me,
By my grace
   one attains
   the everpresent
   eternal dwelling.   56

With one's thought
   having renounced
   all actions in me,
   wholly devoted to me,
Fully taking refuge in
   the yoga of discernment—
   always be thinking of me.   57

With thought on me,
   due to my grace
   you shall transcend
   all difficulties.
Now, if you shall
   not hear because of
   the notion of 'I am acting',
   then you shall be lost.   58

---

3 Comes. Translates *viśate*, which can also
mean "enters into" or "comes back."

When you think,
    having taken shelter
    of the notion of 'I am acting',
    that "I shall not fight"—
This resolve of yours
    is in vain since
    primordial nature
    shall force you.[4]   59

Being bound by what is
    born of your own nature,
    O Son of Kuntī,
    by your own action—
Whatever way you
    desire not to act
    due to bewilderment,
    that way you shall act,
    even against your will.   60

The supreme Lord
    of all beings, O Arjuna,
    is present within the inner
    region of the heart,
Causing all beings
    to move about like riders
    upon a mystical machine,
    by the divine power of Māyā.[5]   61

---

4 "I shall not fight": Translates the phrase, *na yotsya iti*. Note the similar sounding last word of this verse, *niyokṣyati*, which translates the phrase "primordial nature shall force you." This is an example of Krishna's clever play on words.

5 A mystical machine: Translates the word *yantra*, which can refer to "the body" or even to "the complex workings of the whole cosmos."

In that one only,
    take shelter
    with all your heart,
    O Bhārata.
Through his grace
    you shall attain
    supreme peace,
    the eternal dwelling.   62

Thus for you this knowledge,
    which is a greater secret
    than the [previous] secret,
    is made known by me.
Having fully grasped this,
    with nothing overlooked,
    then act as you so choose.[6]   63

The greatest secret of all,
    once more please hear—
    it is my supreme message:
    "You are so much loved by me!"
Thereupon I shall continue
    declaring this message for you,
    which I have set forth into motion.[7]   64

---

6 A greater secret: Translates *guhyatara*. This "greater" secret, more secret than the [previous] secret, constitutes the transcendent state of realizing Brahman and the development of a vision of the "supreme Self," *puruṣa*, or the "supreme Lord," *iśvara*, within one's own heart and the hearts of all living beings. The "greatest secret" of Krishna is introduced in the following verse and expressed in subsequent verses.

The [previous] secret: The first of three secrets, constituting Krishna's words on acting in the outer world according to one's nature, without being attached to the fruits of one's actions. This first secret is to act out of love, and its summary begins with the first verse of this chapter.

7 The greatest secret of all: Translates *sarva-guhyatama*.

Loved: Translates *iṣṭa*, which literally means "wished" or "desired." "You are so much loved by me" therefore conveys the sense of an impassioned love, a divine yearning.

Well-being: translates *hita*, which can also mean "advantage," "welfare," "benefit," or "good."

Be mindful of me
    with love offered to me;
    sacrificing for me,
    act out of reverence for me.
Truly you shall
    come to me—
    this I promise you
    for you are dearly loved by me.   65

Completely relinquishing
    all forms of dharma,
    come to me
    as your only shelter.
I shall grant you
    freedom from
    all misfortune—
    do not despair!⁸   66

This is not to be spoken
    by you at any time
    to one who is
    without discipline,
    nor to one who
    does not offer one's love,
Nor to one who hears
    yet has no desire to follow,
    nor to one who is
    envious of me.   67

---

8 Forms of dharma: Translates the plural
form of dharma.

One who reveals
  this supreme secret
  to those who have
  offered me their love,
Enacting the highest
  offering of love for me—
  that one shall certainly
  come to me, without doubt.   68

And among humans,
  there is no one whose acts
  are more dearly loved by me
  than that one,
Nor shall there be
  any other on earth who
  is more dearly loved by me
  than such a person.   69

Also, whosoever shall study
  this sacred dialogue of ours
  concerning dharma—
By that person, through
  the sacrifice of knowledge,
  I shall be lovingly worshipped;
  this is my conviction.[9]   70

---

9 Lovingly worshipped: This phrase translates *iṣṭa*, which, interestingly, is a past participle derived from two different verbal roots, meaning either "sacrificed, worshipped" (*yaj*) or "loved, desired" (*icch*). Though most scholars understand this participle to be the first of these meanings, I have used "lovingly worshipped" to reflect its expressive ambiguity. It is also interesting to note that this participle bears the sense of "loved" or "desired" several verses earlier, in Krishna's impassioned words, "You are so much loved [*iṣṭa*] by me!" (BG 18.64)

Possessing faith
  and free from envy,
  such a person who
  should only hear it—
Even that one,
  liberated, would attain
  the blissful worlds of
  those whose actions are pure.   71

Has this [teaching] been
  heard by you, O Pārtha,
  with thought focused upon
  the single highest point?
Has this profound
  bewilderment coming
  from the absence of knowledge
  been perfectly destroyed in you,
  O Conqueror of Wealth?   72

Arjuna said:

With confusion destroyed,
  my memory is restored
  by your grace,
  O Achyuta.
I am firmly resolved
  with doubts dispelled—
  I shall act according
  to your guidance.   73

Sanjaya said:

Thus from Vāsudeva
    and Pārtha,
    whose self is exalted,
I have heard this
    wondrous conversation,
    which causes a state
    of rapturous bliss.[10]   74

By the grace of Vyāsa
    I have heard this
    supreme secret of yoga
From Krishna,
    the Supreme Lord of Yoga,
    appearing directly
    before my eyes,
    speaking it himself.[11]   75

O King, remembering—
    remembering over and over
    this wondrous dialogue
Of Keshava and Arjuna,
    which is auspicious,
    I feel rapturous bliss
    moment after moment![12]   76

---

10 Causes a state of rapturous bliss: Translates *romaharshana*, meaning "bodily hairs standing on end" or the "thrilling of bodily hairs."

11 Supreme secret of yoga: Translates *guhyaṁ param yogam*.

12 O King. Refers to Dhritarāshtra.

And remembering—
remembering over and over
that most wondrous
beautiful form of Hari,
My amazement is great,
O King, and I feel
rapturous bliss
again and again![13]   77

Where there is Krishna,
the Supreme Lord of Yoga,
where there is Pārtha,
Holder of the Bow,
There is fortune,
triumph, well-being,
and lasting righteousness—
that is my conclusion.[14]   78

---

13 Hari: A name for Krishna meaning "one who takes away," referring either to one's heart or one's troubles.
14 Fortune: Translates *śrī*, which can also mean "light," "splendor," "beauty," "auspiciousness," "success," or "prosperity."
   Triumph: Translates *vijaya*, which also means "victory" or "conquest."

   Well-being: Translates *bhūti*, which also means "prosperity," "might," "power," "wealth," or "fortune."
   Lasting righteousness: Translates *dhruvā nīti*. The word *nīti* means "wise conduct," "political wisdom," or "moral philosophy."

Textual Illuminations

The Yoga of the Bhagavad Gītā

An essential message concerning yoga pervades the text of the Bhagavad Gītā. Yoga, though taking many forms in the Gītā, acts as a unifying force that ties together all the teachings, practices, philosophies, and analyses presented in Krishna's discourse. The various yogas are meant to lead one to the ultimate form of yoga, what the narrator calls "the supreme secret of yoga." Embedded within the text, unifying its diverse themes, this cohesive message of yoga allows the reader to grasp every aspect of the Bhagavad Gītā through its revealing lens.

Many religious traditions and spiritual or yogic practices claim the Bhagavad Gītā as their own. Commentators from these varied traditions frequently interpret verses in ways that support their doctrines, far too often to the exclusion of the evident meaning of the text as a whole. The voice of the Bhagavad Gītā is powerful, and the text tells us how it wants to be understood. There is no need to superimpose anything that is not presented by the text, as is often done, nor is it necessary to privilege aspects of the text that the text itself does not emphasize. Supplementation is thus required only to bring out what is already emphasized by the text. The imposition of a doctrinal or even esoteric vision onto the verses of the Gītā, ungrounded in the text's essential message of yoga, risks an overly free interpretation. Our task here, therefore, is to offer a vision of the text that is generated from the text itself and a translation that is dedicated to this vision, through which sectarian interpretations of this great work may be better understood and assessed. Such a powerful and embracing vision speaks to those both within and outside traditions that revere this text as sacred.

We can begin to grasp the vision of the Bhagavad Gītā by reviewing the many applications of yoga in the text. The term *yoga* denotes a variety of human practices, disciplines, and even experiences to reach the divine, or a state of perfection that is achieved through rigorous meditational or ascetical discipline. The Bhagavad Gītā explains that these many forms of yoga may be practiced to attain a state of transcendent consciousness and ultimately be united with a specific dimension of the divine. Though the word *yoga* is often used to refer to the human achievement of evolving to higher states of consciousness, the Gītā tells us that it is more than that. At the highest level, yoga is a secret state of union within supreme love, bestowed by divinity, who is also subsumed in this union. Indeed, yoga is the power of love that transforms the heart and to which even divinity submits.

Although yoga generally denotes the soul's union with the divine, the term refers more specifically to the numerous paths for attaining several levels of perfection, as well as the perfections themselves. These paths can be perceived in the prefixed words that modify the term *yoga*, for instance in the compound phrase *buddhi-yoga*, "the yoga of discernment" (BG 2.49). Other prefixed words referring to the different forms of yoga are observable in the titles traditionally given to the eighteen chapters of the Gītā. These traditional presentations of the text are most often read independently from its greater epic context. Although there are no titles in the original text (or for that matter, in the whole of the Mahābhārata), over time, in multiple editions, similar or identical titles have been consistently assigned to its chapters. Most significantly, the word *yoga* always appears in each chapter title. The first group of titles below refers to human practices and philosophical visions that enable souls to reach some aspect of the divine; the second to ways that the divinity manifests himself to allow souls to know particular dimensions of the divine:

Titles Indicating Primary Forms of Yoga for Souls

The Yoga of Action, *karma-yoga* (chapter 3)

The Yoga of Knowledge, *jñāna-yoga* (chapter 4)

The Yoga of Renunciation, *saṁnyāsa-yoga* (chapter 5)

The Yoga of Meditation, *dhyāna-yoga* (chapter 6)

The Yoga of Love, *bhakti-yoga* (chapter 12)

Titles Indicating Primary Forms of Yoga for Divinity

The Yoga of Divine Power, *vibhūti-yoga* (chapter 10)

The Yoga of the Universal Form, *viśva-rūpa-yoga* (chapter 11)

The Yoga of the Ultimate Person, *purushottama-yoga* (chapter 15)

Perhaps the most unexpected form of yoga is indicated in the title of the first chapter, "The Yoga of Arjuna's Despair" (*arjuna-viṣāda-yoga*). Indeed, the concept of yoga is so broad that it even can conceive of despondency as a yoga that connects the practitioner with God.

To understand further the depth of yoga as the Bhagavad Gītā presents it, let us examine the term *yoga* itself. Many introductions to yoga explain that it is a Sanskrit word derived from the verbal root *yuj*, meaning to "yoke," "harness," or "connect." Interestingly, the essential elements as well as the ultimate meaning of yoga are revealed in the English definition of the noun *yoke*. The lexical description of *yoke* is a harness or crossbar by which the heads or necks of two farm animals are joined together. The essential elements derived from this definition could be described as: (1) an overarching powerful element, (2) a particular entity, (3) another distinct entity, and (4) an intimate conjunction between the two entities. Thus, the overarching element of power joins one entity with another in order to create an intimate relationship between the two entities. In the simplest of terms, yoga is the intimacy experienced between two entities who are joined together by a special power (see Figure 1 on the following page).

These four elements found in the yoke are clearly present in the yoga of the Bhagavad Gītā: (1) Yoga-Māyā, abbreviated as Māyā, means literally "the power of yoga."[1] This power can be seen as the potency found in all forms of yoga. Broadly, it is the power that both reveals divinity to souls and conceals divinity from souls. More specifically, it is the divine feminine power that either facilitates intimacy between the two entities of yoga or keeps souls who are not interested in this intimacy from discovering it. Yoga-Māyā thus keeps secret all that is divine, and reveals that secret only to those who are ready to receive it. When this divine power of union is not facilitating intimacy between the soul and the divinity, it is arranging a binding connection between the soul and this world of mixed happiness and suffering, in a state of complete forgetfulness of divinity. (2) Yogeshvara is a name applied to Krishna that

---

1 *Yoga-Māyā* appears in BG 7.25; *Māyā* appears in BG 4.6, 7.14, and 18.61.

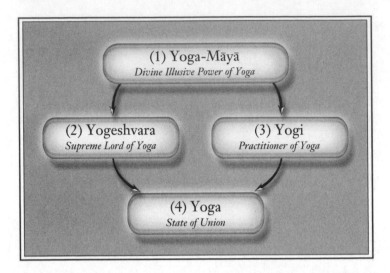

Figure I

means "the Supreme Lord of Yoga."[2] While the name implies that any of Krishna's numerous divine manifestations can be an object of yoga for souls, he himself is the ultimate object. The name also suggests that Krishna is the supreme yogi, that even *he* practices a form of yoga and is himself subsumed by yoga; thus Arjuna addresses Krishna as "O Yogi."[3] When Krishna displays his various manifestations, he is practicing his divine yoga. Arjuna acknowledges this when Krishna reveals his universal form. Moreover, the "ultimate secret," the supreme teaching on yoga, comes from and is sustained by Krishna.[4] (3) A yogi is that soul who practices one of the many forms of yoga presented in the Bhagavad Gītā, of which the primary forms are the yoga of action, the yoga of knowledge, the yoga of meditation, and the yoga of love. Each is a path or discipline that joins the individual self, the yogi, to some dimension of the divine. Thus Krishna tells Arjuna, "Be a yogi!"[5] (4)Yoga here refers to a perfectional union that the soul achieves with a certain level of divinity as the result of yoga practice. In the

---

2 The name Yogeshvara appears in BG 11.4, 11.9, 18.75, and 18.78.
3 The name Yogi for Krishna appears in BG 10.17.
4 The "ultimate secret" is presented in BG 4.3.
5 BG 6.46.

Gītā, this perfectional state of yoga is the supreme love that exists between Yogeshvara and the yogi.

The Bhagavad Gītā demonstrates that, metaphysically, the yoga of divinity has already been achieved, and therefore the divinity is appropriately named Yogeshvara. Krishna expresses his metaphysical achievement of yoga in various ways. He describes the superlatives of this world as his "outer world" manifestations; he presents Brahman, in whom all existences are contained, as his "inner world," or the totality of his spiritual being; and he explains his personal presence as the Purusha in the hearts of living entities, all of which are included within the totality of Brahman, as part of this inner world. Since nothing can exist apart from divinity, and since all living beings are eternally unique and constituent parts of the divine existence, it stands to reason that the only yoga Yogeshvara has yet to achieve is that yoga involving the hearts of humans. In other words, the only thing that God lacks is the personal union with human hearts. Krishna thus beckons souls to come to him in his "innermost" world, the world of his divine heart, where they can offer their love to him freely and fully. The Gītā's ultimate message reflects this choice the human heart makes either to become a part of the intimate world of divinity, or to remain apart from the heart of God in this world of fleeting existence.

The supreme message of the Gītā is revealed gradually in the text, as Krishna discusses the ways in which the hearts of souls can either move toward him, which is the essence of yoga, or away from him, which could be understood as *vi-yoga* ("that which moves one away [*vi-*] from yoga"). The soul that follows the path of *vi-yoga* leads a life of ego-centeredness (*ahaṅkāra*) and selfishness (*mamatva*); whereas the soul that practices some form of yoga focused on divinity leads a life without selfishness and ego-centeredness (*nirmama nirahaṅkāra*). In the former, the self, disconnected from the inner world of the self, becomes entangled in a precarious existence within the outer world of conflict and suffering. In the latter, the self, connected in any number of ways with some dimension of the divine, experiences the inner world of transcendence in which it finds Brahman, "the supreme Spirit," or Purushottama, "the supreme Self." The soul may even see the innermost world of the heart in which it discovers the heart of divinity, as the ultimate human achievement. This concept of the soul moving toward or away from yoga is behind every practice and philosophical discussion presented in the Gītā.

After Krishna has imparted the foundational teaching of the Bhagavad Gītā to Arjuna, and before presenting the ultimate message of his teaching, he boldly declares, "Having fully grasped this, with nothing overlooked, then act as you so choose" (BG 18.63). These words from the final chapter are telling, for they suggest that souls ultimately determine their own destiny. Souls appear to be living in a deterministic universe in which the 'qualities' arising from primordial nature, the *guṇas* (consisting of *sattva, rajas,* and *tamas*), consume them in their daily lives. Souls act according to their unchangeable innate nature, as presented in Krishna's teaching on dharma. No matter what this nature dictates, however, and no matter how forcefully the 'qualities' shape individual lives, when souls have grasped the teachings of the Gītā, they discover that they have a choice—identifying with and serving this temporal world (*vi-yoga*) or identifying with and serving the eternal divine world (*yoga*).

When the soul is bound to this world, it is subject to the powerful conditioning of the 'qualities' of nature. Furthermore, when a soul is reborn, the life of that soul is largely determined by the positive and negative effects arising from the activities of one's previous births. The worldview of the Gītā, however, blends conceptions of free will with this deterministic view. Free will is a necessary ingredient in love; that love cannot be coerced or controlled is axiomatic for the Gītā. This subtle but critical theme shows that souls are given the power of choice, without which there is no possibility of love.

The love call of God, found within his sacred teachings, awakens free will, enabling the soul either to accept the cycle of endless birth and rebirth that binds the soul to this world, or to choose a path leading to the eternal world that frees the soul from the cycle of suffering. This mortal world, the Gītā implies, exists so that souls can exercise choice, without which, again, there is no possibility of love. The implication is that there can be no true love in the divine world without an alternate world. Thus this world, ultimately designed to facilitate love, is brought into being by the divinity to give souls the freedom to love.

The name *Bhagavān* indicates the one from whom love comes and the one who is the most beloved for souls. Wherever Krishna's words are introduced throughout the Gītā, this epithet is utilized. This name also appears as *Bhagavat* (the uninflected stem form of the word) in the title of the work (in which *t* changes to *d* before the word *Gītā*). The word *Bhagavat* embraces many meanings and connotations, one of which is "the one who possesses (*-vat*) his portions (*bhaga-*)," implying that he is the supreme whole, the totality of all portions. The word also means "one who possesses all superlative attributes" or "one who possesses love." The portions (*bhagas*) of the Bhagavat include all souls, each individual soul constituting a bhakta. The metaphysical meaning of *bhakta*, often translated as "devotee," is literally "an apportioned (soul)," and theologically, it denotes a soul who both loves the divinity and is loved by divinity. *Bhakti*, then, refers to the mutual offerings of love intimately shared between the Bhagavat and the bhakta, and bhakti-yoga is the conjunction of Bhagavat and bhakta, achieved through and perfected in love. In bhakti, Bhagavat sends out his love call to all souls, expressed in the deeper theological meaning of the word *Gītā*.

The Beloved Lord already possesses souls metaphysically and loves souls unconditionally, yet he yearns for our hearts to turn toward him, a desire he expresses through his love song. The highest attainment of yoga is therefore reached when the yogi becomes a bhakta, or one who "offers one's love to God." Such a soul unites with Yogeshvara, who is the Bhagavat, in "the yoga of bhakti" (*bhakti-yoga* in chapter 12). The Gītā defines the relationship of yoga to bhakti at the end of chapter 6, where Krishna conclusively states that among all yogis, the one most absorbed in yoga is the bhakta:[6]

> Even among all yogis,
> one whose inner self
> has come to me,

---

[6] For other examples of how yoga is construed with bhakti, see BG 6.31, 8.10, 9.14, 9.34, 12.1, 12.2, 12.14, 13.10, and 14.26.

Who is full of faith,
who offers love to me—
that one is considered by me
to be the most deeply
absorbed in yoga.

(BG. 6.47)

This verse reveals that the highest form of yoga is the soul's offering of love (*bhajate*) to Krishna. The Yoga Sūtra of Patañjali (YS)
also acknowledges the ultimate status of the supreme Lord within
the practice of yoga when it states that "the perfection of *samādhi*
[which itself is the highest perfectional stage of the eight-limbed
yoga system called *aṣṭāṅga*] is dedication to the supreme Lord
[*īśvara-praṇidhāna*]" (YS 2.45). Such dedication to the divinity appears most prominently in the Gītā, in which yoga is conceived as
a practice that ideally involves the heart:

Among these,
    the person of knowledge,
    who is constantly absorbed
    in yoga that is solely
    an offering of love,
    is exceptional.
For I am so dearly loved
    by the person of knowledge,
    and that person
    is dearly loved by me.

(BG 7.17)

The supreme divinity is thus the object of love, or the goal of
yoga, for all souls; the innumerable souls are the object of love, or
the goal of yoga, for the supreme divinity. Because he is unfalter-
ingly receptive to yoga with each and every soul, the divinity is
known as the Supreme Lord of Yoga (*yogeshvara*). These two entities, the Lord and the individual soul, are joined, or harnessed as it
were, by the yoke, the intimate loving union, which subsumes both
the soul and the divinity. We learn from Krishna's teachings that
this power of yoga belongs to divinity but is also something to

which the divinity himself submits, and upon which even he becomes dependent.

Sanjaya: Minister and Visionary

Sanjaya has a central position in the Bhagavad Gītā. Most obviously he plays the role of minister for King Dhritarāshtra, but it is in his capacity as a visionary that he is extraordinary. Sanjaya also represents the consummate teacher, or guru. He epitomizes the "seer of the truth" (BG 4.34), for he sees and hears what transpires privately between Arjuna and Krishna in a remote location. Sanjaya is privy to the secret vision of the universal form that Krishna insists is only for Arjuna's eyes—the exclusive manifestation reserved for Krishna's dearest friend. Sanjaya, then, appears to be as blessed as Arjuna is by Krishna's presence, teachings, and visions.

This fortunate minister and seer clearly has received the grace of God as a devotee, or bhakta. He transmits his visions directly to the troubled king, indirectly to Vyāsa, the author of the text, and finally, through Vyāsa to all readers of the Bhagavad Gītā. Thus Sanjaya simultaneously functions as a teacher. Krishna could easily be speaking about Sanjaya himself in these concluding verses:

> One who reveals
>   this supreme secret
>   to those who have
>   offered me their love,
> Enacting the highest
>   offering of love for me—
>   that one shall certainly
>   come to me, without doubt.

> And among humans,
>   there is no one whose acts
>   are more dearly loved by me
>   than that one,

Nor shall there be
any other on earth who
is more dearly loved by me
than such a person.

(BG 18.68–18.69)

Clearly, Sanjaya, as an ecstatic devotee and transmitter of Krishna's supreme secret, is loved most dearly by the divinity.

The words of Sanjaya fall into three categories: dialogical, narrative, and rapturous. The text begins with the *dialogical,* when the king, Dhritarāshtra, asks Sanjaya in the first verse what is occurring on the battlefield. Sanjaya responds to the king using *narrative* discourse, as he relates the events at Kurukshetra. In the next nine verses he quotes the king's eldest son, who, from the battlefield, reports on the might of the two armies. Throughout the Gītā, while narrating events, Sanjaya occasionally addresses the king in dialogue. His *narrative* words are his dominant form of expression, however, as he transmits either what is taking place on the battlefield or the interactions between Arjuna and his charioteer. Through his special extrasensory power, Sanjaya functions as the visionary minister for the king and the transmitting teacher for the reader of the Gītā. Not until the final verses of the text do we encounter Sanjaya's third type of expression, that of *rapturous* words, in a suite of verses that begins with the following:

Thus from Vāsudeva
and Pārtha,
whose self is exalted,
I have heard this
wondrous conversation,
which causes a state
of rapturous bliss.

(BG 18.74)

These rapturous expressions, along with those of dialogue and narration, demonstrate Sanjaya's powerful presence as a blissful and compassionate deliverer of souls. Sanjaya thus functions as the archetypal guru, a prominent role in India from ancient times.

Sanjaya's central role in the Bhagavad Gītā is understood in the mystical transmission of this personal dialogue between divinity and devotee, achieved through a complex arrangement. It is San-jaya alone, far removed from the battle arena, who directly wit-nesses the dramatic scene:

> By the grace of Vyāsa
> I have heard this
> supreme secret of yoga
> From Krishna,
> the Supreme Lord of Yoga,
> appearing directly
> before my eyes,
> speaking it himself.
>
> (BG 18.75)

The secret dialogue is then received by generations of readers through Vyāsa, the author of the text, from Sanjaya, who is central to its rich delivery (see Figure 2 on the following page).

The Gītā provides us with literary and theological information for understanding the dynamics of the transmission of this sacred dialogue, identified in eight steps: (1) the opening verse of the text, which launches the "outer dialogue," presents Dhritarāshtra, the blind king, who inquires from the enlightened Sanjaya, his minister (BG 1.1); (2) Vyāsa, the famous compiler of the Vedas and other sacred texts, is the renowned sage who grants Sanjaya the power to hear and observe (BG 18.75); (3) what is generally taking place on the battlefield of Kurukshetra (BG 1.2–1.20), specifically the words of Duryodhana (son of Dhritarāshtra) to his teacher, Dronāchārya (BG 1.3–1.11); (4) and, most essentially, the power to transmit the "inner dialogue," those interactions be-tween Arjuna and Krishna (BG 2.11–18.73); (5) Sanjaya narrates what he hears and sees to Dhritarāshtra (BG 18.74–18.78); (6) all of which is then recorded by the author Vyāsa as the complete text of the Bhagavad Gītā (BG 10.13); (7) which is transmitted through teachers of the tradition (BG 4.2); (8) and contemplated by the reader (BG 18.70) either in sacred communities of wor-shippers (BG 10.9, 18.68-18.69) or intellectual traditions, both keeping the inner and outer dialogues of the Bhagavad Gītā alive.

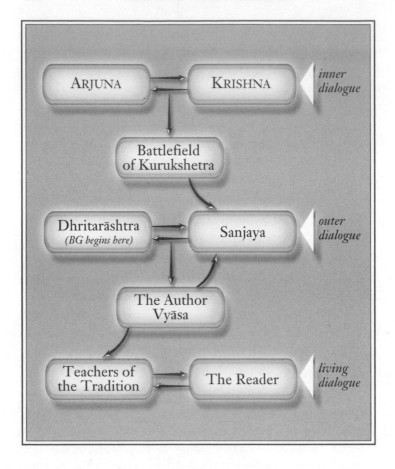

Figure 2

Arjuna:
Warrior and Softhearted Soul

Arjuna exhibits a colorful persona. The types of expression exhibited by Arjuna point to the various dimensions of his relationship with Krishna: the chauffeured general, the troubled and softhearted friend, the humble student, and the paradigmatic devotee. We learn that Arjuna is a leading general of his army, who orders his charioteer, Krishna, to place his chariot between the armies in order to assess the challenge before him. Arjuna is overwhelmed when he sees close relatives, friends, and revered gurus on both sides of the battlefield. His heart is naturally torn between his nature as a warrior, which compels him to protect the innocent and establish righteousness, and his deep affection and respect for so many on the opposing side, as well as on his own side. This conflict causes Arjuna to turn to Krishna as a close friend and confidant.

Very quickly, however, their intimate relationship is transformed into that of a humble student with his wise and compassionate teacher. Now Arjuna has become the archetypal spiritual aspirant, the inquiring disciple who is deeply troubled by insurmountable challenges. The shift in his persona, from a warrior to one seeking counsel to a submissive student, occurs over the first chapter and the beginning of the second. Arjuna's role as a disheartened student who receives Krishna's guidance and teachings dominates the remainder of the text.

Later, however, we discover that Krishna also considers Arjuna to be his loving friend, and elsewhere in the Mahābhārata we learn that Arjuna is a cousin to Krishna, whose aunt, Queen Kuntī, is Arjuna's mother. The final aspect of Arjuna's layered relationship with Krishna is that of a devotee whose softheartedness leads him to dedication, strength, and resolve. The reader observes the softhearted Arjuna as he moves along the path of self-realization, all the way to God realization. After exhibiting these distinct dimensions of identity, he returns to his role as a leading general. Finally Arjuna is able to put his heart fully into his duties, even in this treacherous world, having received strength and counsel from his beloved guru, Krishna.

Arjuna's words within the sacred dialogue show struggle, humility, prayer, inquiry, praise, and resolve. These types of expression paint a full portrait of Arjuna as he confronts his dilemma. They are presented in the text as follows: (1) His words of *struggle* are found primarily within the second part of the first chapter, in what we have already described as his "inner conflict." Arjuna's struggle is further expressed by his confusion and despair at the beginning of the second chapter: "My very being is afflicted by a piteous weakness of spirit. My thoughts on dharma are completely bewildered" (BG 2.7). Arjuna also expresses uneasiness while witnessing Krishna's terrific and frightening universal form in chapter 11: "Yet my mind is distressed and filled with fear." (BG 11.45).

(2) Arjuna speaks words of *humility* when approaching Krishna as a disciple, in the words "I am your student — instruct me, for I have offered myself unto you" (BG 2.7). (3) Arjuna's words are *prayerful* in chapter 11: "O Divinity, allow me to see that very [intimate] form. Bestow upon me your grace, O Lord of Divinities, dwelling place of the universe" (BG 11.45). (4) Words of *inquiry* are Arjuna's dominant form of expression throughout the dialogue, such as these found in chapter 6:

> Arjuna said:
>
> One who does not strive
>   yet possesses faith,
>   whose mind has
>   deviated from yoga
> Without achieving
>   full perfection in yoga—
>   to what destiny does
>   that one go, O Krishna?
>
> (BG 6.37)

Here, Arjuna's questions characterize his relationship with Krishna as a student with his mentor. (5) Arjuna offers words of *praise* or exaltation, as in these worshipful expressions from chapter 10:

> You are the supreme Brahman,
>   the supreme dwelling place,
>   the supreme means of purification;
> You are the eternal divine Person,
>   the original Divinity,
>   the unborn, all-pervading one.
>
> (BG 10.12)

(6) Words of personal *resolve* are found in the last verse spoken by Arjuna. After receiving Krishna's secret teachings, he is resolved to re-enter the outer world of conflict where he now can act with realization and a full heart:

> With confusion destroyed,
>   my memory is restored
>   by your grace,
>   O Achyuta.
> I am firmly resolved,
>   with doubts dispelled—
>   I shall act according
>   to your guidance.
>
> (BG 18.73)

These ways in which Arjuna expresses himself are indicative of his various roles in the Bhagavad Gītā, as he evolves in his spiritual quest.

Krishna:
Intimate and Infinite Divinity

The portrait of Krishna as the divinity in the Bhagavad Gītā is characterized by intimacy, as well as sublimity and infinite might. Krishna exhibits tender and endearing qualities while serving Arjuna as his charioteer, confidant, teacher, and friend; whereas Krishna's magnificence and sublime power become known when he describes his divine attributes and various forms, and proclaims his cosmological and pantheistic manifestations. He even frightens Arjuna when he displays his terrifying "universal form." Although Krishna's intimate and powerful forms differ dramatically, they share a common element. In each manifestation, Krishna embraces souls through his supreme yoga. He embraces the outer world of souls, those who have not yet discovered his inner worlds of transcendence and divine love, with the yoga of his mighty manifestations, and he embraces the inner world of souls with the yoga of his intimate divine form.

Early on, the Gītā reveals Krishna's identity as Arjuna's charioteer. After requesting Krishna to drive his chariot between the two armies (BG 1.21), Arjuna pours his heart out to Krishna, disclosing his torment over the battle that is about to begin. Krishna thus becomes Arjuna's confidant (BG 1.28–2.6). As Arjuna reveals his deep despair to Krishna, who responds with words of wisdom, Arjuna relates to the divinity as his teacher (BG 2.7). Thereafter, Krishna's identity is gradually revealed.

When Krishna begins his philosophical discourse, the narrator identifies him as Bhagavān, which can be taken as simply an honorific for any venerable personage. Moreover, none of Krishna's own words overtly announce his divinity until chapter 4. Krishna's initial role as a charioteer is merely described, but from chapter 2 on he actively plays the part of counselor and teacher. In only a single verse in chapter 2 and one verse in chapter 3 are we given even a hint of Krishna's divinity. These hints take the form of unexpected or even abrupt interjections that express his divine calling, his eternal yearning for souls to come to him. These exhortative expressions give the viewer an underlying powerful message in the form of a communicated subtext. The first hint of Krishna's divinity appears in a verse about yoga:

> Restraining all these [senses],
>   one should be seated
>   while absorbed in yoga,
>   wholly intent on me.
> For one whose senses
>   are under control—
>   for that one,
>   profound knowledge
>   is firmly established.
>
> (BG 2.61)

The phrase "wholly intent on me" introduces the idea that Krishna is not only the charioteer, the confidant, and the teacher, but the object of his own teachings. Furthermore, the phrase provides a brief glimpse into Krishna's divine secret. This idea that Krishna is the object of meditation is without precedent in the text.

In these two earlier chapters, Krishna's interjections prepare the reader for what is to come. Krishna's divine identity remains hidden in chapter 3, and yet is suggested:

> Renouncing all actions in me,
>   with one's thought on
>   the 'principle of self',
> Without longings,
>   without a sense of 'mine'—
> fight, with grief cast off.
>
> (BG 3.30)

Here, Krishna refers to himself in the first person, "renouncing all actions in me," and indirectly in the third person, in the phrase "with one's thought on the 'principle of self'," thus cleverly concealing his identity. We learn later in the text that this 'principle of self' is ultimately Krishna as the Purusha, the divinity dwelling within the hearts of all beings, a form to which he will often refer in the third person.

Krishna openly reveals his divine identity for the first time in chapter 4, after which his interjections seem far less abrupt. Through these interjections Krishna communicates that he is the ultimate end of all actions, disciplines, and spiritual attainments, and also explains that everything metaphysical and cosmic is contained within himself. But most significantly, Krishna includes these exhortative bursts in his teachings as an expression of his impassioned love for humans and his desire for humans to love him, to come to him. Krishna first introduces his divine secret through these hints and later, through bold expressions, until it is fully disclosed in the final chapter.

In Krishna's speaking, which dominates the text, the reader encounters eight types of expression: protective, philosophical, edifying, exhortative, declarative, revelational, compassionate, and affectionate. All facilitate the yoga of the divine heart, in which the divinity desires the love of every soul. Thus, collectively, these types of expression constitute the divinity's love call in the Gītā.

Krishna's *protective* words can take the form of encouragement, as found in an earlier chapter: "Relinquishing this poor faint-heartedness, stand up, O Scorcher of the Enemy!" (BG 2.3). In his climactic words toward the end of the text Krishna is both protective and reassuring: "I shall grant you freedom from all

misfortune—do not despair!" (BG 18.66). Even Krishna's philosophical words can carry an underlying tone of reassurance:

> Never, truly,
>   have I ever not existed—
>   nor you, nor these kings
>   who protect the people,
> And never
>   shall any of us
>   ever cease to be,
>   now or forevermore.
>
> (BG 2.12)

Again, Krishna's words offer refuge and comfort through his bold
declaration of complete protection for souls who never forget
him:

> One who sees me everywhere
>   and sees all things in me,
> To such a person I am never lost
>   nor is such a person ever lost to me.
>
> (BG 6.30)

Krishna's *philosophical* words, the second type of expression, are
most prominent in the Gītā and can exhibit an objective and even
abstract tone:

> Of the impermanent
>   one finds no being;
>   one finds no nonbeing
>   of the permanent.
> Indeed, the certainty
>   of both of these
>   has been perceived
>   by seers of the truth.
>
> (BG 2.16)

However, these words do not remain abstract for long. As he addresses the practical challenges of life, Krishna's words become more supportive, offered by the divinity to elevate the soul to the highest region within his divine realm. He may even combine philosophical teaching with a rhetorical question:

> One who knows this [self]
> to be indestructible,
> eternal, unborn,
> and everpresent—
> How and whom does
> that person slay, O Pārtha?
> And whom does
> that one cause to slay?
>
> (BG 2.21)

Krishna's *edifying* words, another form of expression, are instructive, often addressed to Arjuna in the second person, "you." Here, a certain directional force leads souls ever closer to the ultimate level of Krishna's divinity. Such edifying speech acts in one of three ways: (1) to prepare the soul for elevation to the divine, (2) to encourage particular practices and disciplines that connect the soul to the divine, or (3) to encourage the perfection of offerings and practices, intensifying the soul's intimate connection with the supreme and personal divinity, Krishna. These three types of edifying speech, found throughout the text, typically direct an individual from the outer world of conflict to the inner world of spirit and transcendence, and finally to the innermost world of the heart, in which a soul finds the perfect love of divinity.

Krishna's edifying preparatory remarks emphasize the importance of performing one's "dharma," the right way of acting in this world determined by one's phase of life (*āshrama*) and one's particular capabilities and talents (*varna*). He stresses the importance of acting *according to one's nature*, thus being true to one's dharma:

Better is one's own dharma
    even if imperfect
    than another's dharma
    followed perfectly.
Performing action
    determined by
    one's own nature,
    one does not incur fault.

                                    (BG 18.47)

Here, Krishna reinforces Arjuna's position as a warrior. He also warns Arjuna that he could not act against his nature even if he were to try to do so (BG 18.60). Krishna teaches in the second type of edifying words that the fruits of action produced from following one's dharma are not to be enjoyed; rather, they are to be renounced, resulting in detachment from the outer world and the lifting of consciousness to the inner world of transcendence, where one becomes freed from the cycle of birth and death:

Indeed, those wise ones
    who are absorbed
    in the yoga of discernment,
    relinquishing the fruits
    born of action,
Who are freed
    from the bondage
    of repeated births,
    go to a place beyond suffering.

                                    (BG 2.51)

These edifying statements of Krishna act as encouraging words that gradually elevate the soul *through practice and discipline* to eternal life, beyond this fleeting world of hardship and impermanence. Finally, when action arising from dharma produces fruits that are offered to the divinity *out of love*, then such a soul reaches the innermost world of the heart, in which the love of divinity is discovered:

For them, who are constantly
  absorbed in yoga,
  who offer loving service
  with natural affection,
I offer that yoga
  of discernment
  by which they
  come close to me.
                              (BG 10.10)

These words encouraging souls to perfect such offerings of love
form the third level of edifying speech. All three types of edifying
statements—preparatory, practical, and perfectional—are phases
of yoga that connect the soul more and more intimately with the
divinity.

   The *exhortative* words of Krishna strongly urge souls to know
him, act for him, come to him, or love him. This type of expression, through which Krishna draws souls to himself, often contains, overtly or covertly, the objective pronoun *me*. The following
verse demonstrates the language of reflexive exhortation:

Place your mind on me alone;
  let your discernment
  enter into me.
You shall dwell
  only in me
  from now forevermore—
  of this there is no doubt.
                              (BG 12.8)

This and many other verses exhort souls to take up any of the
contemplative or more active practices presented in the Gītā and
integrate them as an offering to Krishna. Whatever the path or
discipline chosen, Krishna urges souls to tread that path since
it ultimately leads to the heart of the divinity. These exhortations express Krishna's passionate yet patient love for souls. He

proclaims in a great number of verses his desire that souls know, see, and remember him.[7] Similarly, throughout the text, Krishna encourages souls to "meditate" on him and to remain "wholly intent" on him, "with mind deeply attached" to him and "thought focused" upon him.[8] Furthermore, Krishna implores souls to act only for him when he instructs them to take "full refuge" in him and to "renounce all actions" for him.[9]

Krishna's divine love call is most evident in his exhortations to "love" him and "come to" him. First and foremost, he desires that souls "offer their love" to him, as shown in the numerous words derived from the verbal root *bhaj*, meaning "to offer love to the divine," such as the words *bhakti* or *bhakta*. These derivative words appear thirty-eight times and are present in twelve of the Gītā's eighteen chapters. Krishna also speaks of "worshipping" him, "sacrificing" for him, "praising" and "honoring" him, and "acting out of reverence" for him. Krishna describes souls who have "offered their lives" and who are "devoted" to him. The sheer quantity and pervasiveness of these exhortations convey Krishna's ardent desire for the love of souls. This divine yearning is further expressed in exhortations that invite, even entreat, souls to come to him. Indeed, Krishna explains at least twenty-three times the ways in which souls may "come" to him.[10]

In Krishna's *declarations*, another type of expression, he proclaims his divine identity and the manifestations of his divinity. These statements are most often expressed in the first person as "I am" declarations. In numerous places he identifies himself with the superlative dimensions of this world:

---

7 Some verses exhorting souls to remember Krishna are: 7.30, 8.7, 8.13, 8.14; to know Krishna: 5.29, 7.3, 7.10, 7.12, 7.30, 10.24, 10.27, 15.19, 18.55 (twice); to understand Krishna: 4.14, 7.6, 9.6, 10.2, 10.3; to see Krishna: 4.35, 5.18, 6.29, 6.30, 11.3–8, 11.54.

8 Meditating on Krishna: 9.22, 10.8, 12.6; intent on him: 2.61, 6.14, 12.6, 12.20, 18.57; immersed in him: 4.10, 12.10; with thought focused upon him: 6.14, 10.9, 18.57; with mind on him: 5.13, 7.1, 9.13, 9.34, 12.2, 12.8, 12.14, 18.65; with thought on him: 12.7, 12.9, 18.57, 18.58.

9 Taking refuge in Krishna: 4.10, 7.19, 7.29, 9.18, 9.32, 18.56, 18.66; renouncing actions for Krishna: 3.30, 5.13, 12.6, 18.57.

10 Coming to Krishna: 4.9, 4.10, 6.47, 7.14, 7.15, 7.19, 7.23, 8.7, 8.15, 8.16, 9.11, 9.25, 9.28, 9.34, 10.10, 11.55, 13.18, 14.2, 18.55, 18.65, 18.66, 18.68.

I am the taste in water,
O Kaunteya;
I am the radiance
of the moon and the sun,
The sacred utterance
in all the Vedas,
the sound in space,
the prowess in men.

(BG 7.8)

Krishna finally states that all sublime things in this world are but a reflection of his divine splendor:

Whatever form of existence
possesses abounding power,
contains the beautiful,
or is well-endowed
with excellence—
Understand that
every such form
has become fully manifest
from but a part of my splendor.

(BG 10.41)

Thus the superlative aspects of creation function as a medium through which divinity embraces souls. This becomes part of Krishna's yoga. The beautiful and the sublime continuously reveal messages from the heart of divinity, directing us toward him.

Krishna's *revelational* words are found mostly in chapter 11. This form of expression, in which Krishna reveals his manifestation of omnipotence as the Vishva Rūpa, and his intimate divinity as the Bhagavat, also dramatizes the relationship between the two. Arjuna asks to see Krishna's mighty and powerful forms, and Krishna tells him that these forms are innumerable:

Behold my forms,
   O Pārtha,
   by the hundreds,
   or by the thousands—
Divine, of various types,
   and of various colors
   and appearances.

(BG 11.5)

To see these forms would require that Arjuna possess a special
kind of vision:

But you are unable to see me
   with only this, your own eyes.
I [therefore] give divine eyes to you—
   behold my supremely powerful yoga!

(BG 11.8)

This orchestrated vision of the awesome manifestation of Krishna
is described not only by the divinity himself, but also by the narrator, Sanjaya, and by Arjuna, as he witnesses the marvelous display
of divine grandeur.

The juxtaposition of this majestic form with Krishna's preferred form further reveals the supremacy of the divinity's more
intimate form, which has been in dialogue with Arjuna all along.
We learn that Krishna's ultimate form is, paradoxically, concealed
as the manifestation of divine intimacy with whom Arjuna has
interacted but which he has perhaps not fully appreciated until
now, after encountering this starkly contrasting and frightful
form of might. While attempting to comprehend such a display
of overwhelming power, Arjuna implores Krishna to return to the
personal affectionate form that he has always cherished:

As a father is to a son,
   as a friend to a friend,

As a dearly loved one
    to a dearly beloved—
be pleased to show your
    loving kindness, O Divinity.
                                            (BG 11.44cd)

Arjuna is careful to express his gratitude for being granted a vision
of the divinity's universal form, though he yearns to be reunited
with Krishna's intimate form:

Having seen what never
    has been seen before,
    I am exceedingly pleased,
Yet my mind is distressed
    and filled with fear.
O Divinity, allow me to see
    that very [intimate] form.
Bestow upon me your grace,
    O Lord of Divinities,
    dwelling place of the universe.
                                            (BG 11.45)

Many in India, as well as in the West, consider the awesome and
terrifying Vishva Rūpa to be the superior form of divinity. In fact,
some consider chapter 11 as the climactic chapter of the Bhagavad
Gītā because of Krishna's spectacular revelation of the Vishva Rūpa.
One might ask, however, why would the climactic portion of an
eighteen-chapter work be placed in the eleventh chapter?

Arjuna, in his longing for Krishna's personal form, makes a
statement about the superiority of this form. Arjuna's anxious re-
treat from his vision of the Vishva Rūpa, and his corresponding
eagerness to reconnect with Krishna's humanlike form, certainly
confirms the Gītā's emphasis on the intimate divinity. Moreover,
chapter 12 is solely dedicated to the offering of the heart to this
personal form of divinity, leading the reader away from the gran-
diose form of the eleventh chapter, which further expresses the

ultimacy of the intimate deity. Thus the Vishva Rūpa, for Arjuna, functions as an extraordinarily ornate throne that highlights and celebrates Krishna's manifestation as the loving personal deity. And just as Arjuna requires a special vision to see the Vishva Rūpa, he requires a fully devoted heart in order to know the most intimate form of divinity:

> Only by the offering of
>   one's love to none other,
> O Arjuna, am I able,
>   in such a form,
> To be known and
>   to be truly seen,
>   and to be attained,
> O Fighter of the Enemy.
>
> (BG 11.54)

Krishna's words of *compassion*, the next type of expression, demonstrate his loving generosity toward all souls. Krishna clearly is not a jealous God, for out of his infinite compassion he accepts that souls also worship lesser divinities who personify Krishna's divine powers. Krishna even goes so far as to fortify the faith of souls who worship such divinities:

> Whoever, with faith,
>   has offered love
>   to whatever form that
>   person desires to worship—
> Upon every such person,
>   I bestow this
>   immovable faith.
>
> (BG 7.21)

Krishna's openness to the numerous paths by which souls can approach him is an expression of his inclusiveness, as well as his unwavering love:

> In the way they offer
>   themselves to me,
>   in just that way
> I offer my love
>   to them reciprocally.
> Human beings
>   follow my path
>   universally,
>   O Pārtha.
>
> (BG 4.11)

Here, Krishna's words are gentle and accommodating. The divinity's acceptance of all souls is confirmed. Krishna loves souls in whatever ways they are able to love him, directly or indirectly. Moreover, although Krishna states that he is equal toward all souls, he feels especially close to those who offer their hearts directly to him. The following verse demonstrates Krishna's *compassionate* as well as his *affectionate* words:

> I am the same
>   toward all beings;
>   no one is either hated
>   or dearly loved by me.
> Yet those who,
>   with an offering of love,
>   offer their love to me—
>   they are in me
>   and I also am in them.
>
> (BG 9.29)

In this verse Krishna declares, perhaps surprisingly, that no one is dearly loved by him. Such impartiality, as expressed in the first half of the verse, is associated with Krishna's manifestation as the Lord within the hearts of beings. Yet in this and several other verses Krishna states that those who have offered their hearts to him are indeed in him and are dearly loved by him. These verses are examples of the final type of expression, Krishna's *affectionate* words:

> Indeed, this is the immortal
>   essence of dharma,
>   which has been declared;
>   those who participate in
>   this worship fully,
> Who have faith,
>   who are devoted to me,
>   who have offered their love—
> they are most dearly loved by me.
>   (BG 12.20)

This verse is the last one in a grouping of verses found in chapter 12 (BG 12.13–12.20), in which Krishna describes the types of souls who are recipients of his dearest love. As seen above, Krishna emphasizes that there has never been nor will there ever be any soul whom he loves more dearly than the one who reveals his secret of divine love to other souls (BG 18.68–69).

The Secret Love Song

The Bhagavad Gītā is an impassioned expression of divine yearning. Krishna explains that everything is contained in him, that he is the one by whom everything is set forth into motion and sustained, and that he is truly the Bhagavat, the "possessor of all superlatives, existences, and beings." Despite the infinite and absolute fullness of his being, he yearns for one thing that is not within his possession or under his control — the human heart. Thus the divinity experiences some incompleteness within his divine completeness, and longs for what he does not possess. Krishna therefore sends out his secret love call, a song coming from his heart to all hearts, which is the unifying message of the Gītā.

  This essential message of divine love, presented in chapter 18 as "the greatest secret of all," is at once revealed and concealed in the

Gītā. It is secret because Krishna desires souls to know about it only when they are ready to receive it, to preserve the purity of the soul's loving response. The secret nature of this divine longing of God's heart is reflected in its subtle presentation in earlier chapters. It is introduced gradually, then more boldly presented in later chapters, not only because it is secret, but also because Krishna wishes to show how everything is related to this message.

Arjuna is informed of Krishna's divine yearning through his teachings on how souls come to him and how all paths, or dharmas, can lead souls to his inner world. Indeed, the penultimate and final verses of many chapters express this. Krishna's acknowledgment and approval of such paths functions in two ways: one is to demonstrate his compassion in accepting the various ways souls desire to move toward him; and the other is to express his intention to keep his ultimate teachings secret from those who are not yet ready to love him, by diverting them to those paths that are themselves preliminary to realizing the divine secret.

The Gītā opens with an irresolvable ethical conflict in Arjuna's outer world. Through this conflict, which acts as a catalyst, Arjuna attains the highest yoga, the yoga of the heart. By hearing Krishna's call to love, by hearing what the divinity most secretly desires, Arjuna's vision of his overwhelming problems is transformed. He learns to see the embrace of divinity behind all the events of this world, even the most dreadful.

The supreme secret is revealed in key places throughout the text. At the beginning of chapter 4, Krishna claims to deliver the ancient secret of yoga, which had been lost from the lineage that once transmitted it. He specifies who may receive such a secret:

> This same ancient yoga
> is now spoken
> by me to you:
> "Having offered your love,
> you have also
> become my friend"—
> truly, this is the ultimate secret.
>
> (BG 4.3)

This verse introduces the reader to divine secrecy, suggested by the words *ultimate secret*. We hear nothing more of divine secrecy until chapter 9, where Krishna states, "Now I shall reveal to you this greatest secret, for you are without envy" (BG 9.1). Krishna himself speaks highly of this secret of secrets: "This is the king of knowledge, the king of secrets" (BG 9.2), then later declares, "I am the silence of secrets" (BG 10.38). In chapter 11, Arjuna speaks of Krishna's "supreme secret" as the 'principle of self' (BG 11.1). Krishna declares "the greatest secret" to be knowledge of his identity as the "Ultimate Person" (BG 15.18–20). The presentation in chapter 18 of "the secret" constitutes the dramatic finale of the entire work. Here, Krishna speaks about the three levels of "the secret" in the climactic point of the chapter (BG 18.63-64), and explains that one who disseminates this "supreme secret" becomes very dear to him (BG 18.68). Furthermore, Sanjaya describes Krishna's complete teachings as "the supreme secret of yoga" in the last words of the text (BG 18.75).

Krishna's supreme message is positioned within the final chapter of the Gītā as its focal point. Chapter 18 can be divided into four sections, each with its own theme:

1. The Great Secret: The Self's True Actions (vss. 1–49)

2. The Greater Secret: Transcendence and the Supreme Self (vss. 50–63)

3. The Greatest Secret of All: Divine Love (vss. 64–66)

4. Concluding Words: Krishna, Arjuna, and Sanjaya (vss. 67–78)

The first section is dedicated to the capacity of the soul to achieve spiritual transcendence through action in the outer world of conflict. It begins with renunciation of selfish actions by relinquishment of the fruits of action (1–12), then addresses the five causes of action (13–19) and how action is affected by the 'qualities' of primordial nature (19–40). Next, it describes the four general classes of society according to their work: the educators or priests, the rulers or warriors, the business- or tradespeople, and the skilled workers (41–48). Finally, the Gītā explains how attainment of

transcendence is possible in a state of actionlessness, through renunciation (49). This constitutes the great secret.

The second section presents the inner world of transcendence
and moves the reader toward the innermost world of the heart in
bhakti. It presents disciplines of the self to attain Brahman (50–
53), how Brahman leads to bhakti and the nature of bhakti (54–
58), as well as how acting according to one's nature in dharma is
inevitable (59–60). The text then describes how love is offered to
the supreme Self, the indwelling Lord within the heart (61–62).
The transitional and pivotal verse (63) reveals the secret in relation to the greater secret, which anticipates the greatest secret of
all (64).

The third section, only three verses, focuses exclusively on the
innermost world of the heart. In verse 64, Krishna's supreme message is fully disclosed; verse 65 describes the ultimate achievement
of offering one's heart to the divinity and a reaffirmation of how
such a soul is dearly loved. Verse 66 explains the exclusive attention
of the soul for the divinity, a love that goes beyond all forms of
dharma. These three verses, beginning with the revelation of the
divinity's passion for souls, constitute the ultimate message in
Krishna's teachings, the greatest secret of all.

In the fourth section, the voices of Krishna, Arjuna, and Sanjaya are heard. First, the soul who is qualified to receive the supreme secret is presented (67); then comes a declaration that one
who reveals this supreme secret to others possesses the highest love
for divinity, and is more loved by the divinity than any other soul
(68–69). Krishna's words of benediction follow, stating that by
contemplating this dialogue, spiritual achievements will be made
(70–71). In his final words, Krishna inquires from Arjuna if he
has heard "the single highest point" of his teachings, which would
dispel his bewildered state (72), and Arjuna responds in the affir-
mative (73). Sanjaya's ecstatic epilogue then forms the concluding
verses of the text (74–78).

Thus divine secrecy is a theme that runs throughout the Gītā,
building toward Krishna's full disclosure in the final chapter of all
the various forms of secret knowledge that comprise "the supreme
secret of yoga." Krishna identifies the first two phases of secrecy
explicitly, as the "secret" and the "greater secret":

Thus for you this knowledge,
which is a greater secret
than the [previous] secret,
is made known by me.
Having fully grasped this,
with nothing overlooked,
then act as you so choose.

(BG 18.63)

It is clear from this verse that Krishna gives Arjuna the freedom to either act in accordance with this secret knowledge or not, demonstrating free will within supreme love. Then Krishna discloses the third phase of secrecy, his greatest secret among all secrets:

The greatest secret of all,
once more please hear—
it is my supreme message:
"You are so much loved by me!"
Thereupon I shall continue
declaring this message for you,
which I have set forth into motion.

(BG 18.64)

This secret of divine secrets is now revealed: "You are so much loved by me!" The simple message here is that the divinity passionately loves souls, as indicated by the use of the Sanskrit word *iṣṭaḥ*, meaning "desired" or "ardently loved," and the use of the adverbial intensive *so much*. These few words constitute the very essence of the song or "Gītā" of the Beloved Lord. Every verse in the Bhagavad Gītā thus revolves around these words. Krishna underscores this declaration of divine love by calling it his "supreme message," and further emphasizes the message with the use of the Sanskrit equivalent of quotation marks. This ultimate statement establishes the tone of the entire text, the inner intention of the author, and the controlling principle for understanding the text. No other statement in the Gītā receives such attention.

Krishna builds up to the revelation of this greatest secret, as we have seen, with a dramatic summary of his teachings in the first sixty-three verses of the chapter, thus positioning the greatest secret of all as the climax of the work. In verse 65, following this greatest secret, Krishna urges souls to love him, and promises that they will come to him since they are "dearly loved" by him:

> Be mindful of me
>   with love offered to me;
>   sacrificing for me,
>   act out of reverence for me.
> Truly you shall
>   come to me—
>   this I promise you
>   for you are dearly loved by me.
>   (BG 18.65)

This verse reveals that the best possible response of souls to Krishna's greatest of all secrets is bhakti, the love offered by the soul to the supreme divinity. Bhakti, therefore, is not merely a means to reach the divine, but is itself the perfection of all other means for attaining an intimate connection with the divinity in yoga.

Many commentators, beginning with Rāmānuja of the twelfth century, consider the next verse, BG 18.66, to be the Gītā's ultimate statement. Here, Krishna states his desire that souls give up everything and come to him as their only refuge. He provides divine assurance that such souls will be free from all troubles:

> Completely relinquishing
>   all forms of dharma,
>   come to me
>   as your only shelter.
> I shall grant you
>   freedom from
>   all misfortune—
>   do not despair!
>   (BG 18.66)

Krishna presents in this verse a certain irony, even an apparent contradiction, when he directs all forms of dharma to be completely given up, after a significant part of the text has been devoted to establishing the importance of dharma. This request expresses

TEXTUAL ILLUMINATIONS

Krishna's desire for the unmediated love of humans, accentuated by his plea to come to him as one's only shelter. This verse communicates a divine passion for souls, and how such love between the devotee and the divinity is ultimately not limited by dharma. Divine love goes beyond dharma, yet at the same time includes dharma.

Yoga at its highest level is the soul's intimate connection with the divine through the heart. Yoga, for divinity, is the various manifestations of the divine that embrace souls: the all-pervading imperishable Brahman; the presence of divinity in the beautiful and sublime in this world; the powerful and spectacular Vishva Rūpa; the supreme Self dwelling in the hearts of all as the Purusha; and the supreme personal divinity, Krishna, celebrated as Purushottama, the ultimate Person; or Yogeshvara, the supreme Lord of Yoga; or Bhagavān, the Beloved Lord—the most intimate deity for the loving devotee. Through these divine manifestations, the supreme divinity is revealed to souls or concealed from souls according to their desire or lack of desire to come to him, to unite with him.

According to the Gītā, yoga is not a reclusive meditation in some distant mountain hermitage; rather, the hermitage is found within one's heart, and in the hearts of others. The ultimate yoga for souls is to attain a state of full-heartedness — a heart that offers itself in unremitting, unconditional love in response to the divine yearning. This yearning, the greatest secret of all, is pronounced as "You are so much loved by me."

The Bhagavad Gītā is truly the Beloved Lord's "secret love song." This ever-beckoning song urges souls to embrace divinity just as divinity forever embraces souls. The Gītā begins with a question that speaks to every one of us: "How are we to act in this world of conflict and suffering?" The Gītā's answer is simply *to act out of love*. This hidden song of the divinity calls souls to *act out of love* in all that they do, in all that they think, feel, and will. The Gītā insists that human life is meant for hearing this innermost song of the heart. It behooves souls to search for this song, and upon hearing it, to listen to the divine love song as it resonates in everything, everywhere, and at every moment—to hear it through the hearts of all beings and in all of life. Once heard, this secret love song is celebrated as the most blessed gift of divinity to humankind.

Sanskrit Text

On the English Transliteration

The original Sanskrit text is provided here in transliteration. For this I have relied upon the critical edition of the text and its verse divisions presented in the great work of the Bhandarkar Oriental Research Institute (BORI), in Pune, India (see Bibliography). Although popular editions of the BG contain some differences in verse division and numbering in chapters 1 and 13, I have mostly utilized the BORI edition of the text. Readers may find the transliteration helpful in reconciling differences from other translations.

The transliterated text that appears here has been formatted to give nonspecialist readers a visual sense of the versification of the original Sanskrit. The typical eight-syllable quarter-lined metered verses, or *anuṣṭubh*, appear as couplets of Sanskrit text, the quarter lines indicated by commas. For example (1.1):

> dharma-kṣetre kuru-kṣetre, samavetā yuyutsavaḥ
> māmakāḥ pāṇḍavāś caiva, kim akurvata sañjaya

The eleven-syllable quarter-lined verses, or *triṣṭubh*, appear as quatrains, easily distinguishable from the more common two-line *anuṣṭubh* verses by the four lines of embellished metered verses. For example (2.5):

> gurūn ahatvā hi mahānubhāvān
>   śreyo bhoktuṁ bhaikṣyam apīha loke
> hatvārtha-kāmāṁs tu gurūn ihaiva
>   bhuñjīya bhogān rudhira-pradigdhān

The English translation also imitates this visual distinction between the couplets of the *anuṣṭubh* verses and the quatrains of the longer verse form. This is accomplished in the translated *anuṣṭubh* verses by presenting two "leading lines," nonindented lines of text, followed by one or more indented lines. Likewise, for the more complex *triṣṭubh* verses, I have presented four leading lines, each followed by one or more indented lines.

Recitation of Sanskrit Verse

Sanskrit distinguishes between accent and length of syllables. Syllables within words are spoken in either short or long (held twice the length as short) lengths of time, also called light and heavy respectively, and there are numerous varieties of poetic meters for many types of verse lengths. Following are basic rules to acquaint the reader with the recitation of Sanskrit verse, so important to the language.

Accent

1. The first syllable of two-syllable words: e.g., *bhakti, deva*;

2. The penultimate syllable of all words having more than two syllables if the syllable contains a long vowel, a diphthong, or a short vowel followed by two consonants: e.g., *nirvāna*, Ganeśa, *gṛhastha*;

3. The antepenultimate syllable in most other cases: e.g., Mahābhārata, Himālaya, Rāmāyana, Upaniṣad.

Light and Heavy Syllables in Poetic Meter

1. Light syllables (*laghu*) are those made up of short vowels which are not followed by more than one consonant (*anusvāra* "ṁ" and *avagraha* "ḥ" included), either within a word or between words. Light syllables are short, half the length of heavy or long syllables. For example, *nama oṁ viṣṇupādāya* (underlined vowels indicate light syllables).

2. Heavy syllables (*guru*) are those made up of long vowels or those made up of short vowels followed by more than one consonant (*anusvāra* "ṁ" and *avagraha* "ḥ" included), either within a word or between words. For example, *nama oṁ viṣṇupādāya* (underlined vowels indicate heavy syllables).

The Complete Sanskrit Text

I

Dhṛtarāṣṭra uvāca

1 dharma-kṣetre kuru-kṣetre, samavetā yuyutsavaḥ
   māmakāḥ pāṇḍavāś caiva, kim akurvata sañjaya

Sañjaya uvāca

2 dṛṣṭvā tu pāṇḍavānīkaṁ, vyūḍhaṁ duryodhanas tadā
   ācāryam upasaṅgamya, rājā vacanam abravīt
3 paśyaitāṁ pāṇḍu-putrāṇāṁ, ācārya mahatīṁ camūm
   vyūḍhāṁ drupada-putreṇa, tava śiṣyeṇa dhīmatā
4 atra śūrā maheṣv-āsā, bhīmārjuna-samā yudhi
   yuyudhāno virāṭaś ca, drupadaś ca mahā-rathaḥ
5 dhṛṣṭaketuś cekitānaḥ, kāśirājaś ca vīryavān
   purujit kuntibhojaś ca, śaibyaś ca nara-puṅgavaḥ
6 yudhāmanyuś ca vikrānta, uttamaujāś ca vīryavān
   saubhadro draupadeyāś ca, sarva eva mahā-rathāḥ
7 asmākaṁ tu viśiṣṭā ye, tān nibhoda dvijottama
   nāyakā mama sainyasya, saṁjñārthaṁ tān bravīmi te
8 bhavān bhīṣmaś ca karṇaś ca, kṛpaś ca samitiṁ-jayaḥ
   aśvatthāmā vikarṇaś ca, saudamattis tathaiva ca
9 anye ca bahavaḥ śūrā, mad-arthe tyakta-jīvitāḥ
   nānā-śastra-praharaṇāḥ, sarve yuddha-viśāradāḥ
10 aparyāptaṁ tad asmākaṁ, balaṁ bhīṣmābhirakṣitam
   paryāptaṁ tv idam eteṣāṁ, balaṁ bhīmābhirakṣitam
11 ayaneṣu ca sarveṣu, yathā-bhāgam avasthitāḥ
   bhīṣmam evābhirakṣantu, bhavantaḥ sarva eva hi
12 tasya sañjanayan harṣaṁ, kuru-vṛddhaḥ pitāmahaḥ
   siṁha-nādaṁ vinadyoccaiḥ, śaṅkhaṁ dadhmau pratāpavān
13 tataḥ śaṅkhāś ca bheryaś ca, paṇavānaka-gomukhāḥ
   sahasaivābhyahanyanta, sa śabdas tumulo 'bhavat
14 tataḥ śvetair hayair yukte, mahati syandane sthitau
   mādhavaḥ pāṇḍavaś caiva, divyau śaṅkhau pradadhmatuḥ
15 pāñcajanyaṁ hṛṣīkeśo, devadattaṁ dhanañjayaḥ
   pauṇḍraṁ dadhmau mahā-śaṅkhaṁ, bhīma-karmā vṛkodaraḥ
16 anantavijayaṁ rājā, kuntī-putro yudhiṣṭhiraḥ
   nakulaḥ sahadevaś ca, sughoṣa-maṇipuṣpakau
17 kāśyaś ca parameṣv-āsaḥ, śikhaṇḍī ca mahā-rathaḥ
   dhṛṣṭadyumno virāṭaś ca, sātyakiś cāparājitaḥ

18 drupado draupadeyāś ca, sarvaśaḥ pṛthivī-pate
    saubhadraś ca mahā-bāhuḥ, śaṅkhān dadhmuḥ pṛthak pṛthak
19 sa ghoṣo dhārtarāṣṭrāṇāṁ, hṛdayāni vyadārayat
    nabhaś ca pṛthivīṁ caiva, tumulo vyanunādayan
20 atha vyavasthitān dṛṣṭvā, dhārtarāṣṭrān kapi-dhvajaḥ
    pravṛtte śastra-sampāte, dhanur udyamya pāṇḍavaḥ
21 hṛṣīkeśaṁ tadā vākyam, idam āha mahī-pate
    senayor ubhayor madhye, rathaṁ sthāpaya me 'cyuta
22 yāvad etān nirīkṣe 'haṁ, yoddhu-kāmān avasthitān
    kair mayā saha yoddhavyam, asmin raṇa-samudyame
23 yotsyamānān avekṣe 'haṁ, ya ete 'tra samāgatāḥ
    dhārtarāṣṭrasya durbuddher, yuddhe priya-cikīrṣavaḥ
24 evam ukto hṛṣīkeśo, guḍākeśena bhārata
    senayor ubhayor madhye, sthāpayitvā rathottamam
25 bhīṣma-droṇa-pramukhataḥ, sarveṣāṁ ca mahī-kṣitām
    uvāca pārtha paśyaitān, samavetān kurūn iti
26 tatrāpaśyat sthitān pārthaḥ, pitṝn atha pitāmahān
    ācāryān mātulān bhrātṝn, putrān pautrān sakhīṁs tathā
27 śvaśurān suhṛdaś caiva, senayor ubhayor api
    tān samīkṣya sa kaunteyaḥ, sarvān bandhūn avasthitān
28 kṛpayā parayāviṣṭo, viṣīdann idam abravīt
    dṛṣṭvemān sva-janān kṛṣṇa, yuyutsūn samavasthitān
29 sīdanti mama gātrāṇi, mukhaṁ ca pariśuṣyati
    vepathuś ca śarīre me, roma-harṣaś ca jāyate
30 gāṇḍīvaṁ sraṁsate hastāt, tvak caiva paridahyate
    na ca śaknomy avasthātuṁ, bhramatīva ca me manaḥ
31 nimittāni ca paśyāmi, viparītāni keśava
    na ca śreyo 'nupaśyāmi, hatvā sva-janam āhave
32 na kāṅkṣe vijayaṁ kṛṣṇa, na ca rājyaṁ sukhāni ca
    kiṁ no rājyena govinda, kiṁ bhogair jīvitena vā
33 yeṣām arthe kāṅkṣitaṁ no, rājyaṁ bhogāḥ sukhāni ca
    ta ime 'vasthitā yuddhe, prāṇāṁs tyaktvā dhanāni ca
34 ācāryāḥ pitaraḥ putrās, tathaiva ca pitāmahāḥ
    mātulāḥ śvaśurāḥ pautrāḥ, śyālāḥ sambandhinas tathā
35 etān na hantum icchāmi, ghnato 'pi madhusūdana
    api trailokya-rājyasya, hetoḥ kiṁ nu mahī-kṛte
36 nihatya dhārtarāṣṭrān naḥ, kā prītiḥ syāj janārdana
    pāpam evāśrayed asmān, hatvaitān ātatāyinaḥ
37 tasmān nārhā vayaṁ hantuṁ, dhārtarāṣṭrān sa-bāndhavān
    sva-janaṁ hi kathaṁ hatvā, sukhinaḥ syāma mādhava
38 yady apy ete na paśyanti, lobhopahata-cetasaḥ
    kula-kṣaya-kṛtaṁ doṣaṁ, mitra-drohe ca pātakam
39 kathaṁ na jñeyam asmābhiḥ, pāpād asmān nivartitum
    kula-kṣaya-kṛtaṁ doṣaṁ, prapaśyadbhir janārdana

40 kula-kṣaye praṇaśyanti, kula-dharmāḥ sanātanāḥ
    dharme naṣṭe kulaṁ kṛtsnam, adharmo 'bhibhavaty uta
41 adharmābhibhavāt kṛṣṇa, praduṣyanti kula-striyaḥ
    strīṣu duṣṭāsu vārṣṇeya, jāyate varṇa-saṅkaraḥ
42 saṅkaro narakāyaiva, kula-ghnānāṁ kulasya ca
    patanti pitaro hy eṣāṁ, lupta-piṇḍodaka-kriyāḥ
43 doṣair etaiḥ kula-ghnānāṁ, varṇa-saṅkara-kārakaiḥ
    utsādyante jāti-dharmāḥ, kula-dharmāś ca śāśvatāḥ
44 utsanna-kula-dharmāṇāṁ, manuṣyāṇāṁ janārdana
    narake niyataṁ vāso, bhavatīty anuśuśruma
45 aho bata mahat pāpaṁ, kartuṁ vyavasitā vayam
    yad-rājya-sukha-lobhena, hantuṁ sva-janam udyatāḥ
46 yadi mām apratīkāram, aśastraṁ śastra-pāṇayaḥ
    dhārtarāṣṭrā raṇe hanyus, tan me kṣemataraṁ bhavet
47 evam uktvārjunaḥ saṅkhye, rathopastha upāviśat
    visṛjya sa-śaraṁ cāpaṁ, śoka-saṁvigna-mānasaḥ

2

Sañjaya uvāca

1 taṁ tathā kṛpayāviṣṭam, aśru-pūrṇākulekṣaṇam
   viṣīdantam idaṁ vākyam, uvāca madhusūdanaḥ

Śrī-Bhagavān uvāca

2 kutas tvā kaśmalam idaṁ, viṣame samupasthitam
   anārya-juṣṭam asvargyam, akīrti-karam arjuna
3 klaibyaṁ mā sma gamaḥ pārtha, naitat tvayy upapadyate
   kṣudraṁ hṛdaya-daurbalyaṁ, tyaktvottiṣṭha parantapa

Arjuna uvāca

4 kathaṁ bhīṣmam ahaṁ saṅkhye, droṇaṁ ca madhusūdana
   iṣubhiḥ pratiyotsyāmi, pūjārhāv ari-sūdana
5 gurūn ahatvā hi mahānubhāvān
       śreyo bhoktuṁ bhaikṣyam apīha loke
   hatvārtha-kāmāṁs tu gurūn ihaiva
       bhuñjīya bhogān rudhira-pradigdhān
6 na caitad vidmaḥ kataran no garīyo
       yad vā jayema yadi vā no jayeyuḥ
   yān eva hatvā na jijīviṣāmas
       te 'vasthitāḥ pramukhe dhārtarāṣṭrāḥ

7 kārpaṇya-doṣopahata-svabhāvaḥ
   pṛcchāmi tvāṁ dharma-saṁmūḍha-cetāḥ
   yac chreyaḥ syān niścitaṁ brūhi tan me
   śiṣyas te 'haṁ śādhi māṁ tvāṁ prapannam
8 na hi prapaśyāmi mamāpanudyād
   yac chokam ucchoṣaṇam indriyāṇām
   avāpya bhūmāv asapatnam ṛddhaṁ
   rājyaṁ surāṇām api cādhipatyam

Sañjaya uvāca

9 evam uktvā hṛṣīkeśaṁ, guḍākeśaḥ parantapaḥ
   na yotsya iti govindam, uktvā tūṣṇīṁ babhūva ha
10 tam uvāca hṛṣīkeśaḥ, prahasann iva bhārata
   senayor ubhayor madhye, viṣīdantam idam vacaḥ

Śrī-Bhagavān uvāca

11 aśocyān anvaśocas tvaṁ, prajñā-vādāṁś ca bhāṣase
   gatāsūn agatāsūṁś ca, nānuśocanti paṇḍitāḥ
12 na tv evāhaṁ jātu nāsaṁ, na tvaṁ neme janādhipāḥ
   na caiva na bhaviṣyāmaḥ, sarve vayam ataḥ param
13 dehino 'smin yathā dehe, kaumāraṁ yauvanaṁ jarā
   tathā dehāntara-prāptir, dhīras tatra na muhyati
14 mātrā-sparśās tu kaunteya, śītoṣṇa-sukha-duḥkha-dāḥ
   āgamāpāyino 'nityās, tāṁs titikṣasva bhārata
15 yaṁ hi na vyathayanty ete, puruṣaṁ puruṣarṣabha
   sama-duḥkha-sukhaṁ dhīraṁ, so 'mṛtatvāya kalpate
16 nāsato vidyate bhāvo, nābhāvo vidyate sataḥ
   ubhayor api dṛṣṭo 'ntas, tv anayos tattva-darśibhiḥ
17 avināśi tu tad viddhi, yena sarvam idaṁ tatam
   vināśam avyayasyāsya, na kaścit kartum arhati
18 antavanta ime dehā, nityasyoktāḥ śarīriṇaḥ
   anāśino 'prameyasya, tasmād yudhyasva bhārata
19 ya enaṁ vetti hantāraṁ, yaś cainaṁ manyate hatam
   ubhau tau na vijānīto, nāyaṁ hanti na hanyate
20 na jāyate mriyate vā kadācin
   nāyaṁ bhūtvā bhavitā vā na bhūyaḥ
   ajo nityaḥ śāśvato 'yaṁ purāṇo
   na hanyate hanyamāne śarīre
21 vedāvināśinaṁ nityaṁ, ya enam ajam avyayam
   kathaṁ sa puruṣaḥ pārtha, kaṁ ghātayati hanti kam

22 vāsāṁsi jīrṇāni yathā vihāya
   navāni gṛhṇāti naro 'parāṇi
   tathā śarīrāṇi vihāya jīrṇāny
   anyāni saṁyāti navāni dehī
23 nainaṁ chindanti śastrāṇi, nainaṁ dahati pāvakaḥ
   na cainaṁ kledayanty āpo, na śoṣayati mārutaḥ
24 acchedyo 'yam adāhyo 'yam, akledyo 'śoṣya eva ca
   nityaḥ sarva-gataḥ sthāṇur, acalo 'yaṁ sanātanaḥ
25 avyakto 'yam acintyo 'yam, avikāryo 'yam ucyate
   tasmād evaṁ viditvainaṁ, nānuśocitum arhasi
26 atha cainaṁ nitya-jātaṁ, nityaṁ vā manyase mṛtam
   tathāpi tvaṁ mahā-bāho, nainaṁ śocitum arhasi
27 jātasya hi dhruvo mṛtyur, dhruvaṁ janma mṛtasya ca
   tasmād aparihārye 'rthe, na tvaṁ śocitum arhasi
28 avyaktādīni bhūtāni, vyakta-madhyāni bhārata
   avyakta-nidhanāny eva, tatra kā paridevanā
29 āścarya-vat paśyati kaścid enam
   āścarya-vad vadati tathaiva cānyaḥ
   āścarya-vac cainam anyaḥ śṛṇoti
   śrutvāpy enaṁ veda na caiva kaścit
30 dehī nityam avadhyo 'yaṁ, dehe sarvasya bhārata
   tasmāt sarvāṇi bhūtāni, na tvaṁ śocitum arhasi
31 sva-dharmam api cāvekṣya, na vikampitum arhasi
   dharmyād dhi yuddhāc chreyo 'nyat, kṣatriyasya na vidyate
32 yadṛcchayā copapannaṁ, svarga-dvāram apāvṛtam
   sukhinaḥ kṣatriyāḥ pārtha, labhante yuddham īdṛśam
33 atha cet tvam imaṁ dharmyaṁ, saṅgrāmaṁ na kariṣyasi
   tataḥ sva-dharmaṁ kīrtiṁ ca, hitvā pāpam avāpsyasi
34 akīrtiṁ cāpi bhūtāni, kathayiṣyanti te 'vyayām
   sambhāvitasya cākīrtir, maraṇād atiricyate
35 bhayād raṇād uparataṁ, maṁsyante tvāṁ mahā-rathāḥ
   yeṣāṁ ca tvaṁ bahu-mato, bhūtvā yāsyasi lāghavam
36 avācya-vādāṁś ca bahūn, vadiṣyanti tavāhitāḥ
   nindantas tava sāmarthyaṁ, tato duḥkhataraṁ nu kim
37 hato vā prāpsyasi svargaṁ, jitvā vā bhokṣyase mahīm
   tasmād uttiṣṭha kaunteya, yuddhāya kṛta-niścayaḥ
38 sukha-duḥkhe same kṛtvā, lābhālābhau jayājayau
   tato yuddhāya yujyasva, naivaṁ pāpam avāpsyasi
39 eṣā te 'bhihitā sāṅkhye, buddhir yoge tv imāṁ śṛṇu
   buddhyā yukto yayā pārtha, karma-bandhaṁ prahāsyasi
40 nehābhikrama-nāśo 'sti, pratyavāyo na vidyate
   sv-alpam apy asya dharmasya, trāyate mahato bhayāt

41 vyavasāyātmikā buddhir, ekeha kuru-nandana
    bahu-śākhā hy anantāś ca, buddhayo 'vyavasāyinām
42 yām imāṁ puṣpitāṁ vācaṁ, pravadanty avipaścitaḥ
    veda-vāda-ratāḥ pārtha, nānyad astīti vādinaḥ
43 kāmātmānaḥ svarga-parā, janma-karma-phala-pradām
    kriyā-viśeṣa-bahulāṁ, bhogaiśvarya-gatiṁ prati
44 bhogaiśvarya-prasaktānāṁ, tayāpahṛta-cetasām
    vyavasāyātmikā buddhiḥ, samādhau na vidhīyate
45 trai-guṇya-viṣayā vedā, nistrai-guṇyo bhavārjuna
    nirdvandvo nitya-sattva-stho, niryoga-kṣema ātmavān
46 yāvān artha udapāne, sarvataḥ samplutodake
    tāvān sarveṣu vedeṣu, brāhmaṇasya vijānataḥ
47 karmaṇy evādhikāras te, mā phaleṣu kadācana
    mā karma-phala-hetur bhūr, mā te saṅgo 'stv akarmaṇi
48 yoga-sthaḥ kuru karmāṇi, saṅgaṁ tyaktvā dhanañjaya
    siddhy-asiddhyoḥ samo bhūtvā, samatvaṁ yoga ucyate
49 dūreṇa hy avaraṁ karma, buddhi-yogād dhanañjaya
    buddhau śaraṇam anviccha, kṛpaṇāḥ phala-hetavaḥ
50 buddhi-yukto jahātīha, ubhe sukṛta-duṣkṛte
    tasmād yogāya yujyasva, yogaḥ karmasu kauśalam
51 karma-jaṁ buddhi-yuktā, hi phalaṁ tyaktvā manīṣiṇaḥ
    janma-bandha-vinirmuktāḥ, padaṁ gacchanty anāmayam
52 yadā te moha-kalilaṁ, buddhir vyatitariṣyati
    tadā gantāsi nirvedaṁ, śrotavyasya śrutasya ca
53 śruti-vipratipannā te, yadā sthāsyati niścalā
    samādhāv acalā buddhis, tadā yogam avāpsyasi

Arjuna uvāca

54 sthita-prajñasya kā bhāṣā, samādhi-sthasya keśava
    sthita-dhīḥ kiṁ prabhāṣeta, kim āsīta vrajeta kim

Śrī-Bhagavān uvāca

55 prajahāti yadā kāmān, sarvān pārtha mano-gatān
    ātmany evātmanā tuṣṭaḥ, sthita-prajñas tadocyate
56 duḥkheṣv anudvigna-manāḥ, sukheṣu vigata-spṛhaḥ
    vīta-rāga-bhaya-krodhaḥ, sthita-dhīr munir ucyate
57 yaḥ sarvatrānabhisnehas, tat tat prāpya śubhāśubham
    nābhinandati na dveṣṭi, tasya prajñā pratiṣṭhitā
58 yadā saṁharate cāyaṁ, kūrmo 'ṅgānīva sarvaśaḥ
    indriyāṇīndriyārthebhyas, tasya prajñā pratiṣṭhitā
59 viṣayā vinivartante, nirāhārasya dehinaḥ
    rasa-varjaṁ raso 'py asya, paraṁ dṛṣṭvā nivartate

60 yatato hy api kaunteya, puruṣasya vipaścitaḥ
indriyāṇi pramāthīni, haranti prasabhaṁ manaḥ
61 tāni sarvāṇi saṁyamya, yukta āsīta mat-paraḥ
vaśe hi yasyendriyāṇi, tasya prajñā pratiṣṭhitā
62 dhyāyato viṣayān puṁsaḥ, saṅgas teṣūpajāyate
saṅgāt sañjāyate kāmaḥ, kāmāt krodho 'bhijāyate
63 krodhād bhavati sammohaḥ, sammohāt smṛti-vibhramaḥ
smṛti-bhraṁśād buddhi-nāśo, buddhi-nāśāt praṇaśyati
64 rāga-dveṣa-viyuktais tu, viṣayān indriyaiś caran
ātma-vaśyair vidheyātmā, prasādam adhigacchati
65 prasāde sarva-duḥkhānāṁ, hānir asyopajāyate
prasanna-cetaso hy āśu, buddhiḥ paryavatiṣṭhate
66 nāsti buddhir ayuktasya, na cāyuktasya bhāvanā
na cābhāvayataḥ śāntir, aśāntasya kutaḥ sukham
67 indriyāṇāṁ hi caratāṁ, yan mano 'nuvidhīyate
tad asya harati prajñāṁ, vāyur nāvam ivāmbhasi
68 tasmād yasya mahā-bāho, nigṛhītāni sarvaśaḥ
indriyāṇīndriyārthebhyas, tasya prajñā pratiṣṭhitā
69 yā niśā sarva-bhūtānāṁ, tasyāṁ jāgarti saṁyamī
yasyāṁ jāgrati bhūtāni, sā niśā paśyato muneḥ
70 apuryamāṇam acala-pratiṣṭhaṁ
samudram āpaḥ praviśanti yadvat
tadvat kāmā yaṁ praviśanti sarve
sa śāntim āpnoti na kāma-kāmī
71 vihāya kāmān yaḥ sarvān, pumāṁś carati niḥspṛhaḥ
nirmamo nirahaṅkāraḥ, sa śāntim adhigacchati
72 eṣā brāhmī sthitiḥ pārtha, naināṁ prāpya vimuhyati
sthitvāsyām anta-kāle 'pi, brahma-nirvāṇam ṛcchati

3

Arjuna uvāca

1 jyāyasī cet karmaṇas te, matā buddhir janārdana
tat kiṁ karmaṇi ghore māṁ, niyojayasi keśava
2 vyāmiśreṇaiva vākyena, buddhiṁ mohayasīva me
tad ekaṁ vada niścitya, yena śreyo 'ham āpnuyām

Śrī-Bhagavān uvāca

3 loke 'smin dvi-vidhā niṣṭhā, purā proktā mayānagha
jñāna-yogena sāṅkhyānāṁ, karma-yogena yoginām
4 na karmaṇām anārambhan, naiṣkarmyam puruṣo 'snute
na ca saṁnyasanād eva, siddhiṁ samadhigacchati

5 na hi kaścit kṣaṇam api, jātu tiṣṭhaty akarma-kṛt
   kāryate hy avaśaḥ karma, sarvaḥ prakṛti-jair guṇaiḥ

6 karmendriyāṇi saṁyamya, ya āste manasā smaran
   indriyārthān vimūḍhātmā, mithyācāraḥ sa ucyate

7 yas tv indriyāṇi manasā, niyamyārabhate 'rjuna
   karmendriyaiḥ karma-yogam, asaktaḥ sa viśiṣyate

8 niyataṁ kuru karma tvaṁ, karma jyāyo hy akarmaṇaḥ
   śarīra-yātrāpi ca te, na prasiddhyed akarmaṇaḥ

9 yajñārthāt karmaṇo 'nyatra, loko 'yam karma-bandhanaḥ
   tad-arthaṁ karma kaunteya, mukta-saṅgaḥ samācara

10 saha-yajñāḥ prajāḥ sṛṣṭvā, purovāca prajāpatiḥ
   anena prasaviṣyadhvam, eṣa vo 'stv iṣṭa-kāma-dhuk

11 devān bhāvayatānena, te devā bhāvayantu vaḥ
   parasparaṁ bhāvayantaḥ, śreyaḥ param avāpsyatha

12 iṣṭān bhogān hi vo devā, dāsyante yajña-bhāvitāḥ
   tair dattān apradāyaibhyo, yo bhuṅkte stena eva saḥ

13 yajña-śiṣṭāśinaḥ santo, mucyante sarva-kilbiṣaiḥ
   bhuñjate te tv aghaṁ pāpā, ye pacanty ātma-kāraṇāt

14 annād bhavanti bhūtāni, parjanyād anna-sambhavaḥ
   yajñād bhavati parjanyo, yajñaḥ karma-samudbhavaḥ

15 karma brahmodbhavaṁ viddhi, brahmākṣara-samudbhavam
   tasmāt sarva-gataṁ brahma, nityaṁ yajñe pratiṣṭhitam

16 evaṁ pravartitaṁ cakraṁ, nānuvartayatīha yaḥ
   aghāyur indriyārāmo, moghaṁ pārtha sa jīvati

17 yas tv ātma-ratir eva syād, ātma-tṛptaś ca mānavaḥ
   ātmany eva ca santuṣṭas, tasya kāryaṁ na vidyate

18 naiva tasya kṛtenārtho, nākṛteneha kaścana
   na cāsya sarva bhūteṣu, kaścid artha-vyapāśrayaḥ

19 tasmād asaktaḥ satataṁ, kāryaṁ karma samācara
   asakto hy ācaran karma, param āpnoti pūruṣaḥ

20 karmaṇaiva hi saṁsiddhim, āsthitā janakādayaḥ
   loka-saṅgraham evāpi, sampaśyan kartum arhasi

21 yad yad ācarati śreṣṭhas, tat tad evetaro janaḥ
   sa yat pramāṇaṁ kurute, lokas tad anuvartate

22 na me pārthāsti kartavyaṁ, triṣu lokeṣu kiñcana
   nānavāptam avāptavyaṁ, varta eva ca karmaṇi

23 yadi hy ahaṁ na varteyaṁ, jātu karmaṇy atandritaḥ
   mama vartmānuvartante, manuṣyāḥ pārtha sarvaśaḥ

24 utsīdeyur ime lokā, na kuryāṁ karma ced aham
   saṅkarasya ca kartā syām, upahanyām imāḥ prajāḥ

25 saktāḥ karmaṇy avidvāṁso, yathā kurvanti bhārata
   kuryād vidvāṁs tathāsaktaś, cikīrṣur loka-saṅgraham

26 na buddhi-bhedaṁ janayed, ajñānāṁ karma-saṅginām
   joṣayet sarva-karmāṇi, vidvān yuktaḥ samācaran
27 parkṛteḥ kriyamāṇāni, guṇaiḥ karmāṇi sarvaśaḥ
   ahaṅkāra-vimūḍhātmā, kartāham iti manyate
28 tattva-vit tu mahā-bāho, guṇa-karma-vibhāgayoḥ
   guṇā guṇeṣu vartanta, iti matvā na sajjate
29 prakṛter guṇa-sammūḍhāḥ, sajjante guṇa-karmasu
   tān akṛtsna-vido mandān, kṛtsna-vin na vicālayet
30 mayi sarvāṇi karmāṇi, saṁnyasyādhyātma-cetasā
   nirāśīr nirmamo bhūtvā, yudhyasva vigata-jvaraḥ
31 ye me matam idaṁ nityam, anutiṣṭhanti mānavāḥ
   śraddhāvanto 'nasūyanto, mucyante te 'pi karmabhiḥ
32 te tv etad adhyasūyanto, nānutiṣṭhanti me matam
   sarva-jñāna-vimūḍhāṁs tān, viddhi naṣṭān acetasaḥ
33 sadṛśaṁ ceṣṭate svasyāḥ, prakṛter jñānavān api
   prakṛtiṁ yānti bhūtāni, nigrahaḥ kiṁ kariṣyati
34 indriyasyendriyasyārthe, rāga-dveṣau vyavasthitau
   tayor na vaśam āgachet, tau hy asya paripanthinau
35 śreyān sva-dharmo viguṇaḥ, para-dharmāt sv-anuṣṭhitāt
   sva-dharme nidhanaṁ śreyaḥ, para-dharmo bhayāvahaḥ

Arjuna uvāca
36 atha kena prayukto 'yaṁ, pāpaṁ carati pūruṣaḥ
   anicchann api vārṣṇeya, balād iva niyojitaḥ

Śrī-Bhagavān uvāca
37 kāma eṣa krodha eṣa, rajo-guṇa-samudbhavaḥ
   mahāśano mahā-pāpmā, viddhy enam iha vairiṇam
38 dhūmenāvriyate vahnir, yathādarśo malena ca
   yatholbenāvṛto garbhas, tathā tenedam āvṛtam
39 āvṛtaṁ jñānam etena, jñānino nitya-vairiṇā
   kāma-rūpeṇa kaunteya, duṣpūreṇānalena ca
40 indriyāṇi mano buddhir, asyādhiṣṭhānam ucyate
   etair vimohayaty eṣa, jñānam āvṛtya dehinam
41 tasmāt tvam indriyāṇy ādau, niyamya bharatarṣabha
   pāpmānaṁ prajahi hy enam, jñāna-vijñāna-nāśanam
42 indriyāṇi parāṇy āhur, indriyebhyaḥ paraṁ manaḥ
   manasas tu parā buddhir, yo buddheḥ paratas tu saḥ
43 evaṁ buddheḥ paraṁ buddhvā, saṁstabhyātmānam ātmanā
   jahi śatruṁ mahā-bāho, kāma-rūpaṁ durāsadam

4

Śrī-Bhagavān uvāca

1 imaṁ vivasvate yogaṁ, proktavān aham avyayam
vivasvān manave prāha, manur ikṣvākave 'bravīt

2 evaṁ paramparā-prāptam, imaṁ rājarṣayo viduḥ
sa kāleneha mahatā, yogo naṣṭaḥ parantapa

3 sa evāyaṁ mayā te 'dya, yogaḥ proktaḥ purātanaḥ
bhakto 'si me sakhā ceti, rahasyaṁ hy etad uttamam

Arjuna uvāca

4 aparaṁ bhavato janma, paraṁ janma vivasvataḥ
katham etad vijānīyāṁ, tvam ādau proktavān iti

Śrī-Bhagavān uvāca

5 bahūni me vyatītāni, janmāni tava cārjuna
tāny ahaṁ veda sarvāṇi, na tvaṁ vettha parantapa

6 ajo 'pi sann avyayātmā, bhūtānām īśvaro 'pi san
prakṛtiṁ svām adhiṣṭhāya, sambhavāmy ātma-māyayā

7 yadā yadā hi dharmasya, glānir bhavati bhārata
abhyutthānam adharmasya, tadātmānaṁ sṛjāmy aham

8 paritrāṇāya sādhūnāṁ, vināśāya ca duṣkṛtām
dharma-saṁsthāpanārthāya, sambhavāmi yuge yuge

9 janma karma ca me divyam, evaṁ yo vetti tattvataḥ
tyaktvā dehaṁ punar janma, naiti mām eti so 'rjuna

10 vīta-rāga-bhaya-krodhā, man-mayā mām upāśritāḥ
bahavo jñāna-tapasā, pūtā mad-bhāvam āgatāḥ

11 ye yathā māṁ prapadyante, tāṁs tathaiva bhajāmy aham
mama vartmānuvartante, manuṣyāḥ pārtha sarvaśaḥ

12 kāṅkṣantaḥ karmaṇāṁ siddhiṁ, yajanta iha devatāḥ
kṣipraṁ hi mānuṣe loke, siddhir bhavati karma-jā

13 cātur-varṇyaṁ mayā sṛṣṭam, guṇa-karma-vibhāgaśaḥ
tasya kartāram api māṁ, viddhy akartāram avyayam

14 na māṁ karmāṇi limpanti, na me karma-phale spṛhā
iti māṁ yo 'bhijānāti, karmabhir na sa badhyate

15 evaṁ jñātvā kṛtaṁ karma, pūrvair api mumukṣubhiḥ
kuru karmaiva tasmāt tvaṁ, pūrvaiḥ pūrvataraṁ kṛtam

16 kiṁ karma kim akarmeti, kavayo 'py atra mohitāḥ
tat te karma pravakṣyāmi, yaj jñātvā mokṣyase 'śubhāt

17 karmaṇo hy api boddhavyaṁ, boddhavyaṁ ca vikarmaṇaḥ
akarmaṇaś ca boddhavyaṁ, gahanā karmaṇo gatiḥ

18 karmaṇy akarma yaḥ paśyed, akarmaṇi ca karma yaḥ
   sa buddhimān manuṣyeṣu, sa yuktaḥ kṛtsna-karma-kṛt

19 yasya sarve samārambhāḥ, kāma-saṅkalpa-varjitāḥ
   jñānāgni-dagdha-karmāṇaṁ, tam āhuḥ paṇḍitaṁ budhāḥ

20 tyaktvā karma-phalāsaṅgaṁ, nitya-tṛpto nirāśrayaḥ
   karmaṇy abhipravṛtto 'pi, naiva kiñcit karoti saḥ

21 nirāśīr yata-cittātmā, tyakta-sarva-parigrahaḥ
   śārīraṁ kevalaṁ karma, kurvan nāpnoti kilbiṣam

22 yadṛcchā-lābha-santuṣṭo, dvandvātīto vimatsaraḥ
   samaḥ siddhāv asiddhau ca, kṛtvāpi na nibadhyate

23 gata-saṅgasya muktasya, jñānāvasthita-cetasaḥ
   yajñāyācarataḥ karma, samagraṁ pravilīyate

24 brahmārpaṇaṁ brahma havir, brahmāgnau brahmaṇā hutam
   brahmaiva tena gantavyaṁ, brahma-karma-samādhinā

25 daivam evāpare yajñaṁ, yoginaḥ paryupāsate
   brahmāgnāv apare yajñaṁ, yajñenaivopajuhvati

26 śrotrādīnīndriyāṇy anye, saṁyamāgniṣu juhvati
   śabdādīn viṣayān anya, indriyāgniṣu juhvati

27 sarvāṇīndriya-karmāṇi, prāṇa-karmāṇi cāpare
   ātma-saṁyama-yogāgnau, juhvati jñāna-dīpite

28 dravya-yajñās tapo-yajñā, yoga-yajñās tathāpare
   svādhyāya-jñāna-yajñāś ca, yatayaḥ saṁśita-vratāḥ

29 apāne juhvati prāṇaṁ, prāṇe 'pānam tathāpare
   prāṇāpana-gatī ruddhvā, prāṇāyāma-parāyaṇāḥ

30 apare niyatāhārāḥ, prāṇān prāṇeṣu juhvati
   sarve 'py ete yajña-vido, yajña-kṣapita-kalmaṣāḥ

31 yajña-śiṣṭāmṛta-bhujo, yānti brahma sanātanam
   nāyaṁ loko 'sty ayajñasya, kuto 'nyaḥ kuru-sattama

32 evaṁ bahu-vidhā yajñā, vitatā brahmaṇo mukhe
   karma-jān viddhi tān sarvān, evaṁ jñātvā vimokṣase

33 śreyān dravya-mayād yajñāj, jñāna-yajñaḥ parantapa
   sarvaṁ karmākhilaṁ pārtha, jñāne parisamāpyate

34 tad viddhi praṇipātena, paripraśnena sevayā
   upadekṣyanti te jñānaṁ, jñāninas tattva-darśinaḥ

35 yaj jñātvā na punar moham, evaṁ yāsyasi pāṇḍava
   yena bhūtāny āśeṣeṇa, drakṣyasy ātmany atho mayi

36 api ced asi pāpebhyaḥ, sarvebhyaḥ pāpa-kṛt-tamaḥ
   sarvaṁ jñāna-plavenaiva, vṛjinaṁ santariṣyasi

37 yathaidhāṁsi samiddho 'gnir, bhasma-sāt kurute 'rjuna
   jñānāgniḥ sarva-karmāṇi, bhasma-sāt kurute tathā

38 na hi jñānena sadṛśaṁ, pavitram iha vidyate
   tat svayaṁ yoga-saṁsiddhaḥ, kālenātmani vindati

39 śraddhāvāṅl labhate jñānaṁ, tat-paraḥ saṁyatendriyaḥ
    jñānaṁ labdhvā parāṁ śāntim, acireṇādhigacchati
40 ajñaś cāśraddadhānaś ca, saṁśayātmā vinaśyati
    nāyam loko 'sti na paro, na sukhaṁ saṁśayātmanaḥ
41 yoga-saṁnyasta-karmāṇaṁ, jñāna-sañchinna-saṁśayam
    ātmavantaṁ na karmāṇi, nibadhnanti dhanañjaya
42 tasmād ajñāna-sambhūtaṁ, hṛt-sthaṁ jñānāsinātmanaḥ
    chittvainaṁ saṁśayaṁ yogam, ātiṣṭhottiṣṭha bhārata

5

Arjuna uvāca

 1 saṁnyāsaṁ karmaṇāṁ kṛṣṇa, punar yogaṁ ca śaṁsasi
    yac chreya etayor ekaṁ, tan me brūhi su-niścitam

Śrī-Bhagavān uvāca

 2 saṁnyāsaḥ karma-yogaś ca, niḥśreyasa-karāv ubhau
    tayos tu karma-saṁnyāsāt, karma-yogo viśiṣyate
 3 jñeyaḥ sa nitya-saṁnyāsī, yo na dveṣṭi na kāṅkṣati
    nirdvando hi mahā-bāho, sukhaṁ bandhāt pramucyate
 4 sāṅkhya-yogau pṛthag bālāḥ, pravadanti na paṇḍitāḥ
    ekam apy āsthitaḥ samyag, ubhayor vindate phalam
 5 yat sāṅkhyaiḥ prāpyate sthānaṁ, tad yogair api gamyate
    ekaṁ sāṅkhyaṁ ca yogaṁ ca, yaḥ paśyati sa paśyati
 6 saṁnyāsas tu mahā-bāho, duḥkham āptum ayogataḥ
    yoga-yukto munir brahma, na cireṇādhigacchati
 7 yoga-yukto viśuddhātmā, vijitātmā jitendriyaḥ
    sarva-bhūtātma-bhūtātmā, kurvann api na lipyate
 8 naiva kiñcit karomīti, yukto manyeta tattva-vit
    paśyañ śṛṇvan spṛśañ jighrann, aśnan gacchan svapañ śvasan
 9 pralapan visṛjan gṛhṇann, unmiṣan nimiṣann api
    indriyāṇīndriyārtheṣu, vartanta iti dhārayan
10 brahmaṇy ādhāya karmāṇi, saṅgaṁ tyaktvā karoti yaḥ
    lipyate na sa pāpena, padma-patram ivāmbhasā
11 kāyena manasā buddhyā, kevalair indriyair api
    yoginaḥ karma kurvanti, saṅgaṁ tyaktvātma-śuddhaye
12 yuktaḥ karma-phalaṁ tyaktvā, śāntim āpnoti naiṣṭhikīm
    ayuktaḥ kāma-kāreṇa, phale sakto nibadhyate
13 sarva-karmāṇi manasā, saṁnyasyāste sukhaṁ vaśī
    nava-dvāre pure dehī, naiva kurvan na kārayan
14 na kartṛtvaṁ na karmāṇi, lokasya sṛjati prabhuḥ
    na karma-phala saṁyogaṁ, svabhāvas tu pravartate

15 nādatte kasyacit pāpaṁ, na caiva sukṛtaṁ vibhuḥ
   ajñānenāvṛtaṁ jñānaṁ, tena muhyanti jantavaḥ

16 jñānena tu tad ajñānaṁ, yeṣāṁ nāśitam ātmanaḥ
   teṣām āditya-vaj jñānaṁ, prakāśayati tat param

17 tad-buddhayas tad-ātmānas, tan-niṣṭhās tat-parāyaṇāḥ
   gacchanty apunar-āvṛttiṁ, jñāna-nirdhūta-kalmaṣāḥ

18 vidyā-vinaya-sampanne, brāhmaṇe gavi hastini
   śuni caiva śva-pāke ca, paṇḍitāḥ sama-darśinaḥ

19 ihaiva tair jitaḥ sargo, yeṣāṁ sāmye sthitaṁ manaḥ
   nirdoṣaṁ hi samaṁ brahma, tasmād brahmaṇi te sthitāḥ

20 na prahṛṣyet priyaṁ prāpya, nodvijet prāpya cāpriyam
   sthira-buddhir asammūḍho, brahma-vid brahmaṇi sthitaḥ

21 bāhya-sparśeṣv asaktātmā, vindaty ātmani yat sukham
   sa brahma-yoga-yuktātmā, sukham akṣayam aśnute

22 ye hi saṁsparśa-jā bhogā, duḥkha-yonaya eva te
   ādy-antavantaḥ kaunteya, na teṣu ramate budhaḥ

23 śaknotīhaiva yaḥ soḍhuṁ, prāk śarīra-vimokṣaṇāt
   kāma-krodhodbhavaṁ vegaṁ, sa yuktaḥ sa sukhī naraḥ

24 yo 'ntaḥ-sukho 'ntar-ārāmas, tathāntar-jyotir eva yaḥ
   sa yogī brahma-nirvāṇaṁ, brahma-bhūto 'dhigacchati

25 labhante brahma-nirvāṇam, ṛṣayaḥ kṣīṇa-kalmaṣāḥ
   chinna-dvaidhā yatātmānaḥ, sarva-bhūta-hite ratāḥ

26 kāma-krodha-viyuktānāṁ, yatīnāṁ yata-cetasām
   abhito brahma-nirvāṇaṁ, vartate viditātmanām

27 sparśān kṛtvā bahir bāhyāṁś, cakṣuś caivāntare bhruvoḥ
   prāṇāpānau samau kṛtvā, nāsābhyantara-cāriṇau

28 yatendriya-mano-buddhir, munir mokṣa-parāyaṇaḥ
   vigatecchā-bhaya-krodho, yaḥ sadā mukta eva saḥ

29 bhoktāraṁ yajña-tapasāṁ, sarva-loka-maheśvaram
   suhṛdaṁ sarva-bhūtānāṁ, jñātvā māṁ śāntim ṛcchati

6

Śrī-Bhagavān uvāca

1 anāśritaḥ karma-phalaṁ, kāryaṁ karma karoti yaḥ
   sa saṁnyāsī ca yogī ca, na niragnir na cākriyaḥ

2 yaṁ saṁnyāsam iti prāhur, yogaṁ taṁ viddhi pāṇḍava
   na hy asaṁnyasta-saṅkalpo, yogī bhavati kaścana

3 ārurukṣor muner yogaṁ, karma kāraṇam ucyate
   yogārūḍhasya tasyaiva, śamaḥ kāraṇam ucyate

4 yadā hi nendriyārtheṣu, na karmasv anuṣajjate
   sarva-saṅkalpa-saṁnyāsī, yogārūḍhas tadocyate

5 uddhared ātmanātmānaṁ, nātmānam avasādayet
  ātmaiva hy ātmano bandhur, ātmaiva ripur ātmanaḥ

6 bandhur ātmātmanas tasya, yenātmaivātmanā jitaḥ
  anātmanas tu śatrutve, vartetātmaiva śatru-vat

7 jitātmanaḥ praśāntasya, paramātmā samāhitaḥ
  śītoṣṇa-sukha-duḥkheṣu, tathā mānāpamānayoḥ

8 jñāna-vijñāna-tṛptāmā, kūṭa-stho vijitendriyaḥ
  yukta ity ucyate yogī, sama-loṣṭrāśma-kāñcanaḥ

9 suhṛn-mitrāry-udāsīna-, madhyastha-dveṣya-bandhuṣu
  sādhuṣv api ca pāpeṣu, sama-buddhir viśiṣyate

10 yogī yuñjīta satatam, ātmānaṁ rahasi sthitaḥ
   ekākī yata-cittātmā, nirāśīr aparigrahaḥ

11 śucau deśe pratiṣṭhāpya, sthiram āsanam ātmanaḥ
   nāty-ucchritaṁ nāti-nīcaṁ, cailājina-kuśottaram

12 tatraikāgraṁ manaḥ kṛtvā, yata-cittendriya-kriyaḥ
   upaviśyāsane yuñjyād, yogam ātma-viśuddhaye

13 samaṁ kāya-śiro-grīvaṁ, dhārayann acalaṁ sthiraḥ
   samprekṣya nāsikāgraṁ svaṁ, diśaś cānavalokayan

14 praśāntātmā vigata-bhīr, brahmacāri-vrate sthitaḥ
   manaḥ saṁyamya mac-citto, yukta āsīta mat-paraḥ

15 yuñjann evaṁ sadātmānaṁ, yogī niyata-mānasaḥ
   śāntiṁ nirvāṇa-paramāṁ, mat-saṁsthām adhigacchati

16 nāty-aśnatas tu yogo 'sti, na caikāntam anaśnataḥ
   na cāti-svapna-śīlasya, jāgrato naiva cārjuna

17 yuktāhāra-vihārasya, yukta-ceṣṭasya karmasu
   yukta-svapnāvabodhasya, yogo bhavati duḥkha-hā

18 yadā viniyataṁ cittam, ātmany evāvatiṣṭhate
   niḥspṛhaḥ sarva-kāmebhyo, yukta ity ucyate tadā

19 yathā dīpo nivāta-stho, neṅgate sopamā smṛtā
   yogino yata-cittasya, yuñjato yogam ātmanaḥ

20 yatroparamate cittaṁ, niruddhaṁ yoga-sevayā
   yatra caivātmanātmānaṁ, paśyann ātmani tuṣyati

21 sukham ātyantikaṁ yat tad, buddhi-grāhyam atīndriyam
   vetti yatra na caivāyaṁ, sthitaś calati tattvataḥ

22 yaṁ labdhvā cāparaṁ lābhaṁ, manyate nādhikaṁ tataḥ
   yasmin sthito na duḥkhena, guruṇāpi vicālyate

23 taṁ vidyād duḥkha-saṁyoga-, viyogaṁ yoga-saṁjñitam
   sa niścayena yoktavyo, yogo 'nirviṇṇa-cetasā

24 saṅkalpa-prabhavān kāmāṁs, tyaktvā sarvān aśeṣataḥ
   manasaivendriya-grāmaṁ, viniyamya samantataḥ

25 śanaiḥ śanair uparamed, buddhyā dhṛti-gṛhītayā
   ātma-saṁsthaṁ manaḥ kṛtvā, na kiñcid api cintayet

26 yato yato niścarati, manaś cañcalam asthiram
   tatas tato niyamyaitad, ātmany eva vaśaṁ nayet
27 praśānta-manasaṁ hy enaṁ, yoginaṁ sukham uttamam
   upaiti śānta-rajasaṁ, brahma-bhūtam akalmaṣam
28 yuñjann evaṁ sadātmānaṁ, yogī vigata-kalmaṣaḥ
   sukhena brahma-saṁsparśam, atyantaṁ sukham aśnute
29 sarva-bhūta-stham ātmānaṁ, sarva-bhūtāni cātmani
   īkṣate yoga-yuktātmā, sarvatra sama-darśanaḥ
30 yo māṁ paśyati sarvatra, sarvaṁ ca mayi paśyati
   tasyāhaṁ na praṇaśyāmi, sa ca me na praṇaśyati
31 sarva-bhūta-sthitaṁ yo māṁ, bhajaty ekatvam āsthitaḥ
   sarvathā vartamāno 'pi, sa yogī mayi vartate
32 ātmaupamyena sarvatra, samaṁ paśyati yo 'rjuna
   sukhaṁ vā yadi vā duḥkhaṁ, sa yogī paramo mataḥ

Arjuna uvāca

33 yo 'yaṁ yogas tvayā proktaḥ, sāmyena madhusūdana
   etasyāhaṁ na paśyāmi, cañcalatvāt sthitiṁ sthirām
34 cañcalaṁ hi manaḥ kṛṣṇa, pramāthi balavad dṛḍham
   tasyāhaṁ nigrahaṁ manye, vāyor iva su-duṣkaram

Śrī-Bhagavān uvāca

35 asaṁśayaṁ mahā-bāho, mano durnigrahaṁ calam
   abhyāsena tu kaunteya, vairāgyeṇa ca gṛhyate
36 asaṁyatātmanā yogo, duṣprāpa iti me matiḥ
   vaśyātmanā tu yatatā, śakyo 'vāptum upāyataḥ

Arjuna uvāca

37 ayatiḥ śraddhayopeto, yogāc calita-mānasaḥ
   aprāpya yoga-saṁsiddhiṁ, kāṁ gatiṁ kṛṣṇa gacchati
38 kaccin nobhaya-vibhraṣṭaś, chinnābhram iva naśyati
   apratiṣṭho mahā-bāho, vimūḍho brahmaṇaḥ pathi
39 etan me saṁśayaṁ kṛṣṇa, chettum arhasy aśeṣataḥ
   tvad-anyaḥ saṁśayasyāsya, chettā na hy upapadyate

Śrī-Bhagavān uvāca

40 pārtha naiveha nāmutra, vināśas tasya vidyate
   na hi kalyāṇa-kṛt kaścid, durgatiṁ tāta gacchati
41 prāpya puṇya-kṛtāṁ lokān, uṣitvā śāśvatīḥ samāḥ
   śucīnāṁ śrīmatāṁ gehe, yoga-bhraṣṭo 'bhijāyate

42 atha vā yogināṁ eva, kule bhavati dhīmatām
   etad dhi durlabhataraṁ, loke janma yad īdṛśam
43 tatra taṁ buddhi-saṁyogaṁ, labhate paurva-dehikam
   yatate ca tato bhūyaḥ, saṁsiddhau kuru-nandana
44 pūrvābhyāsena tenaiva, hriyate hy avaśo 'pi saḥ
   jijñāsur api yogasya, śabda-brahmātivartate
45 prayatnād yatamānas tu, yogī saṁśuddha-kilbiṣaḥ
   aneka-janma-saṁsiddhas, tato yāti paraṁ gatim
46 tapasvibhyo 'dhiko yogī, jñānibhyo 'pi mato 'dhikaḥ
   karmibhyaś cādhiko yogī, tasmād yogī bhavārjuna
47 yogināṁ api sarveṣāṁ, mad-gatenāntar-ātmanā
   śraddhāvān bhajate yo māṁ, sa me yuktatamo mataḥ

7

Śrī-Bhagavān uvāca

1 mayy āsakta-manāḥ pārtha, yogaṁ yuñjan mad-āśrayaḥ
  asaṁśayaṁ samagraṁ māṁ, yathā jñāsyasi tac chṛṇu
2 jñānaṁ te 'haṁ sa-vijñānam, idaṁ vakṣyāmy aśeṣataḥ
  yaj jñātvā neha bhūyo 'nyaj, jñātavyam avaśiṣyate
3 manuṣyāṇāṁ sahasreṣu, kaścid yatati siddhaye
  yatatām api siddhānāṁ, kaścin māṁ vetti tattvataḥ
4 bhūmir āpo 'nalo vāyuḥ, khaṁ mano buddhir eva ca
  ahaṅkāra itīyaṁ me, bhinnā prakṛtir aṣṭadhā
5 apareyam itas tv anyāṁ, prakṛtiṁ viddhi me parām
  jīva-bhūtāṁ mahā-bāho, yayedaṁ dhāryate jagat
6 etad-yonīni bhūtāni, sarvāṇīty upadhāraya
  ahaṁ kṛtsnasya jagataḥ, prabhavaḥ pralayas tathā
7 mattaḥ parataraṁ nānyat, kiñcid asti dhanañjaya
  mayi sarvam idaṁ protaṁ, sūtre maṇi-gaṇā iva
8 raso 'ham apsu kaunteya, prabhāsmi śaśi-sūryayoḥ
  praṇavaḥ sarva-vedeṣu, śabdaḥ khe pauruṣaṁ nṛṣu
9 puṇyo gandhaḥ pṛthivyāṁ, ca tejaś cāsmi vibhāvasau
  jīvanaṁ sarva-bhūteṣu, tapaś cāsmi tapasviṣu
10 bījaṁ māṁ sarva-bhūtānāṁ, viddhi pārtha sanātanam
   buddhir buddhimatām asmi, tejas tejasvinām aham
11 balaṁ balavatāṁ cāhaṁ, kāma-rāga-vivarjitam
   dharmāviruddho bhūteṣu, kāmo 'smi bharatarṣabha
12 ye caiva sāttvikā bhāvā, rājasās tāmasāś ca ye
   matta eveti tān viddhi, na tv ahaṁ teṣu te mayi
13 tribhir guṇa-mayair bhāvair, ebhiḥ sarvam idaṁ jagat
   mohitaṁ nābhijānāti, mām ebhyaḥ param avyayam

14 daivī hy eṣā guṇa-mayī, mama māyā duratyayā
    mām eva ye prapadyante, māyām etāṁ taranti te
15 na māṁ duṣkṛtino mūḍhāḥ, prapadyante narādhamāḥ
    māyayāpahṛta-jñānā, āsuraṁ bhāvam āśritāḥ
16 catur-vidhā bhajante māṁ, janāḥ sukṛtino 'rjuna
    ārto jijñāsur arthārthī, jñānī ca bharatarṣabha
17 teṣāṁ jñānī nitya-yukta, eka-bhaktir viśiṣyate
    priyo hi jñānino 'tyartham, ahaṁ sa ca mama priyaḥ
18 udārāḥ sarva evaite, jñānī tv ātmaiva me matam
    āsthitaḥ sa hi yuktātmā, mām evānuttamāṁ gatim
19 bahūnāṁ janmanām ante, jñānavān māṁ prapadyate
    vāsudevaḥ sarvam iti, sa mahātmā su-durlabhaḥ
20 kāmais tais tair hṛta-jñānāḥ, prapadyante 'nya-devatāḥ
    taṁ taṁ niyamam āsthāya, prakṛtyā niyatāḥ svayā
21 yo yo yāṁ yāṁ tanuṁ bhaktaḥ, śraddhayārcitum icchati
    tasya yasyācalāṁ śraddhāṁ, tām eva vidadhāmy aham
22 sa tayā śraddhayā yuktas, tasyārādhanam īhate
    labhate ca tataḥ kāmān, mayaiva vihitān hi tān
23 antavat tu phalaṁ teṣāṁ, tad bhavaty alpa-medhasām
    devān deva-yajo yānti, mad-bhaktā yānti mām api
24 avyaktaṁ vyaktim āpannaṁ, manyante mām abuddhayaḥ
    paraṁ bhāvam ajānanto, mamāvyayam anuttamam
25 nāhaṁ prakāśaḥ sarvasya, yoga-māyā-samāvṛtaḥ
    mūḍho 'yaṁ nābhijānāti, loko mām ajam avyayam
26 vedāhaṁ samatītāni, vartamānāni cārjuna
    bhaviṣyāṇi ca bhūtāni, māṁ tu veda na kaścana
27 icchā-dveṣa-samutthena, dvandva-mohena bhārata
    sarva-bhūtāni sammohaṁ, sarge yānti parantapa
28 yeṣāṁ tv anta-gataṁ pāpaṁ, janānāṁ puṇya-karmaṇām
    te dvandva-moha-nirmuktā, bhajante māṁ dṛḍha-vratāḥ
29 jarā-maraṇa-mokṣāya, mām āśritya yatanti ye
    te brahma tad viduḥ kṛtsnam, adhyātmaṁ karma cākhilam
30 sādhibhūtādhidaivaṁ māṁ, sādhiyajñaṁ ca ye viduḥ
    prayāṇa-kāle 'pi ca māṁ, te vidur yukta-cetasaḥ

8

Arjuna uvāca

1 kiṁ tad brahma kim adhyātmaṁ, kiṁ karma puruṣottama
   adhibhūtaṁ ca kiṁ proktam, adhidaivaṁ kim ucyate
2 adhiyajñaḥ kathaṁ ko 'tra, dehe 'smin madhusūdana
   prayāṇa-kāle ca kathaṁ, jñeyo 'si niyatātmabhiḥ

Śrī-Bhagavān uvāca

3 akṣaraṁ brahma paramaṁ, svabhāvo 'dhyātmam ucyate
    bhūta-bhāvodbhava-karo, visargaḥ karma-saṁjñitaḥ

4 adhibhūtaṁ kṣaro bhāvaḥ, puruṣaś cādhidaivatam
    adhiyajño 'ham evātra, dehe deha-bhṛtāṁ vara

5 anta-kāle ca mām eva, smaran muktvā kalevaram
    yaḥ prayāti sa mad-bhāvaṁ, yāti nāsty atra saṁśayaḥ

6 yaṁ yaṁ vāpi smaran bhāvaṁ, tyajaty ante kalevaram
    taṁ tam evaiti kaunteya, sadā tad-bhāva-bhāvitaḥ

7 tasmāt sarveṣu kāleṣu, mām anusmara yudhya ca
    mayy arpita-mano-buddhir, mām evaiṣyasy asaṁśayaḥ

8 abhyāsa-yoga-yuktena, cetasā nānya-gāminā
    paramaṁ puruṣaṁ divyaṁ, yāti pārthānucintayan

9 kaviṁ purāṇam anuśāsitāram
      aṇor aṇīyāṁsam anusmared yaḥ
    sarvasya dhātāram acintya-rūpam
      āditya-varṇaṁ tamasaḥ parastāt

10 prayāṇa-kāle manasācalena
      bhaktyā yukto yoga-balena caiva
    bhruvor madhye prāṇam āveśya samyak
      sa taṁ paraṁ puruṣam upaiti divyam

11 yad akṣaraṁ veda-vido vadanti
      viśanti yad yatayo vīta-rāgāḥ
    yad icchanto brahmacaryaṁ caranti
      tat te padaṁ saṅgraheṇa pravakṣye

12 sarva-dvārāṇi saṁyamya, mano hṛdi nirudhya ca
    mūrdhny ādhāyātmanaḥ prāṇam, āsthito yoga-dhāraṇām

13 om ity ekākṣaraṁ brahma, vyāharan mām anusmaran
    yaḥ prayāti tyajan dehaṁ, sa yāti paramāṁ gatim

14 ananya-cetāḥ satataṁ, yo māṁ smarati nityaśaḥ
    tasyāhaṁ sulabhaḥ pārtha nitya-yuktasya yoginaḥ

15 mām upetya punar janma, duḥkhālayam aśāśvatam
    nāpnuvanti mahātmānaḥ, saṁsiddhiṁ paramāṁ gatāḥ

16 ā-brahma-bhuvanāl lokāḥ, punar āvartino 'rjuna
    mām upetya tu kaunteya, punar janma na vidyate

17 sahasra-yuga-paryantam, ahar yad brahmaṇo viduḥ
    rātriṁ yuga-sahasrāntāṁ, te 'ho-rātra-vido janāḥ

18 avyaktād vyaktayaḥ sarvāḥ, prabhavanty ahar-āgame
    rātry-āgame pralīyante, tatraivāvyakta-saṁjñake

19 bhūta-grāmaḥ sa evāyaṁ, bhūtvā bhūtvā pralīyate
    rātry-āgame 'vaśaḥ pārtha, prabhavaty ahar-āgame

20 paras tasmāt tu bhāvo 'nyo, 'vyakto 'vyaktāt sanātanaḥ
    yaḥ sa sarveṣu bhūteṣu, naśyatsu na vinaśyati
21 avyakto 'kṣara ity uktas, tam āhuḥ paramāṁ gatim
    yaṁ prāpya na nivartante, tad dhāma paramaṁ mama
22 puruṣaḥ sa paraḥ pārtha, bhaktyā labhyas tv ananyayā
    yasyāntaḥ-sthāni bhūtāni, yena sarvam idaṁ tatam
23 yatra kāle tv anāvṛttim, āvṛttiṁ caiva yoginaḥ
    prayātā yānti taṁ kālaṁ, vakṣyāmi bharatarṣabha
24 agnir jyotir ahaḥ śuklaḥ, ṣaṇ-māsā uttarāyaṇam
    tatra prayātā gacchanti, brahma brahma-vido janāḥ
25 dhūmo rātris tathā kṛṣṇaḥ, ṣaṇ-māsā dakṣiṇāyanam
    tatra cāndramasaṁ jyotir, yogī prāpya nivartate
26 śukla-kṛṣṇe gatī hy ete, jagataḥ śāśvate mate
    ekayā yāty anāvṛttim, anyayāvartate punaḥ
27 naite sṛtī pārtha jānan, yogī muhyati kaścana
    tasmāt sarveṣu kāleṣu, yoga-yukto bhavārjuna
28 vedeṣu yajñeṣu tapaḥsu caiva
    dāneṣu yat puṇya-phalaṁ pradiṣṭam
    atyeti tat sarvam idaṁ viditvā
    yogī paraṁ sthānam upaiti cādyam

9

Śrī-Bhagavān uvāca

I idaṁ tu te guhyatamaṁ, pravakṣyāmy anasūyave
    jñānaṁ vijñāna-sahitaṁ, yaj jñātvā mokṣyase 'śubhāt
2 rāja-vidyā rāja-guhyaṁ, pavitram idam uttamam
    pratyakṣāvagamaṁ dharmyaṁ, su-sukhaṁ kartum avyayam
3 aśraddadhānāḥ puruṣā, dharmasyāsya parantapa
    aprāpya māṁ nivartante, mṛtyu-saṁsāra-vartmani
4 mayā tatam idaṁ sarvaṁ, jagad avyakta-mūrtinā
    mat-sthāni sarva-bhūtāni, na cāhaṁ teṣv avasthitaḥ
5 na ca mat-sthāni bhūtāni, paśya me yogam aiśvaram
    bhūta-bhṛn na ca bhūta-stho, mamātmā bhūta-bhāvanaḥ
6 yathākāśa-sthito nityaṁ, vāyuḥ sarvatra-go mahān
    tathā sarvāṇi bhūtāni, mat-sthānīty upadhāraya
7 sarva-bhūtāni kaunteya, prakṛtiṁ yānti māmikām
    kalpa-kṣaye punas tāni, kalpādau visṛjāmy aham
8 prakṛtiṁ svām avaṣṭabhya, visṛjāmi punaḥ punaḥ
    bhūta-grāmam imaṁ kṛtsnam, avaśaṁ prakṛter vaśāt

9 na ca māṁ tāni karmāṇi, nibadhnanti dhanañjaya
udāsīna-vad āsīnam, asaktaṁ teṣu karmasu

10 mayādhyakṣeṇa prakṛtiḥ, sūyate sa-carācaram
hetunānena kaunteya, jagad viparivartate

11 avajānanti māṁ mūḍhā, mānuṣīṁ tanum āśritam
paraṁ bhāvam ajānanto, mama bhūta-maheśvaram

12 moghāśā mogha-karmāṇo, mogha-jñānā vicetasaḥ
rākṣasīm āsurīṁ caiva, prakṛtiṁ mohinīṁ śritāḥ

13 mahātmānas tu māṁ pārtha, daivīṁ prakṛtim āśritāḥ
bhajanty ananya-manaso, jñātvā bhūtādim avyayam

14 satataṁ kīrtayanto māṁ, yatantaś ca dṛḍha-vratāḥ
namasyantaś ca māṁ bhaktyā, nitya-yuktā upāsate

15 jñāna-yajñena cāpy anye, yajanto māṁ upāsate
ekatvena pṛthaktvena, bahudhā viśvato-mukham

16 ahaṁ kratur ahaṁ yajñaḥ, svadhāham aham auṣadham
mantro 'ham aham evājyam, aham agnir ahaṁ hutam

17 pitāham asya jagato, mātā dhātā pitāmahaḥ
vedyaṁ pavitram oṁkāra, ṛk sāma yajur eva ca

18 gatir bhartā prabhū sākṣī, nivāsaḥ śaraṇaṁ suhṛt
prabhavaḥ pralayaḥ sthānam, nidhānaṁ bījam avyayam

19 tapāmy aham ahaṁ varṣam, nigṛhṇāmy utsṛjāmi ca
amṛtaṁ caiva mṛtyuś ca, sad asac cāham arjuna

20 trai-vidyā māṁ soma-pāḥ pūta-pāpā
yajñair iṣṭvā svar-gatiṁ prārthayante
te puṇyam āsādya surendra-lokam
aśnanti divyān divi deva-bhogān

21 te taṁ bhuktvā svarga-lokaṁ viśālaṁ
kṣīṇe puṇye martya-lokaṁ viśanti
evaṁ trayī-dharmam anuprapannā
gatāgataṁ kāma-kāmā labhante

22 ananyāś cintayanto māṁ, ye janāḥ paryupāsate
teṣāṁ nityābhiyuktānāṁ, yoga-kṣemaṁ vahāmy aham

23 ye 'py anya-devatā-bhaktā, yajante śraddhayānvitāḥ
te 'pi mām eva kaunteya, yajanty avidhi-pūrvakam

24 ahaṁ hi sarva-yajñānāṁ, bhoktā ca prabhur eva ca
na tu mām abhijānanti, tattvenātaś cyavanti te

25 yānti deva-vratā devān, pitṛ yānti pitṛ-vratāḥ
bhūtāni yānti bhūtejyā, yānti mad-yājino 'pi mām

26 patraṁ puṣpaṁ phalaṁ toyam, yo me bhaktyā prayacchati
tad ahaṁ bhakty-upahṛtam, aśnāmi prayatātmanaḥ

27 yat karoṣi yad aśnāsi, yaj juhoṣi dadāsi yat
yat tapasyasi kaunteya, tat kuruṣva mad-arpaṇam

28 śubhāśubha-phalair evaṁ, mokṣyase karma-bandhanaiḥ
   saṁnyāsa-yoga-yuktātmā, vimukto mām upaiṣyasi

29 samo 'haṁ sarva-bhūteṣu, na me dveṣyo 'sti na priyaḥ
   ye bhajanti tu māṁ bhaktyā, mayi te teṣu cāpy aham

30 api cet su-durācāro, bhajate mām ananya-bhāk
   sādhur eva sa mantavyaḥ, samyag vyavasito hi saḥ

31 kṣipraṁ bhavati dharmātmā, śaśvac-chāntiṁ nigacchati
   kaunteya pratijānīhi, na me bhaktaḥ praṇaśyati

32 māṁ hi pārtha vyapāśritya, ye 'pi syuḥ pāpa-yonayaḥ
   striyo vaiśyās tathā śūdrās, te 'pi yānti parāṁ gatim

33 kiṁ punar brāhmaṇāḥ puṇyā, bhaktā rājarṣayas tathā
   anityam asukhaṁ lokam, imaṁ prāpya bhajasva mām

34 man-manā bhava mad-bhakto, mad-yājī māṁ namaskuru
   mām evaiṣyasi yuktvaivam, ātmānaṁ mat-parāyaṇaḥ

10

Śrī-Bhagavān uvāca

1 bhūya eva mahā-bāho, śṛṇu me paramaṁ vacaḥ
  yat te 'haṁ prīyamāṇāya, vakṣyāmi hita-kāmyayā

2 ne me viduḥ sura-gaṇāḥ, prabhavaṁ na maharṣayaḥ
  aham ādir hi devānāṁ, maharṣīṇāṁ ca sarvaśaḥ

3 yo mām ajam anādiṁ ca, vetti loka-maheśvaram
  asammūḍhaḥ sa martyeṣu, sarva-pāpaiḥ pramucyate

4 buddhir jñānam asammohaḥ, kṣamā satyaṁ damaḥ śamaḥ
  sukhaṁ duḥkhaṁ bhavo 'bhāvo, bhayaṁ cābhayam eva ca

5 ahiṁsā samatā tuṣṭis, tapo dānaṁ yaśo 'yaśaḥ
  bhavanti bhāvā bhūtānāṁ, matta eva pṛthag-vidhāḥ

6 maharṣayaḥ sapta pūrve, catvāro manavas tathā
  mad-bhāvā mānasa jata, yeṣāṁ loka imāḥ prajāḥ

7 etāṁ vibhūtiṁ yogaṁ ca, mama yo vetti tattvataḥ
  so 'vikampena yogena, yujyate nātra saṁśayaḥ

8 aham sarvasya prabhavo, mattaḥ sarvaṁ pravartate
  iti matvā bhajante mām, budhā bhāva-samanvitāḥ

9 mac-cittā mad-gata-prāṇā, bodhayantaḥ parasparam
  kathayantaś ca māṁ nityaṁ, tuṣyanti ca ramanti ca

10 teṣāṁ satata-yuktānāṁ, bhajatāṁ prīti-pūrvakam
   dadāmi buddhi-yogaṁ taṁ, yena mām upayānti te

11 teṣām evānukampārtham, aham ajñāna-jaṁ tamaḥ
   nāśayāmy ātma-bhāva-stho, jñāna-dīpena bhāsvatā

Arjuna uvāca

12 param brahma param dhāma, pavitram paramam bhavān
    puruṣam śāśvatam divyam, ādi-devam ajam vibhum
13 āhus tvām ṛṣayaḥ sarve, devarṣir nāradas tathā
    asito devalo vyāsaḥ, svayam caiva bravīṣi me
14 sarvam etad ṛtam manye, yan mām vadasi keśava
    na hi te bhagavan vyaktim, vidur devā na dānavāḥ
15 svayam evātmanātmānam, vettha tvam puruṣottama
    bhūta-bhāvana bhūteśa, deva-deva jagat-pate
16 vaktum arhasy aśeṣeṇa, divyā hy ātma-vibhūtayaḥ
    yābhir vibhūtibhir lokān, imāṃs tvam vyāpya tiṣṭhasi
17 katham vidyām aham yogiṃs, tvām sadā paricintayan
    keṣu keṣu ca bhāveṣu, cintyo 'si bhagavan mayā
18 vistareṇātmano yogam, vibhūtim ca janārdana
    bhūyaḥ kathaya tṛptir hi, śṛṇvato nāsti me 'mṛtam

Śrī-Bhagavān uvāca

19 hanta te kathayiṣyāmi, divyā hy ātma-vibhūtayaḥ
    prādhānyataḥ kuru-śreṣṭha, nāsty anto vistarasya me
20 aham ātmā guḍākeśa, sarva-bhūtāśaya-sthitaḥ
    aham ādiś ca madhyam ca, bhūtānām anta eva ca
21 ādityānām aham viṣṇur, jyotiṣām ravir aṃśumān
    marīcir marutām asmi, nakṣatrāṇām aham śaśī
22 vedānām sāma-vedo 'smi, devānām asmi vāsavaḥ
    indriyāṇām manaś cāsmi, bhūtānām asmi cetanā
23 rudrāṇām śaṅkaraś cāsmi, vitteśo yakṣa-rakṣasām
    vasūnām pāvakaś cāsmi, meruḥ śikhariṇām aham
24 purodhasām ca mukhyam mām, viddhi pārtha bṛhaspatim
    senānīnām aham skandaḥ, sarasām asmi sāgaraḥ
25 maharṣīṇām bhṛgur aham, girām asmy ekam akṣaram
    yajñānām japa-yajño 'smi, sthāvarāṇām himālayaḥ
26 aśvatthaḥ sarva-vṛkṣāṇām, devarṣīṇām ca nāradaḥ
    gandharvāṇām citrarathaḥ, siddhānām kapilo muniḥ
27 uccaiḥśravasam aśvānām, viddhi mām amṛtodbhavam
    airāvatam gajendrāṇām, narāṇām ca narādhipam
28 āyudhānām aham vajram, dhenūnām asmi kāmadhuk
    prajanaś cāsmi kandarpaḥ, sarpāṇām asmi vāsukiḥ
29 anantaś cāsmi nāgānām, varuṇo yādasām aham
    pitṝṇām aryamā cāsmi, yamaḥ saṃyamatām aham
30 prahlādaś cāsmi daityānām, kālaḥ kalayatām aham
    mṛgāṇām ca mṛgendro 'ham, vainateyaś ca pakṣiṇām

31 pavanaḥ pavatām asmi, rāmaḥ śastra-bhṛtām aham
  jhaṣāṇāṁ makaraś cāsmi, srotasām asmi jāhnavī

32 sargāṇām ādir antaś ca, madhyaṁ caivāham arjuna
  adhyātma-vidyā vidyānāṁ, vādaḥ pravadatām aham

33 akṣarāṇām a-kāro 'smi, dvandvaḥ sāmāsikasya ca
  aham evākṣayaḥ kālo, dhātāhaṁ viśvato-mukhaḥ

34 mṛtyuḥ sarva-haraś cāham, udbhavaś ca bhaviṣyatām
  kīrtiḥ śrīr vāk ca nārīṇāṁ, smṛtir medhā dhṛtiḥ kṣamā

35 bṛhat-sāma tathā sāmnāṁ, gāyatrī chandasām aham
  māsānāṁ mārga-śīrṣo 'ham, ṛtūnāṁ kusumākaraḥ

36 dyūtaṁ chlayatām asmi, tejas tejasvinām aham
  jayo 'smi vyavasāyo 'smi, sattvaṁ sattvavatām aham

37 vṛṣṇīnāṁ vāsudevo 'smi, pāṇḍavānāṁ dhanañjayaḥ
  munīnām apy ahaṁ vyāsaḥ, kavīnām uśanā kaviḥ

38 daṇḍo damayatām asmi, nītir asmi jigīṣatām
  maunaṁ caivāsmi guhyānāṁ, jñānaṁ jñānavatām aham

39 yac cāpi sarva-bhūtānāṁ, bījaṁ tad aham arjuna
  na tad asti vinā yat syān, mayā bhūtaṁ carācaram

40 nānto 'sti mama divyānāṁ, vibhūtīnāṁ parantapa
  eṣa tūddeśataḥ prokto, vibhūter vistaro mayā

41 yad yad vibhūtimat sattvaṁ, śrīmad ūrjitam eva vā
  tat tad evāvagaccha tvaṁ, mama tejo-'ṁśa-sambhavam

42 atha vā bahunaitena, kiṁ jñātena tavārjuna
  viṣṭabhyāham idaṁ kṛtsnam, ekāṁśena sthito jagat

11

Arjuna uvāca

1 mad-anugrahāya paramaṁ, guhyam adhyātma-saṁjñitam
  yat tvayoktaṁ vacas tena, moho 'yaṁ vigato mama

2 bhavāpyayau hi bhūtānāṁ, śrutau vistaraśo mayā
  tvattaḥ kamala-patrākṣa, māhātmyam api cāvyayam

3 evam etad yathāttha tvam, ātmānaṁ parameśvara
  draṣṭum icchāmi te rūpam, aiśvaraṁ puruṣottama

4 manyase yadi tac chakyaṁ, mayā draṣṭum iti prabho
  yogeśvara tato me tvaṁ, darśayātmānam avyayam

Śrī-Bhagavān uvāca

5 paśya me pārtha rūpāṇi, śataśo 'tha sahasraśaḥ
  nānā-vidhāni divyāni, nānā-varṇākṛtīni ca

6 paśyādityān vasūn rudrān, aśvinau marutas tathā
   bahūny adṛṣṭa-pūrvāṇi, paśyāścaryāṇi bhārata
7 ihaika-sthaṁ jagat kṛtsnaṁ, paśyādya sa-carācaram
   mama dehe guḍākeśa, yac cānyad draṣṭum icchasi
8 na tu māṁ śakyase draṣṭum, anenaiva sva-cakṣuṣā
   divyaṁ dadāmi te cakṣuḥ, paśya me yogam aiśvaram

Sañjaya uvāca

9 evam uktvā tato rājan, mahā-yogeśvaro hariḥ
   darśayām āsa pārthāya, paramaṁ rūpam aiśvaram
10 aneka-vaktra-nayanam, anekādbhuta-darśanam
   aneka-divyābharaṇaṁ, divyānekodyatāyudham
11 divya-mālyāmbara-dharaṁ, divya-gandhānulepanam
   sarvāścarya-mayaṁ devam, anantaṁ viśvato-mukham
12 divi sūrya-sahasrasya, bhaved yugapad utthitā
   yadi bhāḥ sadṛśī sā syād, bhāsas tasya mahātmanaḥ
13 tatraika-sthaṁ jagat kṛtsnaṁ, pravibhaktam anekadhā
   apaśyad deva-devasya, śarīre pāṇḍavas tadā
14 tataḥ sa vismayāviṣṭo, hṛṣṭa-romā dhanañjayaḥ
   praṇamya śirasā devaṁ, kṛtāñjalir abhāṣata

Arjuna uvāca

15 paśyāmi devāṁs tava deva dehe
      sarvāṁs tathā bhūta-viśeṣa-saṅghān
   brahmāṇam īśaṁ kamalāsana-stham
      ṛṣīṁś ca sarvān uragāṁś ca divyān
16 aneka-bāhūdara-vaktra-netraṁ
      paśyāmi tvā sarvato 'nanta-rūpam
   nāntaṁ na madhyaṁ na punas tavādiṁ
      paśyāmi viśveśvara viśva-rūpa
17 kirīṭinaṁ gadinaṁ cakriṇaṁ ca
      tejo-rāśiṁ sarvato dīptimantam
   paśyāmi tvāṁ durnirīkṣyaṁ samantād
      dīptānalārka-dyutim aprameyam
18 tvam akṣaraṁ paramaṁ veditavyaṁ
      tvam asya viśvasya paraṁ nidhānam
   tvam avyayaḥ śāśvata-dharma-goptā
      sanātanas tvaṁ puruṣo mato me
19 anādi-madyāntam ananta-vīryam
      ananta-bāhuṁ śaśi-sūrya-netram
   paśyāmi tvāṁ dīpta-hutāśa-vaktraṁ
      sva-tejasā viśvam idaṁ tapantam

20 dyāv ā-pṛthivyor idam antaraṁ hi
    vyāptaṁ tvayaikena diśaś ca sarvāḥ
    dṛṣṭvābhutaṁ rūpam idaṁ tavogram
    loka-trayaṁ pravyathitaṁ mahātman

21 amī hi tvā sura-saṅghā viśanti
    kecid bhītāḥ prāñjalayo gṛṇanti
    svastīty uktvā maharṣi-siddha-saṅghāḥ
    stuvanti tvāṁ stutibhiḥ puṣkalābhiḥ

22 rudrādityā vasavo ye ca sādhyā
    viśve 'svinau marutaś coṣmapāś ca
    gandharva-yakṣāsura-siddha-saṅghā
    vīkṣante tvaṁ vismitāś caiva sarve

23 rūpaṁ mahat te bahu-vaktra-netraṁ
    mahā-bāho bahu-bāhūru-pādam
    bahūdaraṁ bahu-daṁṣṭrā-karālaṁ
    dṛṣṭvā lokāḥ pravyathitās tathāham

24 nabhaḥ-spṛśaṁ dīptam aneka-varṇaṁ
    vyāttānanaṁ dīpta-viśāla-netram
    dṛṣṭvā hi tvāṁ pravyathitāntar-ātmā
    dhṛtiṁ na vindāmi śamaṁ ca viṣṇo

25 daṁṣṭrā-karālāni ca te mukhāni
    dṛṣṭvaiva kālānala-sannibhāni
    diśo na jāne na labhe ca śarma
    prasīda deveśa jagan-nivāsa

26 amī ca tvāṁ dhṛtarāṣṭrasya putrāḥ
    sarve sahaivāvani-pāla-saṅghaiḥ
    bhīṣmo droṇaḥ sūta-putras tathāsau
    sahāsmadīyair api yodha-mukhyaiḥ

27 vaktrāṇi te tvaramāṇā viśanti
    daṁṣṭrā-karālāni bhayānakāni
    kecid vilagnā daśanāntareṣu
    sandṛśyante cūrṇitair uttamāṅgaiḥ

28 yathā nadīnāṁ bahavo 'mbu-vegāḥ
    samudram evābhimukhā dravanti
    tathā tavāmī nara-loka-vīrā
    viśanti vaktrāṇy abhivijvalanti

29 yathā pradīptaṁ jvalanaṁ pataṅgā
    viśanti nāśāya samṛddha-vegāḥ
    tathaiva nāśāya viśanti lokās
    tavāpi vaktrāṇi samṛddha-vegāḥ

30 lelihyase grasamānaḥ samantāl
    lokān samagrān vadanair jvaladbhiḥ
    tejobhir āpūrya jagat samagraṁ
    bhāsas tavogrāḥ pratapanti viṣṇo

31   ākhyāhi me ko bhavān ugra-rūpo
        namo 'stu te deva-vara prasīda
      vijñātum icchāmi bhavantam ādyaṁ
        na hi prajānāmi tava pravṛttim

Śrī-Bhagavān uvāca

32   kālo 'smi loka-kṣaya-kṛt pravṛddho
        lokān samāhartum iha pravṛttaḥ
      ṛte 'pi tvāṁ na bhaviṣyanti sarve
        ye 'vasthitāḥ pratyanīkeṣu yodhāḥ
33   tasmāt tvam uttiṣṭha yaśo labhasva
        jitvā śatrūn bhuṅkṣva rājyaṁ samṛddham
      mayaivaite nihatāḥ pūrvam eva
        nimitta-mātraṁ bhava savya-sācin
34   droṇaṁ ca bhīṣmaṁ ca jayadrathaṁ ca
        karṇaṁ tathānyān api yodha-vīrān
      mayā hatāṁs tvaṁ jahi mā vyathiṣṭhā
        yudhyasva jetāsi raṇe sapatnān

Sañjaya uvāca

35   etac chrutvā vacanaṁ keśavasya
        kṛtāñjalir vepamānaḥ kirīṭī
      namaskṛtvā bhūya evāha kṛṣṇaṁ
        sa-gadgadaṁ bhīta-bhītaḥ praṇamya

Arjuna uvāca

36   sthāne hṛṣīkeśa tava prakīrtyā
        jagat prahṛṣyaty anurajyate ca
      rakṣāṁsi bhītāni diśo dravanti
        sarve namasyanti ca siddha-saṅghāḥ
37   kasmāc ca te na nameran mahātman
        garīyase brahmaṇo 'py ādi-kartre
      ananta deveśa jagan-nivāsa
        tvam akṣaraṁ sad-asat tat paraṁ yat
38   tvam ādi-devaḥ puruṣaḥ purāṇas
        tvam asya viśvasya paraṁ nidhānam
      vettāsi vedyaṁ ca paraṁ ca dhāma
        tvayā tataṁ viśvam ananta-rūpa
39   vāyur yamo 'gnir varuṇaḥ śaśāṅkaḥ
        prajāpatis tvaṁ prapitāmahaś ca
      namo namas te 'stu sahasra-kṛtvaḥ
        punaś ca bhūyo 'pi namo namas te

40 namaḥ purastād atha pṛṣṭhatas te
      namo 'stu te sarvata eva sarva
   ananta-vīryāmita-vikramas tvaṁ
      sarvaṁ samāpnoṣi tato 'si sarvaḥ

41 sakheti matvā prasabhaṁ yad uktaṁ
      he kṛṣṇa he yādava he sakheti
   ajānatā mahimānaṁ tavedaṁ
      mayā pramādāt praṇayena vāpi

42 yac cāvahāsārtham asat-kṛto 'si
      vihāra-śayyāsana-bhojaneṣu
   eko 'tha vāpy acyuta tat-samakṣaṁ
      tat kṣāmaye tvām aham aprameyam

43 pitāsi lokasya carācarasya
      tvam asya pūjyaś ca gurur garīyān
   na tvat-samo 'sty abhyadhikaḥ kuto 'nyo
      loka-traye 'py apratima-prabhāva

44 tasmāt praṇamya praṇidhāya kāyaṁ
      prasādaye tvām aham īśam īḍyam
   piteva putrasya sakheva sakhyuḥ
      priyaḥ priyāyārhasi deva soḍhum

45 adṛṣṭa-pūrvaṁ hṛṣito 'smi dṛṣṭvā
      bhayena ca pravyathitaṁ mano me
   tad eva me darśaya deva-rūpaṁ
      prasīda deveśa jagan-nivāsa

46 kirīṭinaṁ gadinaṁ cakra-hastam
      icchāmi tvāṁ draṣṭum ahaṁ tathaiva
   tenaiva rūpeṇa catur-bhujena
      sahasra-bāho bhava viśva-mūrte

Śrī-Bhagavān uvāca

47 mayā prasannena tavārjunedaṁ
      rūpaṁ paraṁ darśitam ātma-yogāt
   tejo-mayaṁ viśvam anantam ādyaṁ
      yan me tvad anyena na dṛṣṭa-pūrvam

48 na veda-yajñādhyayanair na dānair
      na ca kriyābhir na tapobhir ugraiḥ
   evaṁ-rūpaḥ śakya ahaṁ nṛ-loke
      draṣṭuṁ tvad anyena kuru-pravīra

49 mā te vyathā mā ca vimūḍha-bhāvo
      dṛṣṭvā rūpaṁ ghoram īdṛṅ mamedam
   vyapeta-bhīḥ prīta-manāḥ punas tvaṁ
      tad eva me rūpam idaṁ prapaśya

Sañjaya uvāca

50 ity arjunaṁ vāsudevas tathoktvā
     svakaṁ rūpaṁ darśayām āsa bhūyaḥ
     āśvāsayām āsa ca bhītam enaṁ
     bhūtvā punaḥ saumya-vapur mahātmā

Arjuna uvāca

51 dṛṣṭvedaṁ mānuṣaṁ rūpaṁ, tava saumyaṁ janārdana
     idānīm asmi saṁvṛttaḥ, sa-cetāḥ prakṛtiṁ gataḥ

Śrī-Bhagavān uvāca

52 su-durdarśam idaṁ rūpaṁ, dṛṣṭavān asi yan mama
     devā apy asya rūpasya, nityaṁ darśana-kāṅkṣiṇaḥ
53 nāhaṁ vedair na tapasā, na dānena na cejyayā
     śakya evaṁ-vidho draṣṭuṁ, dṛṣṭavān asi māṁ yathā
54 bhaktyā tv ananyayā śakya, aham evaṁ-vidho 'rjuna
     jñātuṁ draṣṭuṁ ca tattvena, praveṣṭuṁ ca parantapa
55 mat-karma-kṛn mat-paramo, mad-bhaktaḥ saṅga-varjitaḥ
     nirvairaḥ sarva-bhūteṣu, yaḥ sa mām eti pāṇḍava

12

Arjuna uvāca

1 evaṁ satata-yuktā ye, bhaktās tvāṁ paryupāsate
    ye cāpy akṣaram avyaktaṁ, teṣāṁ ke yoga-vittamāḥ

Śrī-Bhagavān uvāca

2 mayy āveśya mano ye māṁ, nitya-yuktā upāsate
    śraddhayā parayopetās, te me yuktatamā matāḥ
3 ye tv akṣaram anirdeśyam, avyaktaṁ paryupāsate
    sarvatra-gam acintyaṁ ca, kūṭa-stham acalaṁ dhruvam
4 sanniyamyendriya-grāmaṁ, sarvatra sama-buddhayaḥ
    te prāpnuvanti mām eva, sarva-bhūta-hite ratāḥ
5 kleśo 'dhikataras teṣām, avyaktāsakta-cetasām
    avyaktā hi gatir duḥkhaṁ, dehavadbhir avāpyate
6 ye tu sarvāṇi karmāṇi, mayi saṁnyasya mat-parāḥ
    ananyenaiva yogena, māṁ dhyāyanta upāsate
7 teṣām ahaṁ samuddhartā, mṛtyu-saṁsāra-sāgarāt
    bhavāmi na cirāt pārtha, mayy āveśita-cetasām
8 mayy eva mana ādhatsva, mayi buddhiṁ niveśaya
    nivasiṣyasi mayy eva, ata ūrdhvaṁ na saṁśayaḥ

9   atha cittaṁ samādhātuṁ, na śaknoṣi mayi sthiram
    abhyāsa-yogena tato, mām icchāptuṁ dhanañjaya

10 abhyāse 'py asamartho 'si, mat-karma-paramo bhava
    mad-artham api karmāṇi, kurvan siddhim avāpsyasi

11 athaitad apy aśakto 'si, kartuṁ mad-yogam āśritaḥ
    sarva-karma-phala-tyāgaṁ, tataḥ kuru yatātmavān

12 śreyo hi jñānam abhyāsāj, jñānād dhyānaṁ viśiṣyate
    dhyānāt karma-phala-tyāgas, tyāgāc chāntir anantaram

13 adveṣṭā sarva-bhūtānāṁ, maitraḥ karuṇa eva ca
    nirmamo nirahaṅkāraḥ, sama-duḥkha-sukhaḥ kṣamī

14 santuṣṭaḥ satataṁ yogī, yatātmā dṛḍha-niścayaḥ
    mayy arpita-mano-budhir, yo mad-bhaktaḥ sa me priyaḥ

15 yasmān nodvijate loko, lokān nodvijate ca yaḥ
    harṣāmarṣa-bhayodvegair, mukto yaḥ sa ca me priyaḥ

16 anapekṣaḥ śucir dakṣa, udāsīno gata-vyathaḥ
    sarvārambha-parityāgī, yo mad-bhaktaḥ sa me priyaḥ

17 yo na hṛṣyati na dveṣṭi, na śocati na kāṅkṣati
    śubhāśubha-parityāgī, bhaktimān yaḥ sa me priyaḥ

18 samaḥ śatrau ca mitre ca, tathā mānāpamānayoḥ
    śitoṣṇa-sukha-duḥkheṣu, samaḥ saṅga-vivarjitaḥ

19 tulya-nindā-stutir maunī, santuṣṭo yena kenacit
    aniketaḥ sthira-matir, bhaktimān me priyo naraḥ

20 ye tu dharmyāmṛtam idaṁ, yathoktaṁ paryupāsate
    śraddadhānā mat-paramā, bhaktās te 'tīva me priyāḥ

13

Arjuna uvāca

    prakṛtiṁ puruṣaṁ caiva, kṣetraṁ kṣetra-jñam eva ca
    etad veditum icchāmi, jñānaṁ jñeyaṁ ca keśava

Śrī-Bhagavān uvāca

1   idaṁ śarīraṁ kaunteya, kṣetram ity abhidhīyate
    etad yo vetti taṁ prāhuḥ, kṣetra-jña iti tad-vidaḥ

2   kṣetra-jñaṁ cāpi mām viddhi, sarva-kṣetreṣu bhārata
    kṣetra-kṣetrajñayor jñānaṁ, yat taj jñānaṁ mataṁ mama

3   tat kṣetraṁ yac ca yādṛk ca, yad-vikāri yataś ca yat
    sa ca yo yat-prabhāvaś ca, tat samāsena me śṛṇu

4   ṛṣibhir bahudhā gītaṁ, chandobhir vividhaiḥ pṛthak
    brahma-sūtra-padaiś caiva, hetumadbhir viniścitaiḥ

5   mahā-bhūtāny ahaṅkāro, buddhir avyaktam eva ca
    indriyāṇi daśaikaṁ ca, pañca cendriya-gocarāḥ

6 icchā dveṣaḥ sukhaṁ duḥkhaṁ, saṅghātaś cetanā dhṛtiḥ
　　etat kṣetraṁ samāsena, sa-vikāram udāhṛtam
7 amānitvam adambhitvam, ahiṁsā kṣāntir ārjavam
　　ācāryopāsanaṁ śaucaṁ, sthairyam ātma-vinigrahaḥ
8 indriyārtheṣu vairāgyam, anahaṅkāra eva ca
　　janma-mṛtyu-jarā-vyādhi-, duḥkha-doṣānudarśanam
9 asaktir anabhiṣvaṅgaḥ, putra-dāra-gṛhādiṣu
　　nityaṁ ca sama-cittatvam, iṣṭāniṣṭopapattiṣu
10 mayi cānanya-yogena, bhaktir avyabhicāriṇī
　　vivikta-deśa-sevitvam, aratir jana-saṁsadi
11 adhyātma-jñāna-nityatvaṁ, tattva-jñānārtha-darśanam
　　etaj jñānam iti proktam, ajñānaṁ yad ato 'nyathā
12 jñeyaṁ yat tat pravakṣyāmi, yaj jñātvāmṛtam aśnute
　　anādi mat-paraṁ brahma, na sat tan nāsad ucyate
13 sarvataḥ pāṇi-pādaṁ tat, sarvato 'kṣi-śiro-mukham
　　sarvataḥ śrutimal loke, sarvam āvṛtya tiṣṭhati
14 sarvendriya-guṇābhāsaṁ, sarvendriya-vivarjitam
　　asaktaṁ sarva-bhṛc caiva, nirguṇaṁ guṇa-bhoktṛ ca
15 bahir antaś ca bhūtānām, acaraṁ caram eva ca
　　sūkṣmatvāt tad avijñeyaṁ, dūra-sthaṁ cāntike ca tat
16 avibhaktaṁ ca bhūteṣu, vibhaktam iva ca sthitam
　　bhūta-bhartṛ ca taj jñeyaṁ, grasiṣṇu prabhaviṣṇu ca
17 jyotiṣām api taj jyotis, tamasaḥ param ucyate
　　jñānaṁ jñeyaṁ jñāna-gamyaṁ, hṛdi sarvasya viṣṭhitam
18 iti kṣetraṁ tathā jñānaṁ, jñeyaṁ coktaṁ samāsataḥ
　　mad-bhakta etad vijñāya, mad-bhāvāyopapadyate
19 prakṛtiṁ puruṣaṁ caiva, viddhy anādī ubhāv api
　　vikārāṁś ca guṇāṁś caiva, viddhi prakṛti-sambhavān
20 kārya-kāraṇa-kartṛtve, hetuḥ prakṛtir ucyate
　　puruṣaḥ sukha-duḥkhānāṁ, bhoktṛtve hetur ucyate
21 puruṣaḥ prakṛti-stho hi, bhuṅkte prakṛti-jān guṇān
　　kāraṇaṁ guṇa-saṅgo 'sya, sad-asad-yoni-janmasu
22 upadraṣṭānumantā ca, bhartā bhoktā maheśvaraḥ
　　paramātmeti cāpy ukto, dehe 'smin puruṣaḥ paraḥ
23 ya evaṁ vetti puruṣaṁ, prakṛtiṁ ca guṇaiḥ saha
　　sarvathā vartamāno 'pi, na sa bhūyo 'bhijāyate
24 dhyānenātmani paśyanti, kecid ātmānam ātmanā
　　anye sāṅkhyena yogena, karma-yogena cāpare
25 anye tv evam ajānantaḥ, śrutvānyebhya upāsate
　　te 'pi cātitaranty eva, mṛtyuṁ śruti-parāyaṇāḥ
26 yāvat sañjāyate kiñcit, sattvaṁ sthāvara-jaṅgamam
　　kṣetra-kṣetrajña-saṁyogāt, tad viddhi bharatarṣabha

27 samaṁ sarveṣu bhūteṣu, tiṣṭhantaṁ parameśvaram
   vinaśyatsv avinaśyantaṁ, yaḥ paśyati sa paśyati
28 samaṁ paśyan hi sarvatra, samavasthitam īśvaram
   na hinasty ātmanātmānaṁ, tato yāti parāṁ gatim
29 prakṛtyaiva ca karmāṇi, kriyamāṇāni sarvaśaḥ
   yaḥ paśyati tathātmānam, akartāraṁ sa paśyati
30 yadā bhūta-pṛthag-bhāvam, eka-stham anupaśyati
   tata eva ca vistāraṁ, brahma sampadyate tadā
31 anāditvān nirguṇatvāt, paramātmāyam avyayaḥ
   śarīra-stho 'pi kaunteya, na karoti na lipyate
32 yathā sarva-gataṁ saukṣmyād, ākāśaṁ nopalipyate
   sarvatrāvasthito dehe, tathātmā nopalipyate
33 yathā prakāśayaty ekaḥ, kṛtsnaṁ lokam imaṁ raviḥ
   kṣetraṁ kṣetrī tathā kṛtsnaṁ, prakāśayati bhārata
34 kṣetra-kṣetrajñayor evam, antaraṁ jñāna-cakṣuṣā
   bhūta-prakṛti-mokṣaṁ ca, ye vidur yānti te param

14

Śrī-Bhagavān uvāca

1 paraṁ bhūyaḥ pravakṣyāmi, jñānānāṁ jñānam uttamam
  yaj jñātvā munayaḥ sarve, parāṁ siddhim ito gatāḥ
2 idaṁ jñānam upāśritya, mama sādharmyam āgatāḥ
  sarge 'pi nopajāyante, pralaye na vyathanti ca
3 mama yonir mahad brahma, tasmin garbhaṁ dadhāmy aham
  sambhavaḥ sarva-bhūtānāṁ, tato bhavati bhārata
4 sarva-yoniṣu kaunteya, mūrtayaḥ sambhavanti yāḥ
  tāsāṁ brahma mahad yonir, ahaṁ bīja-pradaḥ pitā
5 sattvaṁ rajas tama iti, guṇāḥ prakṛti-sambhavāḥ
  nibadhnanti mahā-bāho, dehe dehinam avyayam
6 tatra sattvaṁ nirmalatvāt, prakāśakam anāmayam
  sukha-saṅgena badhnāti, jñāna-saṅgena cānagha
7 rajo rāgātmakaṁ viddhi, tṛṣṇā-saṅga-samudbhavam
  tan nibadhnāti kaunteya, karma-saṅgena dehinam
8 tamas tv ajñāna-jaṁ viddhi, mohanaṁ sarva-dehinām
  pramādālasya-nidrābhis, tan nibadhnāti bhārata
9 sattvaṁ sukhe sañjayati, rajaḥ karmaṇi bhārata
  jñānam āvṛtya tu tamaḥ, pramāde sañjayaty uta
10 rajas tamaś cābhibhūya, sattvaṁ bhavati bhārata
   rajaḥ sattvaṁ tamaś caiva, tamaḥ sattvaṁ rajas tathā
11 sarva-dvāreṣu dehe 'smin, prakāśa upajāyate
   jñānaṁ yadā tadā vidyād, vivṛddhaṁ sattvam ity uta

12 lobhaḥ pravṛttir ārambhaḥ, karmaṇām aśamaḥ spṛhā
     rajasy etāni jāyante, vivṛddhe bharatarṣabha
13 aprakāśo 'pravṛttiś ca, pramādo moha eva ca
     tamasy etāni jāyante, vivṛddhe kuru-nandana
14 yadā sattve pravṛddhe tu, pralayaṁ yāti deha-bhṛt
     tadottama-vidāṁ lokān, amalān pratipadyate
15 rajasi pralayaṁ gatvā, karma-saṅgiṣu jāyate
     tathā pralīnas tamasi, mūḍha-yoniṣu jāyate
16 karmaṇaḥ sukṛtasyāhuḥ, sāttvikaṁ nirmalaṁ phalam
     rajasas tu phalaṁ duḥkham, ajñānaṁ tamasaḥ phalam
17 sattvāt sañjāyate jñānaṁ, rajaso lobha eva ca
     pramāda-mohau tamaso, bhavato 'jñānam eva ca
18 ūrdhvaṁ gacchanti sattva-sthā, madhye tiṣṭhanti rājasāḥ
     jaghanya-guṇa-vṛtta-sthā, adho gacchanti tāmasāḥ
19 nānyaṁ guṇebhyaḥ kartāraṁ, yadā draṣṭānupaśyati
     guṇebhyaś ca paraṁ vetti, mad-bhāvaṁ so 'dhigacchati
20 guṇān etān atītya trīn, dehī deha-samudbhavān
     janma-mṛtyu-jarā-duḥkhair, vimukto 'mṛtam aśnute

Arjuna uvāca

21 kair liṅgais trīn guṇān etān, atīto bhavati prabho
     kim ācāraḥ kathaṁ caitāṁs, trīn guṇān ativartate

Śrī-Bhagavān uvāca

22 prakāśaṁ ca pravṛttiṁ ca, moham eva ca pāṇḍava
     na dveṣṭi sampravṛttāni, na nivṛttāni kāṅkṣati
23 udāsīna-vad āsīno, guṇair yo na vicālyate
     guṇā vartanta ity eva, yo 'vatiṣṭhati neṅgate
24 sama-duḥkha-sukhaḥ sva-sthaḥ, sama-loṣṭāśma-kāñcanaḥ
     tulya-priyāpriyo dhīras, tulya-nindātma-saṁstutiḥ
25 mānāvamānayos tulyas, tulyo mitrāri-pakṣayoḥ
     sarvārambha-parityāgī, guṇātītaḥ sa ucyate
26 māṁ ca yo 'vyabhicāreṇa, bhakti-yogena sevate
     sa guṇān samatītyaitān, brahma-bhūyāya kalpate
27 brahmaṇo hi pratiṣṭhāham, amṛtasyāvyayasya ca
     śāśvatasya ca dharmasya, sukhasyaikāntikasya ca

15

Śrī-Bhagavān uvāca

1 ūrdhva-mūlam adhaḥ-śākham, aśvatthaṁ prāhur avyayam
    chandāṁsi yasya parṇāni, yas taṁ veda sa veda-vit

2 adhaś cordhvaṁ prasṛtās tasya śākhā
    guṇa-pravṛddhā viṣaya-pravālāḥ
 adhaś ca mūlāny anusantatāni
    karmānubandhīni manuṣya-loke
3 na rūpam asyeha tathopalabhyate
    nānto na cādir na ca sampratiṣṭhā
 aśvattham enaṁ su-virūḍha-mūlam
    asaṅga-śastreṇa dṛḍhena chittvā
4 tataḥ padaṁ tat parimārgitavyaṁ
    yasmin gatā na nivartanti bhūyaḥ
 tam eva cādyaṁ puruṣaṁ prapadye
    yataḥ pravṛttiḥ prasṛtā purāṇī
5 nirmāna-mohā jita-saṅga-doṣā
    adhyātma-nityā vinivṛtta-kāmāḥ
 dvandvair vimuktāḥ sukha-duḥkha-saṁjñair
    gacchanty amūḍhāḥ padam avyayaṁ tat
6 na tad bhāsayate sūryo, na śaśāṅko na pāvakaḥ
 yad gatvā na nivartante, tad dhāma paramaṁ mama
7 mamaivāṁśo jīva-loke, jīva-bhūtaḥ sanātanaḥ
 manaḥ-ṣaṣṭhānīndriyāṇi, prakṛti-sthāni karṣati
8 śarīraṁ yad avāpnoti, yac cāpy utkrāmatīśvaraḥ
 gṛhītvaitāni saṁyāti, vāyur gandhān ivāśayāt
9 śrotraṁ cakṣuḥ sparśanaṁ ca, rasanaṁ ghrāṇameva ca
 adhiṣṭhāya manaś cāyaṁ, viṣayān upasevate
10 utkrāmantaṁ sthitaṁ vāpi, bhuñjānaṁ vā guṇānvitam
 vimūḍhā nānupaśyanti, paśyanti jñāna-cakṣuṣaḥ
11 yatanto yoginaś cainaṁ, paśyanty ātmany avasthitam
 yatanto 'py akṛtātmāno, nainaṁ paśyanty acetasaḥ
12 yad āditya-gataṁ tejo, jagad bhāsayate 'khilam
 yac candramasi yac cāgnau, tat tejo viddhi māmakam
13 gām āviśya ca bhūtāni, dhārayāmy aham ojasā
 puṣṇāmi causadhīḥ sarvāḥ, somo bhūtvā rasātmakaḥ
14 ahaṁ vaiśvānaro bhūtvā, prāṇināṁ deham āśritaḥ
 prāṇāpāna-samāyuktaḥ, pacāmy annaṁ catur-vidham
15 sarvasya cāhaṁ hṛdi sanniviṣṭo
    mattaḥ smṛtir jñānam apohanaṁ ca
 vedaiś ca sarvair aham eva vedyo
    vedānta-kṛd veda-vid eva cāham
16 dvāv imau puruṣau loke, kṣaraś cākṣara eva ca
 kṣaraḥ sarvāṇi bhūtāni, kūṭa-stho 'kṣara ucyate
17 uttamaḥ puruṣas tv anyaḥ, paramātmety udāhṛtaḥ
 yo loka-trayam āviśya, bibharty avyaya īśvaraḥ

18 yasmāt kṣaram atīto 'ham, akṣarād api cottamaḥ
   ato 'smi loke vede ca, prathitaḥ puruṣottamaḥ
19 yo mām evam asammūḍho, jānāti puruṣottamam
   sa sarva-vid bhajati mām, sarva-bhāvena bhārata
20 iti guhyatamaṁ śāstram, idam uktaṁ mayānagha
   etad buddhvā buddhimān syāt, kṛta-kṛtyaś ca bhārata

16

Śrī-Bhagavān uvāca

1 abhayaṁ sattva-saṁśuddhir, jñāna-yoga-vyavasthitiḥ
  dānaṁ damaś ca yajñaś ca, svādhyāyas tapa ārjavam
2 ahiṁsā satyam akrodhas, tyāgaḥ śāntir apaiśunam
  dayā bhūteṣv aloluptvaṁ, mārdavaṁ hrīr acāpalam
3 tejaḥ kṣamā dhṛtiḥ śaucam, adroho nāti-mānitā
  bhavanti sampadaṁ daivīm, abhijātasya bhārata
4 dambho darpo 'timānaś ca, krodhaḥ pāruṣyam eva ca
  ajñānaṁ cābhijātasya pārtha sampadam āsurīm
5 daivī sampad vimokṣāya, nibandhāyāsurī matā
  mā śucaḥ sampadaṁ daivīm, abhijāto 'si pāṇḍava
6 dvau bhūta-sargau loke 'smin, daiva āsura eva ca
  daivo vistaraśaḥ prokta, āsuraṁ pārtha me śṛṇu
7 pravṛttiṁ ca nivṛttiṁ ca, janā na vidur āsurāḥ
  na śaucaṁ nāpi cācāro, na satyaṁ teṣu vidyate
8 asatyam apratiṣṭhaṁ te, jagad āhur anīśvaram
  aparaspara-sambhūtaṁ, kim anyat kāma-haitukam
9 etāṁ dṛṣṭim avaṣṭabhya, naṣṭātmāno 'lpa-buddhayaḥ
  prabhavanty ugra-karmāṇaḥ, kṣayāya jagato 'hitāḥ
10 kāmam āśritya duṣpūraṁ, dambha māna-madānvitāḥ
   mohād gṛhītvāsad-grāhān, pravartante 'śuci-vratāḥ
11 cintām aparimeyāṁ ca, pralayāntām upāśritāḥ
   kāmopabhoga-paramā, etāvad iti niścitāḥ
12 āśā-pāśa-śatair baddhāḥ, kāma-krodha-parāyaṇāḥ
   īhante kāma-bhogārtham, anyāyenārtha-sañcayān
13 idam adya mayā labdham, idaṁ prāpsye manoratham
   idam astīdam api me, bhaviṣyati punar dhanam
14 asau mayā hataḥ śatrur, haniṣye cāparān api
   īśvaro 'ham ahaṁ bhogī, siddho 'haṁ balavān sukhī
15 āḍhyo 'bhijanavān asmi, ko 'nyo 'sti sadṛśo mayā
   yakṣye dāsyāmi modiṣya, ity ajñāna-vimohitāḥ
16 aneka-citta-vibhrāntā, moha-jāla-samāvṛtāḥ
   prasaktāḥ kāma-bhogeṣu, patanti narake 'śucau

17 ātma-sambhāvitāḥ stadbhā, dhana-māna-madānvitāḥ
    yajante nāma-yajñais te, dambhenāvidhi-pūrvakam

18 ahaṅkāraṁ balaṁ darpaṁ, kāmaṁ krodhaṁ ca saṁśritāḥ
    mām ātma-para-deheṣu, pradviṣanto 'bhyasūyakāḥ

19 tān ahaṁ dviṣataḥ krūrān, saṁsāreṣu narādhamān
    kṣipāmy ajasram aśubhān, āsurīṣv eva yoniṣu

20 āsurīṁ yonim āpannā, mūḍhā janmani janmani
    mām aprāpyaiva kaunteya, tato yānty adhamāṁ gatim

21 tri-vidhaṁ narakasyedaṁ, dvāraṁ nāśanam ātmanaḥ
    kāmaḥ krodhas tathā lobhas, tasmād etat trayaṁ tyajet

22 etair vimuktaḥ kaunteya, tamo-dvārais tribhir naraḥ
    ācaraty ātmanaḥ śreyas, tato yāti parāṁ gatim

23 yaḥ śāstra-vidhim utsṛjya, vartate kāma-kārataḥ
    na sa siddhim avāpnoti, na sukhaṁ na parāṁ gatim

24 tasmāc chāstraṁ pramāṇaṁ te, kāryākārya-vyavasthitau
    jñātvā śāstra-vidhānoktaṁ, karma kartum ihārhasi

17

Arjuna uvāca

  1 ye śāstra-vidhim utsṛjya, yajante śraddhayānvitāḥ
     teṣāṁ niṣṭhā tu kā kṛṣṇa, sattvam āho rajas tamaḥ

Śrī-Bhagavān uvāca

  2 tri-vidhā bhavati śraddhā, dehināṁ sā svabhāva-jā
     sāttvikī rājasī caiva, tāmasī ceti tāṁ śṛṇu

  3 sattvānurūpā sarvasya, śraddhā bhavati bhārata
     śraddhā-mayo 'yaṁ puruṣo, yo yac-chraddhaḥ sa eva saḥ

  4 yajante sāttvikā devān, yakṣa-rakṣāṁsi rājasāḥ
     pretān bhūta-gaṇāṁś cānye, yajante tāmasā janāḥ

  5 aśāstra-vihitaṁ ghoraṁ, tapyante ye tapo janāḥ
     dambhāhaṅkāra-saṁyuktāḥ, kāma-rāga-balānvitāḥ

  6 karśayantaḥ śarīra-sthaṁ, bhūta-grāmam acetasaḥ
     māṁ caivāntaḥ śarīra-sthaṁ, tān viddhy āsura-niścayān

  7 āhāras tv api sarvasya, tri-vidho bhavati priyaḥ
     yajñas tapas tathā dānaṁ, teṣāṁ bhedam imaṁ śṛṇu

  8 āyuḥ-sattva-balārogya-, sukha-prīti-vivardhanāḥ
     rasyāḥ snigdhāḥ sthirā hṛdyā, āhārāḥ sāttvika-priyāḥ

  9 kaṭv-amla-lavaṇāty-uṣṇa-, tīkṣṇa-rūkṣa-vidāhinaḥ
     āhārā rājasasyeṣtā, duḥkha-śokāmaya-pradāḥ

 10 yāta-yāmaṁ gata-rasaṁ, pūti paryuṣitaṁ ca yat
     ucchiṣṭam api cāmedhyaṁ, bhojanaṁ tāmasa-priyam

11 aphalākāṅkṣibhir yajño, vidhi-dṛṣṭo ya ijyate
   yaṣṭavyam eveti manaḥ, samādhāya sa sāttvikaḥ
12 abhisandhāya tu phalaṁ, dambhārtham api caiva yat
   ijyate bharata-śreṣṭha, taṁ yajñaṁ viddhi rājasam
13 vidhi-hīnam asṛṣṭānnaṁ, mantra-hīnam adakṣiṇam
   śraddhā-virahitaṁ yajñaṁ, tāmasaṁ paricakṣate
14 deva-dvija-guru-prājña-, pūjanaṁ śaucam ārjavam
   brahmacaryam ahiṁsā ca, śarīraṁ tapa ucyate
15 anudvega-karaṁ vākyaṁ, satyaṁ priya-hitaṁ ca yat
   svādhyāyābhyasanaṁ caiva, vāṅ-mayaṁ tapa ucyate
16 manaḥ-prasādaḥ saumyatvaṁ, maunam ātma-vinigrahaḥ
   bhāva-saṁśuddhir ity etat, tapo mānasam ucyate
17 śraddhayā parayā taptaṁ, tapas tat tri-vidhaṁ naraiḥ
   aphalākāṅkṣibhir yuktaiḥ, sāttvikaṁ paricakṣate
18 satkāra-māna-pūjārthaṁ, tapo dambhena caiva yat
   kriyate tad iha proktaṁ, rājasaṁ calam adhruvam
19 mūḍhā-grāheṇātmano yat, pīḍayā kriyate tapaḥ
   parasyotsādanārthaṁ vā, tat tāmasam udāhṛtam
20 dātavyam iti yad dānaṁ, dīyate 'nupakāriṇe
   deśe kāle ca pātre ca, tad dānaṁ sāttvikaṁ smṛtam
21 yat tu pratyupakārārthaṁ, phalam uddiśya vā punaḥ
   dīyate ca parikliṣṭaṁ, tad dānaṁ rājasaṁ smṛtam
22 adeśa-kāle yad dānam, apātrebhyaś ca dīyate
   asat-kṛtam avajñātaṁ, tat tāmasam udāhṛtam
23 oṁ tat sad iti nirdeśo, brahmaṇas tri-vidhaḥ smṛtaḥ
   brāhmaṇās tena vedāś ca, yajñāś ca vihitāḥ purā
24 tasmād oṁ ity udāhṛtya, yajña-dāna-tapaḥ-kriyāḥ
   pravartante vidhānoktāḥ, satataṁ brahma-vādinām
25 tad ity anabhisandhāya, phalaṁ yajña-tapaḥ-kriyāḥ
   dāna-kriyāś ca vividhāḥ, kriyante mokṣa-kāṅkṣibhiḥ
26 sad-bhāve sādhu-bhāve ca, sad ity etat prayujyate
   praśaste karmaṇi tathā, sac-chabdaḥ pārtha yujyate
27 yajñe tapasi dāne ca, sthitiḥ sad iti cocyate
   karma caiva tad-arthīyaṁ, sad ity evābhidhīyate
28 aśraddhayā hutaṁ dattaṁ, tapas taptaṁ kṛtaṁ ca yat
   asad ity ucyate pārtha, na ca tat pretya no iha

18

Arjuna uvāca

1 saṁnyāsasya mahā-bāho, tattvam icchāmi veditum
  tyāgasya ca hṛṣīkeśa, pṛthak keśi-niṣūdana

Śrī-Bhagavān uvāca

2 kāmyānāṁ karmaṇāṁ nyāsaṁ, saṁnyāsaṁ kavayo viduḥ
   sarva-karma-phala-tyāgaṁ, prāhus tyāgaṁ vicakṣaṇāḥ

3 tyājyaṁ doṣa-vad ity eke, karma prāhur manīṣiṇaḥ
   yajña-dāna-tapaḥ-karma, na tyājyam iti cāpare

4 niścayaṁ śṛṇu me tatra, tyāge bharata-sattama
   tyāgo hi puruṣa-vyāghra, tri-vidhaḥ samprakīrtitaḥ

5 yajña-dāna-tapaḥ-karma, na tyājyaṁ kāryam eva tat
   yajño dānaṁ tapaś caiva, pāvanāni manīṣiṇām

6 etāny api tu karmāṇi, saṅgaṁ tyaktvā phalāni ca
   kartavyānīti me pārtha, niścitaṁ matam uttamam

7 niyatasya tu saṁnyāsaḥ, karmaṇo nopapadyate
   mohāt tasya parityāgas, tāmasaḥ parikīrtitaḥ

8 duḥkham ity eva yat karma, kāya-kleśa-bhayāt tyajet
   sa kṛtvā rājasaṁ tyāgaṁ, naiva tyāga-phalaṁ labhet

9 kāryam ity eva yat karma, niyataṁ kriyate 'rjuna
   saṅgaṁ tyaktvā phalaṁ caiva, sa tyāgaḥ sāttviko mataḥ

10 na dveṣṭy akuśalaṁ karma, kuśale nānuṣajjate
   tyāgī sattva-samāviṣṭo, medhāvī chinna-saṁśayaḥ

11 na hi deha-bhṛtā śakyaṁ, tyaktuṁ karmāṇy aśeṣataḥ
   yas tu karma-phala-tyāgī, sa tyāgīty abhidhīyate

12 amiṣṭam iṣṭaṁ miśraṁ ca, tri-vidhaṁ karmaṇaḥ phalam
   bhavaty atyāginām pretya, na tu saṁnyāsināṁ kvacit

13 pañcaitāni mahā-bāho, kāraṇāni nibodha me
   sāṅkhye kṛtānte proktāni, siddhaye sarva-karmaṇām

14 adhiṣṭhānaṁ tathā kartā, karaṇaṁ ca pṛthag-vidham
   vividhāś ca pṛthak ceṣṭā, daivaṁ caivātra pañcamam

15 śarīra-vāṅ-manobhir yat, karma prārabhate naraḥ
   nyāyyaṁ vā viparītaṁ vā, pañcaite tasya hetavaḥ

16 tatraivaṁ sati kartāram, ātmānaṁ kevalaṁ tu yaḥ
   paśyaty akṛta-buddhitvān, na sa paśyati durmatiḥ

17 yasya nāhaṅkṛto bhāvo, buddhir yasya na lipyate
   hatvāpi sa imāṅl lokān, na hanti na nibadhyate

18 jñānaṁ jñeyaṁ parijñātā, tri-vidhā karma-codanā
   karaṇaṁ karma karteti, tri-vidhaḥ karma-saṅgrahaḥ

19 jñānaṁ karma ca kartā ca, tridhaiva guṇa-bhedataḥ
   procyate guṇa-saṅkhyāne, yathāvac chṛṇu tāny api

20 sarva-bhūteṣu yenaikaṁ, bhāvam avyayam īkṣate
   avibhaktaṁ vibhakteṣu, taj jñānaṁ viddhi sāttvikam

21 pṛthaktvena tu taj jñānaṁ, nānā-bhāvān pṛthag-vidhān
   vetti sarveṣu bhūteṣu, taj jñānaṁ viddhi rājasam

22 yat tu kṛtsna-vad ekasmin, kārye saktam ahaitukam
   atattvārtha-vad alpaṁ ca, tat tāmasam udāhṛtam

23 niyataṁ saṅga-rahitam, arāga-dveṣataḥ kṛtam
    aphala-prepsunā karma, yat tat sāttvikam ucyate

24 yat tu kāmepsunā karma, sāhaṅkāreṇa vā punaḥ
    kriyate bahulāyāsaṁ, tad rājasam udāhṛtam

25 anubandhaṁ kṣayaṁ hiṁsām, anapekṣya ca pauruṣam
    mohād ārabhyate karma, yat tat tāmasam ucyate

26 mukta-saṅgo 'nahaṁ-vādī, dhṛty-utsāha-samanvitaḥ
    siddhy-asiddhyor nirvikāraḥ, kartā sāttvika ucyate

27 rāgī karma-phala-prepsur, lubdho hiṁsātmako 'śuciḥ
    harṣa-śokānvitaḥ kartā, rājasaḥ parikīrtitaḥ

28 ayuktaḥ prākṛtaḥ stabdhaḥ, śaṭho naikṛtiko 'lasaḥ
    viṣādī dīrgha-sūtrī ca, kartā tāmasa ucyate

29 buddher bhedaṁ dhṛteś caiva, guṇatas tri-vidhaṁ śṛṇu
    procyamānam aśeṣeṇa, pṛthaktvena dhanañjaya

30 pravṛttiṁ ca nivṛttiṁ ca, kāryākārye bhayābhaye
    bandhaṁ mokṣaṁ ca yā vetti, buddhiḥ sā pārtha sāttvikī

31 yayā dharmam adharmaṁ ca, kāryaṁ cākāryam eva ca
    ayathāvat prajānāti, buddhiḥ sā pārtha rājasī

32 adharmaṁ dharmam iti yā, manyate tamasāvṛtā
    sarvārthān viparītāṁś ca, buddhiḥ sā pārtha tāmasī

33 dhṛtyā yayā dhārayate, manaḥ-prāṇendriya-kriyāḥ
    yogenāvyabhicāriṇyā, dhṛtiḥ sā pārtha sāttvikī

34 yayā tu dharma-kāmārthān, dhṛtyā dhārayate 'rjuna
    prasaṅgena phalākāṅkṣī, dhṛtiḥ sā pārtha rājasī

35 yayā svapnaṁ bhayaṁ śokaṁ, viṣādaṁ madam eva ca
    na vimuñcati durmedhā, dhṛtiḥ sā pārtha tāmasī

36 sukhaṁ tv idānīṁ tri-vidhaṁ, śṛṇu me bharatarṣabha
    abhyāsād ramate yatra, duḥkhāntaṁ ca nigacchati

37 yat tad agre viṣam iva, pariṇāme 'mṛtopamam
    tat sukhaṁ sāttvikaṁ proktam, ātma-buddhi-prasāda-jam

38 viṣayendriya-saṁyogād, yat tad agre 'mṛtopamam
    pariṇāme viṣam iva, tat sukhaṁ rājasaṁ smṛtam

39 yad agre cānubandhe ca, sukhaṁ mohanam ātmanaḥ
    nidrālasya-pramādotthaṁ, tat tāmasam udāhṛtam

40 na tad asti pṛthivyāṁ vā, divi deveṣu vā punaḥ
    sattvaṁ prakṛti-jair muktam, yad ebhiḥ syāt tribhir guṇaiḥ

41 brāhmaṇa-kṣtratriya-viśāṁ, śūdrāṇāṁ ca parantapa
    karmāṇi pravibhaktāni, svabhāva-prabhavair guṇaiḥ

42 śamo damas tapaḥ śaucam, kṣāntir ārjavam eva ca
    jñānaṁ vijñānam āstikyaṁ, brahma-karma svabhāva-jam

43 śauryaṁ tejo dhṛtir dākṣyaṁ, yuddhe cāpy apalāyanam
    dānam īśvara-bhāvaś ca, kṣātra-karma svabhāva-jam

44 kṛṣi-go-rakṣya-vāṇijyaṁ, vaiśya-karma svabhāva-jam
    paricaryātmakaṁ karma, śūdrasyāpi svabhāva-jam
45 sve sve karmaṇy abhirataḥ, saṁsiddhiṁ labhate naraḥ
    sva-karma-nirataḥ siddhiṁ, yathā vindati tac chṛṇu
46 yataḥ pravṛttir bhūtānāṁ, yena sarvam idaṁ tatam
    sva-karmaṇā tam abhyarcya, siddhiṁ vindati mānavaḥ
47 śreyān sva-dharmo viguṇaḥ, para-dharmāt sv-anuṣṭhitāt
    svabhāva-niyataṁ karma, kurvan nāpnoti kilbiṣam
48 saha-jaṁ karma kaunteya, sa-doṣam api na tyajet
    sarvārambhā hi doṣeṇa, dhūmenāgnir ivāvṛtāḥ
49 asakta-buddhiḥ sarvatra, jitātmā vigata-spṛhaḥ
    naiṣkarmya-siddhiṁ paramāṁ, saṁnyāsenādhigacchati
50 siddhiṁ prāpto yathā brahma, tathāpnoti nibodha me
    samāsenaiva kaunteya, niṣṭhā jñānasya yā parā
51 buddhyā viśuddhayā yukto, dhṛtyātmānaṁ niyamya ca
    śabdādīn viṣayāṁs tyaktvā, rāga-dveṣau vyudasya ca
52 vivikta-sevī laghv-āśī, yata-vāk-kāya-mānasaḥ
    dhyāna-yoga-paro nityaṁ, vairāgyaṁ samupāśritaḥ
53 ahaṅkāraṁ balaṁ darpaṁ, kāmaṁ krodhaṁ parigraham
    vimucya nirmamaḥ śānto, brahma-bhūyāya kalpate
54 brahma-bhūtaḥ prasannātmā, na śocati na kāṅkṣati
    samaḥ sarveṣu bhūteṣu, mad-bhaktiṁ labhate parām
55 bhaktyā mām abhijānāti, yāvān yaś cāsmi tattvataḥ
    tato māṁ tattvato jñātvā, viśate tad-anantaram
56 sarva-karmāṇy api sadā, kurvāṇo mad-vyapāśrayaḥ
    mat-prasādād avāpnoti, śāśvataṁ padam avyayam
57 cetasā sarva-karmāṇi, mayi saṁnyasya mat-paraḥ
    buddhi-yogam upāśritya, mac-cittaḥ satataṁ bhava
58 mac-cittaḥ sarva-durgāṇi, mat-prasādāt tariṣyasi
    atha cet tvam ahaṅkārān, na śroṣyasi vinaṅkṣyasi
59 yad ahaṅkāram āśritya, na yotsya iti manyase
    mithyaiṣa vyavasāyas te, prakṛtis tvāṁ niyokṣyati
60 svabhāva-jena kaunteya, nibaddhaḥ svena karmaṇā
    kartuṁ necchasi yan mohāt, kariṣyasy avaśo 'pi tat
61 īśvaraḥ sarva-bhūtānāṁ, hṛd-deśe 'rjuna tiṣṭhati
    bhrāmayan sarva-bhūtāni, yantrārūḍhāni māyayā
62 tam eva śaraṇaṁ gaccha, sarva-bhāvena bhārata
    tat-prasādāt parāṁ śāntiṁ, sthānaṁ prāpsyasi śāśvatam
63 iti te jñānam ākhyātaṁ, guhyād guhyataraṁ mayā
    vimṛśyaitad aśeṣeṇa, yathecchasi tathā kuru
64 sarva-guhyatamaṁ bhūyaḥ, śṛṇu me paramaṁ vacaḥ
    iṣṭo 'si me dṛḍham iti, tato vakṣyāmi te hitam

65 man-manā bhava mad-bhakto, mad-yājī māṁ namaskuru
    mām evaiṣyasi satyaṁ te, pratijāne priyo 'si me
66 sarva-dharmān parityajya, mām ekaṁ śaraṇaṁ vraja
    ahaṁ tvā sarva-pāpebhyo, mokṣayiṣyāmi mā śucaḥ
67 idaṁ te nātapaskāya, nābhaktāya kadācana
    na cāśuśrūṣave vācyaṁ, na ca māṁ yo 'bhyasūyati
68 ya idaṁ paramaṁ guhyaṁ, mad-bhakteṣv abhidhāsyati
    bhaktiṁ mayi parāṁ kṛtvā, mām evaiṣyaty asaṁśayaḥ
69 na ca tasmān manuṣyeṣu, kaścin me priya-kṛttamaḥ
    bhavitā na ca me tasmād, anyaḥ priyataro bhuvi
70 adhyeṣyate ca ya imaṁ, dharmyaṁ saṁvādam āvayoḥ
    jñāna-yajñena tenāham, iṣṭaḥ syām iti me matiḥ
71 śraddhāvān anasūyaś ca, śṛṇuyād api yo naraḥ
    so 'pi muktaḥ śubhāṅl lokān, prāpnuyāt puṇya-karmaṇām
72 kaccid etac chrutaṁ pārtha, tvayaikāgreṇa cetasā
    kaccid ajñāna-sammohaḥ, praṇaṣṭas te dhanañjaya

Arjuna uvāca

73 naṣṭo mohaḥ smṛtir labdhā, tvat-prasādān mayācyuta
    sthito 'smi gata-sandehaḥ, kariṣye vacanaṁ tava

Sañjaya uvāca

74 ity ahaṁ vāsudevasya, pārthasya ca mahātmanaḥ
    saṁvādam imam aśrauṣam, adbhutaṁ roma-harṣaṇam
75 vyāsa-prasādāc chrutavān, etad guhyam ahaṁ param
    yogaṁ yogeśvarāt kṛṣṇāt, sākṣāt kathayataḥ svayam
76 rājan saṁsmṛtya saṁsmṛtya, saṁvādam imam adbhutam
    keśavārjunayoḥ puṇyaṁ, hṛṣyāmi ca muhur muhuḥ
77 tac ca saṁsmṛtya saṁsmṛtya, rūpam aty-adbhutaṁ hareḥ
    vismayo me mahān rājan, hṛṣyāmi ca punaḥ punaḥ
78 yatra yogeśvaraḥ kṛṣṇo, yatra pārtho dhanur-dharaḥ
    tatra śrīr vijayo bhūtir, dhruvā nītir matir mama

Appendices

Pronunciation of Sanskrit

Sanskrit words and names in the translated verses are given in a phonetic spelling utilizing a macron for alternate pronunciations of the vowels *a*, *i*, and *u* (see the pronunciation table below for the distinct sounds these six vowels make). The standardized full transliteration system for the Sanskrit alphabet is utilized for Sanskrit words in the notes and other parts of this book. Below are the vowels and consonants that require clarification. Transliterated consonants not listed below are pronounced as in English.

Vowels

a	like *a* in *about*
ā	like *a* in *yacht*
ai	like *ai* in *aisle* (*ai* represents a single transliterated vowel)
au	like *ow* in *cow* (*au* represents a single transliterated vowel)
e	like *e* in *prey*
i	like *i* in *bit*
ī	like *i* in *magazine*
ḷ	like *lree* (this vowel is rarely found; it is pronounced by combining the English *l* and *r* with an *ee* sound following)
o	like *o* in *home*
ṛ	like *ri* in *rich*
ṝ	like *rea* in *reach* (this vowel is rarely found)
u	like *u* in *put*
ū	like *u* in *rude*

Consonants

c	like *ch* in *chart* (never pronounced like the English *k* or *s*)
d	like *d* in *lude*
ḍ	like *d* in *red*

g   like *g* in *gate* (the soft *g* as pronounced in the word *germane* is found only in the Sanskrit letter *j*)

h   like *h* in *hot* (standing alone or followed by a vowel, without following a consonant)

_+h   any consonant followed by *h* is merely aspirated, like the subtle aspirated breath sound naturally occurring in the word *pot* (whereas aspiration is naturally absent from *dot*); thus *ph* sounds like the letter in the word *loophole* (never an *f* sound as in *pharmacy*); and *th* sounds like the *t* in the word *torn* (never the *th* sound as in *thorn*)

ḥ   is the silent consonant often found at the end of words; when the word is at the end of a sentence, the short form of the vowel of the last syllable is duplicated: for example, *rāmaḥ* sounds like *rāmaha*, and *śaktiḥ* sounds like *śaktihee* (underscored letters indicate duplicated syllable)

j   like *j* in *joy*

ṁ   like *n* in the French word *bon*

n   like *n* in *soon*

ṅ   like *n* in *song*

ñ   like *n* in *staunch*

ṇ   like *n* in *sand*

ph   like *p* in *pan* (with aspirated breath; it never makes the sound of *f* as in English, for example, the *ph* in the word *phase*)

ṛ   (is a vowel; see *ṛ* in the section above entitled "Vowels")

s   like *s* in *suit*

ś   like *sh* in *shoot* (this sibilant and the following are commonly pronounced by English speakers without any discernable distinction)

ṣ   like *sh* in *shout*

t   like *t* in *tool* (with tip of tongue near the place where the teeth meet the roof of the mouth)

ṭ   like *t* in *lute* (with tip of tongue toward the middle of the roof of the mouth)

In most compound consonants, each consonant retains its original sound in combination with the others. However, the combination *jñ* as found in the word *jñāna* is often pronounced like the *gy* in the English compound *dog-yard*.

On This Translation

Every verse of the Bhagavad Gītā is a meditation. Each verse is translated so as to bring out its meditative richness, as well as its place within the continuum of verses. I have attempted to make this English translation a "reincarnation" of the mood and feeling of the original Sanskrit verse. My goal is for the reader to receive a powerful experience of the original, to be able to hear something of the poetic form and qualities of the Sanskrit verse in the English rendering.

My approach to translation, aided by the inclusion of supplementary notes, is meant to give the reader an immediate grasp of the ideas of the Gītā. In the notes, readers will find the meanings of untranslated Sanskrit words retained in the translation and further explanation of names and ideas found in the verses. The reader will seldom need to leave the page to consult any other part of the book for better understanding, even during a first reading of the translation, although a comprehensive index has been provided. With the new reader of the text in mind, as well as spiritual aspirants and students or scholars of religion, I have presented the Bhagavad Gītā in a translation that is very faithful to the original text and reflects some of the literary qualities of the original, yet which can be easily read and grasped.

My approach to translating this famous work can be explained in contrast with the two other most common approaches. Other translations often either *free* the original text, in what I call "free prose" style, or *constrict* the original Sanskrit verse, in what I call "constricted quatrain" verse. The result is too often a translation that either ignores the poetic qualities of the original by treating verses as if they were loosely assembled ideas, or one that loses important senses of the original in fitting the translation into a verse form that is necessarily constricting. The free prose approach loosely embodies, at best, only a small sense of the rhythms and ordering of meanings and ideas as they present themselves, giving the text a loose and random form very different from that of the original. On the other hand, the quatrain verse approach attempts to force the English translation to be as concise as the original inflected words of the Sanskrit. This approach proves ineffective precisely because Sanskrit is a highly inflected language that requires more breathing room when reincarnated in English.

The poetics and ideas of each verse demand a unique treatment when translated into English—a very specific type of lineation that is sensitive to the subtleties of phrasing and cadence in the original Sanskrit verse. My approach could be described as "dedicated free verse translation," which preserves as much of the poetic sense as possible, while incorporating the full meaning of the original. This approach seeks to reap the advantages of the other two approaches yet avoid their shortcomings, thus attempting to reincarnate something of the power and spirit of the original verse. Here, "free verse" is not as "free" as we might indicate in the Western poetic sense of the term. Rather, verse lines in the English are strictly and carefully "dedicated," or tied to the verse's original rhythms of meaning and epiphanic qualities. The ordering of ideas and words in the original is retained as much as is possible without sacrificing their meaning in English. This approach gives the English reader a much fuller sense of the actual meaning of the verse. For example, the original Sanskrit in the English transliteration of the first verse of the text appears in the following form:

dhṛtarāṣṭra uvāca
dharma-kṣetre kuru-kṣetre, samavetā yuyutsavaḥ
māmakāḥ pāṇḍavāś caiva, kim akurvata sañjaya

This verse in dedicated free verse translation is presented below, juxtaposed to the corresponding transliterated words of the verse:

Dhritarāshtra said:	*dhṛtarāṣṭra uvāca*
On the field of dharma,	*dharma-kṣetre*
on the field of Kuru,	*kuru-kṣetre*
assembled together	*samavetā*
desiring to fight,	*yuyutsavaḥ*
Were my armies	*māmakāḥ*
and indeed those	*pāṇḍavāś*
of the sons of Pāndu—	*caiva*
how did they act, O Sanjaya?	*kim akurvata sañjaya*

Note that the translation is dedicated to the original ordering of the words in the transliteration. One can also observe that it takes more English words to translate the Sanskrit words. This first verse of the Gītā is the most common verse form found in the work, known as *anuṣṭubh*, with eight syllables per quarter line. The two leading lines mirror the structure of the original. Under the leading lines, indented lines generally present the meanings that appear in the first and second halves of the verses, whenever possible, in the same order in which they appear in the original. The leading lines and respective indented lines are carefully crafted to capture the feeling and phrasing of the Sanskrit verse and to "trans-create" an overall sense of the original poetic form.

Additionally, I have retained a few key Sanskrit words, some of which have made their way into the English lexicon (e.g., *yoga*, *dharma*), in what is meant to be a literal but poetically sensitive English translation, as these untranslated words carry a certain lexical power and richness all their own that is too difficult to convey in English. Their usage allows me to avoid either protracted or reductive glosses of such significant words within the verses themselves. Note that the word *yoga* is retained in the translation of the word's past participle form of *yukta*, which derives from the verbal root *yuj*, consistently translated as "absorbed in yoga." The word *yoga* is often translated as "discipline" and the verbal form as "disciplined" or "engaged," which loses the sense that yoga is actively experienced. I engage the word *absorbed* to intimate the ultimate act in yoga, which is *samādhi*, a state of total *absorption* in the object of meditation.

In this translation, personal names are either given in the original Sanskrit, with the meaning provided in a note, or are translated within the verse. The various names for Arjuna and Krishna reveal intriguing aspects of their identities, as well as contributing added meaning or even irony to the verses. For example, Arjuna addresses Krishna as Madhusūdana, "slayer of the Madhu demon," when expressing his dismay over the prospect of slaying others: "I do not wish to slay them—even those who are about to slay, O Madhusūdana" (BG I.35). To illuminate the fullness of the original, these special names are not simply replaced with antecedent primary names, as is often done; instead they are preserved.

Pronouns are not replaced by personal names as is often done. I believe the Gītā's poetry and expression are very deliberate, conscious, and erudite, and the ordering and presentation of the original words must be respected and preserved as much as possible. For easier reading, the Sanskrit names as well as all Sanskrit words are spelled phonetically, and only a few diacritics are utilized (see "Pronunciation of Sanskrit"). Furthermore, most of the pronouns in the text, though technically masculine in the original (or, in some verses, unspecified but implied third-person masculine), have been changed to gender-free language. The following verse demonstrates this:

> One who sees me everywhere
>   and sees all things in me,
> To such a person I am never lost
>   nor is such a person ever lost to me.
>   (BG 6.30)

Note how I have avoided the gender specificity of *he* by replacing it with words such as *one* and *such a person*. I translate verses in this gender-neutral way in order to preserve the universality that is subtly present in the masculine pronouns of the Sanskrit but lacking in the English.

As a translator, I have not hesitated to repeat words or meanings that are repeated in the original verse. In Sanskrit, repetition is a powerful means of inducing a meditative-like state in the reader. Repetition conveys the depth and pursuit of a vision, but most translations simply avoid this repetitive element. In this translation synonyms are not sought for words that are repeated in the Sanskrit, or even for words that are repeated by virtue of being derivative forms, either from a common verbal root or a noun stem. Instead, I use the same or a similar English word to render the Sanskrit word or its derivative that is repeated in the original:

> One should raise
>   the self by the self;
>   one should not
>   degrade the self.

Indeed, the self alone
is the self's friend;
the self alone
is the self's enemy.

(BG 6.5)

In this verse, the word *self* is used to translate the important Sanskrit word *ātman*, which appears in this verse seven times, more
than any other word in any verse. This word is translated throughout as "self." Because in Sanskrit the term can mean "soul," "body,"
"mind," or "heart," I have selected a word that embraces all these
meanings. It has been the tendency of translators to abandon these
repetitions so as to reflect specific shades of meaning, make philosophical sense, or avoid repetition. However, one hears and feels
the power of the repetition of such a monumental word in the
original language. I believe my choice of translation both satisfies
the requirements of meaning and retains the power of repetition.

Even in instances in which there is great temptation to translate
differently two words with the same noun stem or words related to
the same verbal root, Krishna's play on words would be lost if I
chose to ignore their close relationship. In the verse BG 6.6, the
word *shatru*, "enemy," occurs twice. First the abstract form of *sha-
tru-tva* is found, translated in the verse as "enmity," and then the
adverbial comparative form of *shatru-vat*, translated as "like an
enemy." Again, in BG 4.42, Krishna tells Arjuna to "ascend to
yoga," using the verb *ātiṣṭha*, and then immediately tells him to
"stand up," using the same verb but with a different prefix, *uttiṣṭha*.
Therefore my translation is: "rise in yoga!/Rise up, O Bhārata!"
By retaining the word *rise* in both imperative statements, while pro-
viding different prepositions to express the force of the different
prefixes, we can respect the original effect of the repetition.

Words with a negative prefix in the Sanskrit are not translated
into English as if they were a positive form; rather, such words
reflect the absence of the word's positive noun stem. For example,
the word *sukha* is "happiness," and its negative *a-sukha* is "unhappi-
ness" or "without happiness." This negative form of the word is
often translated, however, as "misery" or "suffering," meanings
more suitable for the positive word *duḥkha*. Another example would
be *a-siddha*, the negation of *siddha*, "success." I translate *asiddha* as

"without success," rather than the often used translation of "fail-ure." Again, when a reader hears the word *a-jñāna*, he or she does not hear "ignorance," as it is often translated, but rather "without knowledge." When translators employ antonyms to translate nega-tives, a very different sense is conveyed.

Wherever possible I have used English cognates for Sanskrit words. Thus the word *sama*, often translated as "equal" or "impar-tial," I translate as "same." The word's abstract forms, *samatva* and *samatā*, retain the cognate sense of *sama* in the translation of "same-ness" rather than the more removed senses of "equanimity" or "equality" so often used.

Because some Sanskrit words are laden with meaning, it often takes several English words to convey their sense. Frequently trans-lators provide a simple translation for such words, which reduces the power of the word's presence or presents a meaning that does not reflect the word's complete sense. For example, the two cosmo-logical words *prabhava* and *pralaya*, antonyms referring to the mani-festing and unmanifesting of the universe, are typically translated simply as "origin" and "dissolution," respectively. To convey the richness of the language in the original, and characterize cosmo-logically the referents for these words, I have translated *prabhava* as "the coming forth into being" and *pralaya* as "the going forth into cosmic absorption," accurately reflecting the purānic cosmology.[1]

With the English word *love*, one finds the opposite challenge. The word *love* incorporates all varieties and intensities of affection, tenderness, endearment, passion, and compassion, and only its context indicates the specific nuance of love, whereas in Sanskrit a great array of words and phrases are used to convey the many nuances of love. Therefore any attempt to translate such words and phrases into English is problematic, since there are no compa-rable English words that relate the specific experience of love described by such Sanskrit terms. In English, we use the word *love* constantly as the ultimate way to express our hearts, and there is no other word that can be substituted for it; therefore its usage is indispensible in the expression of the human heart.

---

1 See BG 7.6 and 9.18; in BG 10.8, the word *prabhava* is presented without *pralaya*, but is jux-taposed in the next line with the verb *pravartate*, meaning "is set forth into motion," further continuing the cosmological idea of *prabhava*.

This translation resorts to the ultimate English word *love* when translating any of the numerous Sanskrit words that express particular dimensions of love, so that the English translation is not deprived of the absolute sense intended by the more specific Sanskrit words. Therefore, the word *bhakta*, often translated as "devotee" or "the devoted one," is translated here as "one who has offered love" (see the first instance of this word in BG 4.3), utilizing *offered* along with *love*. The word's related verbal form *bhajāmi*, typically translated as "I worship" or "I honor," is translated as "I offer my love" (BG 4.11). The word *priya*, usually translated as "dear," is translated as "dearly loved," and in the Sanskrit carries a sense of the purity of love (BG 7.17). And the word *bhāva*, literally "feeling," is translated as "feelings of love" (BG 10.8). The word *iṣṭa*, often translated as "desired," here appears as "loved" (BG 18.64). The result of this approach is that one discovers that the Bhagavad Gītā says much more about love than what we perhaps have appreciated up until now.

Finally, particle words such as *and, even,* and *but* are never ignored, passed off as mere verse fillers or convenient words to complete the verse rhythm or meter. The assumption here is that each of these verses is a jewel that does not need to be altered in any way; rather, each jewel needs only to be polished until its natural glow is revealed.

Select Bibliography

Source for the Sanskrit Text

The Bhagavadgītā, critically edited by Shripad Krishna Belvalkar et al. Poona: Bhandarkar Oriental Research Institute, 1968.

Works on or Related to the Bhagavad Gītā

Minor, Robert N. *Bhagavad-Gītā: An Exegetical Commentary.* New Delhi: Heritage Publishers, 1991.

_____, ed. *Modern Indian Interpreters of the Bhagavadgita.* Albany: State University of New York, 1986.

Rosen, Steven J., ed. *Holy War: Violence and the Bhagavad Gita.* Hampton, VA: Deepak Heritage Books, 2002.

Schweig, Graham M. *Dance of Divine Love: India's Classic Sacred Love Story: The Rāsa Līlā of Krishna from the Bhāgavata Purāṇa.* Princeton, NJ: Princeton University Press, 2005.

_____. "The Essential Meaning of the Bhagavad-gītā According to Caitanyite Vaishnavism." *Journal of Vaishnava Studies* 9, no. 2 (Spring 2001): 227–39.

Sharma, Arvind. *The Hindu Gita: Ancient and Classical Interpretations of the 'Bhagavadgita.'* La Salle, IL: Open Court Publishing, 1986.

Sharpe, Eric J. *The Universal Gītā: Western Images of the Bhagavad Gītā.* La Salle, IL: Open Court Publishing, 1985.

Translations of the Bhagavad Gītā

Bhaktivedanta Swami Prabhupāda, A. C., trans. and comm. *Bhagavad-gita As It Is.* 2nd ed. Los Angeles: Bhaktivedanta Book Trust, 1989.

Edgerton, Franklin, trans. *The Bhagavad Gītā.* Cambridge, MA: Harvard University Press, 1944.

Patton, Laurie, trans. *The Bhagavad Gītā.* Harmondsworth, UK: Penguin Press, 2007.

Van Buitenen, J. A. B., trans. and ed. *The Bhagavadgītā in the Mahābhārata, A Bilingual Edition.* Chicago: University of Chicago Press, 1981.

Zaehner, R. C., ed. *The Bhagavad-Gītā.* Oxford: Oxford University Press, 1969.

Word References for the Bhagavad Gītā

Apte, Vaman Shivaram. *The Practical Sanskrit-English Dictionary* (Revised and Enlarged Reprint Edition). Kyoto: Rinsen Book Company, [1957] 1978.

Macdonell, Arthur Anthony. *A Practical Sanskrit Dictionary* (with transliteration, accentuation, and etymological analysis). New Delhi: Munshiram Manoharlal Publishers Pvt. Ltd., 1996.

Monier-Williams, Monier. *A Sanskrit-English Dictionary.* Oxford: Clarendon Press, [1899] 1974.

Schweig, Graham M. *Bhagavad Gītā Concordance: Comprehensive Word Reference with Sanskrit and English Indexes.* New York: Columbia University Press, forthcoming.

Index to Verses and Text

God. *See* Bhagavān; Brahman; Divinity;
　　Krishna; Person; Purushottama; Self;
　　Universal form
Goddesses, presiding, 10.34. *See also*
　　women
godless, the, 9.12
gods. *See* deities; divinities
gold, 6.8, 14.24
Govinda [Krishna], 12, 1.32, 2.9
grandfathers, 1.26, 1.34.
　　　See also fathers
grandsons, 1.26, 1.34
Great-Grandfather [Brahmā], 11.39
greed, 1.45, 14.12, 14.17, 16.21, 18.27
grief, 2.11, 2.25, 2.27, 2.30, 3.30
Gudākesha [Arjuna], 1.24, 2.9, 10.20, 11.7
guṇa(s). See 'qualities'
guru(s), 2.5, 11.43, 13.7, 17.14, 253, 254, 257

happiness [*sukha*], 1.36, 1.45, 247
　in absorption in yoga, 5.23
　action in, 2.38
　attachment to, 14.6, 14.9
　and Brahman, 6.28
　and ethical treatment of relatives, 1.37
　as extraordinary, 14.27
　and the field, 13.6
　freedom from, 2.56, 15.5
　and Krishna, 10.4, 14.27
　lack of attainment of, 16.23
　and peace, 2.66
　and *rajas*, 18.38
　and *sattva*, 18.37
　in self, 5.21
　and self-conquest, 6.7
　and senses, 2.14, 6.21
　and suffering, 2.15, 2.38, 6.32, 12.13,
　　12.18, 14.24
　and *tamas*, 18.39
　through discernment, 6.21
　as translation of *sukha*, 333
　types of, 18.36, 18.37, 18.38, 18.39
　and the ungodly, 16.14
　as within, 5.24
Hari [Krishna], 11.9, 18.77
harm, 18.25
hatred, 5.3, 6.9, 7.27, 16.19
head, 8.12, 13.13
hearing, 2.52, 4.26, 13.13, 15.9
heart(s)
　Brahman as seated within, 13.17
　hermitage within, 278
　innermost world of, 11, 275
　Krishna within, 10.11, 10.20, 15.15, 18.61,
　　261
　mind stopped within, 8.12
　offered to Krishna, 269

offered to the divinity, 275
offering of, 125n
vision of supreme Lord within,
　237n
vision of supreme Self within, 237n
and yoga, 249, 252, 273, 278
heat, 2.14, 6.7, 12.18
heavenly bodies, 10.21
hermitage, 278
heroes, 11.28, 18.43
Hero of the Kurus [Arjuna], 11.48
highest heaven, 86n
Himalayas, 10.25
Hinduism, 4
honesty, 13.7
honor, 6.7, 12.18, 14.25, 266
hope, 16.12
horses, 10.27
Hrishīkesha [Krishna], 1.15, 1.21, 1.24, 2.9,
　2.10, 11.36, 18.1
humility, 16.2, 258
hymns, 12, 10.35, 13.4, 15.1

'I am acting', notion of, 2.71, 7.4, 12.13,
　13.5, 13.8, 16.18, 17.5, 18.24, 18.53,
　18.58, 18.59
'I have acted', notion of, 18.17
identity, mistaken, 55n
Ikshvāku, 4.1
illumination, 14.22
illusion, 4.35, 7.14, 7.15, 10.4
immortality, 2.15, 4.31, 9.19, 10.18, 13.12,
　14.20, 14.27, 18.37, 18.38
immovable, the, 12.3
impartiality, 12.16
impatience, 12.15
imperishable, the, 3.15, 8.11, 12.1, 12.3,
　15.16, 15.18
impermanence, 2.14, 2.16
impurity, 3.16, 6.27, 6.28, 6.45, 16.10, 16.19,
　17.10. *See also* purity; taint
inaction/actionlessness, 2.47, 3.8, 4.16, 4.18,
　14.13, 16.7, 18.49, 275. *See also* action
inauspiciousness, 9.1
inconceivable, the, 12.3
indestructible, the, 8.21, 11.18, 11.37
Indra, 144n
injunction, 9.23, 16.23, 16.24, 17.1, 17.11,
　17.24. *See also* prescribed actions
injustice, 16.12
intelligence, 7.23, 10.34. *See also* discern-
　ment; knowledge; mind; thought

Jahnu, 10.31
Janaka, King, 3.20
Janārdana [Krishna], 1.36, 1.39, 1.44, 3.1,
　10.18, 11.51

About the Author-Translator

Graham M. Schweig received his doctorate from Harvard University in comparative religion. He did his graduate work in Indic studies and sacred Sanskrit literature at both the University of Chicago and Harvard. His scholarly work focuses on the philosophy and history of yoga, the devotional bhakti traditions of India, as well as love mysticism in world religions, comparative theology, and interfaith dialogue.

Schweig is currently a professor of philosophy and religion at Christopher Newport University, Virginia. Schweig first taught at Harvard as a teaching fellow, and then at the University of North Carolina and Duke University. Schweig was a visiting professor of Sanskrit at the University of Virginia and a visiting fellow at the Oxford Centre of Hindu Studies of Oxford University. He has mentored theses and examined doctoral dissertations in Europe, Australia, and the United States.

Schweig is an internationally sought-out speaker and has delivered over three dozen invited lectures at the Smithsonian Institution in Washington, DC. He also regularly offers workshops and seminars at major yoga centers and conferences. Since his early teens, he studied ashtānga and bhakti yoga under the guidance of traditional teachers and has been practicing various forms of meditation and heart-centered yoga for over forty-five years.

Schweig has written over one hundred publications, including articles for professional journals and encyclopedias, reviews and chapters for books in his field, and several books. His book *Dance of Divine Love: India's Classic Sacred Love Story* (Princeton) focuses on the yoga of the heart and a translation from the Sanskrit of one of the most celebrated sacred love stories in the world. Schweig is also senior editor of the international periodical *Journal of Vaishnava Studies* and director of theology for the Avanti Schools Trust in England.